SOCIAL DREAMING

The idea of social dreaming argues that dreams are relevant to the wider social sphere and have a collective resonance that goes beyond the personal narrative.

In this fascinating collection, the principles of social dreaming are explored to uncover shared anxieties and prejudices, suggest likely responses, enhance cultural surveys, inform managerial policies and embody community affiliation. Including, for the first time, a coherent epistemology to support the theoretical principles of the field, the book reflects upon and extends the theory and philosophy behind the method, as well as discussing new research in the area, and how social dreaming practice is conducted in a range of localities, situations and circumstances.

The book will appeal to anyone interested in the idea that social dreaming can help us to delve deeper into the question of what it means to be human, from psychoanalysts to sociologists and beyond.

Dr. Susan Long is Director of Research at the National Institute for Organisation Dynamics Australia. She conducts research in organisational change and collaborative dynamics, and supervises research candidates. She is president of the Gordon Lawrence Foundation for the promotion of social dreaming and a past president of the International Society for the Psychoanalytic Study of Organisations. She is also an organisational consultant in private practice.

Dr. Julian Manley works at the University of Central Lancashire, UK. His research focusses on psychosocial applications of visual methods and Deleuzian perspectives, with a particular emphasis on social dreaming. He is Vice-Chair and Academic Research Lead of the Gordon Lawrence Foundation for the Promotion of Social Dreaming.

"This is an important book that extends the horizons envisioned by Gordon Lawrence. Dreams are overdetermined events that condense many divergent strands of thought into one remarkable internal event. 'Social dreaming' theorists analyze the way dreams include social events in their matrix. At a time when there is widespread distress in societies around the globe, a work such as this is timely and useful."

– Christopher Bollas

SOCIAL DREAMING

Philosophy, Research, Theory and Practice

Edited by Susan Long and Julian Manley

Routledge
Taylor & Francis Group

LONDON AND NEW YORK

First published 2019
by Routledge
2 Park Square, Milton Park, Abingdon, Oxon OX14 4RN

and by Routledge
52 Vanderbilt Avenue, New York, NY 10017

Routledge is an imprint of the Taylor & Francis Group, an informa business

British Library Cataloguing in Publication Data
A catalogue record for this book is available from the British Library

Library of Congress Cataloging-in-Publication Data
A catalog record has been requested for this book

ISBN: 978-1-138-32733-7 (hbk)
ISBN: 978-1-138-32735-1 (pbk)
ISBN: 978-0-429-44927-7 (ebk)

Typeset in Bembo
by Taylor & Francis Books

Dedicated to the memory of Gordon Lawrence

For in that sleep of death what dreams may come
When we have shuffled off this mortal coil...[1]

1. (Hamlet, Act III, Scene 1, lines 66–67, p. 886. The Oxford Shakespeare, 1943)

CONTENTS

SECTION III
Social dreaming practice   **129**

FIGURES

AUTHOR BIOGRAPHIES

Domenico Agresta

Domenico is a Trustee of the Gordon Lawrence Foundation and works with social dreaming studying rites of passage, religious rites, and cultural contexts linked with historical events. He has used social dreaming in clinical fields and psycho-oncology vocational training in public health. He is a clinical psychologist, group-analyst and psycho-oncologist. He works as a group-analyst in private practice and teaches at university and at schools of psychotherapy. He is president of the Centre for the Study of Psychology and Psychosomatic Medicine (CSPP) and studies the correlation between mind and body, links to anthropology and group processes using dream icons. He is Chair of Family Section in IAGP and OPUS. He is an Academic Member of AGPA (American Group Psychotherapy Association) and Board Member of SIMP (Italian Society of Psychosom Med). He lives and works in Pescara, Italy.

Ruth Balogh Ph.D.

Ruth studied psychology at Bristol University as an undergraduate, modern social and cultural studies at Chelsea College, London University and was awarded her doctorate in 1993 from University of London Institute of Education. It was there that she gained her first opportunity to practise action research. As Ruth Davies she edited the anti-psychology journal '*Red Rat*' in the 1970s. She has continued to support the rights of mental health service users whenever the opportunity has arisen in her long career as a social researcher at various higher education institutions in the UK, eventually becoming a Reader in Health Research & Practice Development. She is currently Associate Senior Research Fellow at Glasgow University and Co-ordinator of the international Collaborative Action Research Network (CARN), the scholarly association linked with the international journal *Educational Action Research*. A long-time environmental campaigner, she was awarded the Friends of the Earth (England Wales & Northern Ireland) Earthmover Award 2017 for Exceptional campaigning on nuclear waste and sustainable economies based on renewables.

Hanni Biran

Hanni is a clinical psychologist, a training psychoanalyst and a group analyst teaching at the Tel Aviv Institute for Contemporary Psychoanalysis. She is a lecturer at the program for psychotherapy of the Tel Aviv University, and at Magid Institute, the Hebrew University. She is a lecturer at the Israeli Institute of Group Analysis. She supervises many teams and staff members in public clinics and hospitals involved in group psychotherapy. Hanni worked for many years with Gordon Lawrence and together with a group of colleagues, she hosted the first SDM in Israel in 1988. Hanni has published many papers and also chapters in books dealing with social issues. She published the book *The Courage of Simplicity* (Karnac, 2015) about Bion's ideas.

Angela Eden

Angela works as an organisational consultant from her own practice EDEN EVOLUTION. Through her original training in theatre, education and organisational consultancy, she has used metaphor, symbols and dreams. Over the last fifteen years working with social dreaming she has developed training workshops with the Gordon Lawrence Foundation. Through ISPSO annual meetings, she has hosted a series of social dreaming matrices in Philadelphia, Toledo, San Diego and recently in Copenhagen. Additionally, she has opened another creative stream, working as an artist with a range of mixed media and abstract images.

Judith Ezra

Judith is a social worker, a group analyst, a staff member at the Bar Ilan School of Social Work and an individual, couple and family therapist. She is the former co-head of the Israeli Association of Group Psychotherapy. She was a member of the Editorial Board and published papers in *The International Journal of Group Analytic Psychotherapy* and in "*Mikbatz*", The Israeli Journal of Group Psychotherapy.

Franca Fubini

Franca is the newly elected Chair of the Gordon Lawrence Foundation and Vice Chair of Il Nodo Group. She trained and worked with Gordon Lawrence since the 1980s: together they developed social dreaming in Italy. She has published articles about social dreaming and its applications, she has also taught social dreaming at universities and hosted social dreaming programs internationally and in a variety of work contexts as a consultant to the organisations. She has designed a one-year social dreaming training. She is an experienced and qualified psychoanalytic psychotherapist, organizational consultant and group analyst, who works both privately and for the public administrations.

Francesca La Nave MA AP GAP HCPC UKCP

Francesca La Nave is an art psychotherapist and group analytic psychotherapist with a background combining science and fine arts and over twenty years of clinical experience in both, adult mental health and special education. She works for the NHS, with patients with complex needs, integrating her interest and experience in attachment theory, object relations, creativity and mentalization. She also manages all arts therapies training placements for her Trust. She has a private practice providing art psychotherapy for adults and children, as well as supervision and training. She is a visiting lecturer on a number of art psychotherapy and group analytic psychotherapy training courses, in the UK and in Europe. She trained as a Social Dreaming host with Gordon Lawrence and Angela Eden.

Nuala Flynn

Nuala is a depth psychologist, clinical supervisor, dream-worker, artist and social dreaming matrix host. She has an MA in Imaginal Studies from Chichester University, completed Marion Woodman Foundation Body-soul Leadership training, and is an Embodied Imagination therapist in training with Robert Bosnak. She runs dream workshops and an ongoing dream group for therapists, combining personal and professional development via dreamwork. She is in private practice in East London and works as a designated "Towards Healing" trauma therapist, working with Irish survivors of clerical and institutional abuse. www.nualaflynn.co.uk

Jonathan Gosling

Jonathan Gosling is co-founder of One Planet Education Networks (OPEN) and of the One Planet MBA at Exeter University where he is Emeritus Professor of Leadership. He is currently supporting malaria control and elimination efforts in Southern Africa and is faculty of The Forward Institute in the UK. He holds visiting positions at universities in Australia, Canada, China, Denmark, India and Slovenia, and recently completed a study of leadership development in healthcare in these and other countries. He has designed and directed programs for many commercial and humanitarian organisations. He is co-author of *Sustainable Business: A one planet approach* (Wiley, 2017) and several other books and articles. Jonathan has an ongoing interest in social dreaming and has conducted social dreaming matrices at academic conferences and integrated within leadership development programs.

Ruth E. Jones

Ruth first trained as an art therapist, and is now a UKCP registered Psychoanalytic Psychotherapist and Clinical Supervisor, and an Energy Psychotherapist (DCEP). Publications include *Foreshoring the Unconscious, Living Psychoanalytic Practice* (2010) and *Psychodynamic Art Therapy Practice with People on the Autistic Spectrum* (2014). At the time of writing, Ruth was working primarily in private practice in North Kent. www.ruthejones.co.uk

Susan Long Ph.D.

Susan is Director of Research at the National Institute of Organisation Dynamics in Melbourne, Australia. She is also a visiting professor at INSEAD in Singapore and supervises doctoral candidates in Melbourne. She is president of the Gordon Lawrence Foundation and has been involved with social dreaming since the 1990s, hosting matrices in a variety of settings. She is a past president of the International Society for the Psychoanalytic Study of Organisations and founding president of Group Relations Australia. Her interests lie in the study of organisations. Together with Maurita Harney, she has outlined the "Associative Unconscious" as a philosophic foundation to psychoanalytic and socioanalytic studies.

Julian Manley Ph.D.

Julian works at the University of Central Lancashire (UCLan), England. He holds qualifications from Cambridge University, Middlesex University and the University of the West of England (UWE), where he completed a PhD on social dreaming. He was awarded college and university prizes for academic excellence at both Cambridge and UWE. Since then, he has pursued research using psychosocial methods applied to a diverse range of research areas, including climate change, the socially engaged arts, substance misuse and co-operative principles and values. He is Module Leader for Psychosocial Studies at UCLan. He has previously worked in organisational consultancy, and was founder and Director of Ecowaves, an organisational and ecological consultancy business in Spain. He is Vice Chair and Trustee of the Gordon Lawrence Foundation for the Promotion of Social Dreaming; Executive Committee member of the Climate Psychology Alliance (CPA); Co-Chair of CPA Scotland; and Chair of the Preston Co-operative Development Network.

Rose Redding Mersky Ph.D.

Rose has been an organisational development consultant and executive coach for over 25 years. She offers workshops in various socioanalytic methodologies, such as Organisational Role Analysis, Social Dream-Drawing, Organisational Observation, Social Photo-Matrix and Social Dreaming. She is an Honorary Trustee of the Gordon Lawrence Foundation for the Promotion of Social Dreaming. She has been a member of the International Society for the Psychoanalytic Study of Organizations (ISPSO) for almost 30 years and served as its first female president. Her publications have focused primarily on the practice of consultation and the utilisation of these methodologies in both organisational and research practice. She recently received her doctorate from the Centre for Psycho-Social Studies at the University of West England in Bristol, UK She lives and works in Germany. E-Mail: rose.merky@dream-drawing.com; website: www.dream-drawing.com.

Richard Morgan-Jones

Richard is involved in group relations, organizational consulting and executive coaching. He is a supervising and training psychoanalytic psychotherapist with British Psychotherapy Foundation; a registered member of British Psychoanalytic Council (BPC); elected board member of International Society for Psychoanalytic Society of Organizations (ISPSO); mentor and member of the AK Rice Institute (USA); member of the Organization for Promoting the Understanding of Society (OPUS); visiting faculty member at the Indian Institute of Management at Ahmedabad, India and associate consultant of Work Lab, New York. He is director of Work Force Health: Consulting and Research. His work is explored in consultancies, an international workshop and a book entitled: *The Body of the Organisation and its Health* which explores on how organisations get under the skin and reveal personal and team development opportunities and organisational strategic choices.

Or Netanelyis

Or is a psychologist in clinical internship and an online blogger. In his private practice in Tel Aviv, he combines psychoanalytic psychotherapy with practical counselling. In his online writing, he is interested with current readings of psychoanalytic texts, and the applicability of psychoanalytic logic to mechanised forms of therapy. He is one of the younger generation partners in the initiative to bring social dreaming to Israeli communities, in order to allow dialogue in a split society. He views his work in hosting these matrices as a vital personal need to talk about the reality beyond politics.

Hanan Sabah-Teicher

Hanan is a clinical psychologist who works with children and adults. He combines his practice of psychoanalytic psychotherapy in a variety of settings, including mental health services, educational institutions, and his private clinic. Hanan promotes socially engaged psychological work. He is one of the founders of the therapist's cooperative "Mekomi" in Tel-Aviv - a democratic and egalitarian collegial clinic that provides an accessible psychotherapy for the public. He is also one of the initiators of social dreaming matrices gatherings which are open to the community, offering a facilitating space for dialogue in the complex political reality of Israel.

Mannie Sher Ph.D., TQAP, FBAP

Mannie is Principal Researcher and Consultant in Organisational Development and Change; executive coach; former Director of the Group Relations Programme, The Tavistock Institute of Human Relations, London; trustee of the Gordon Lawrence Foundation for the Promotion of Social Dreaming; a psychoanalytical psychotherapist; a member of OFEK, Israel and a former board member of ISPSO. Relying on a total systems approach of open systems thinking, socio-technical systems theory and systems psychodynamics, integrated with action learning, group relations and traditional organisational and culture change methods, Mannie has delivered successful change programmes to many private and public sector organisations in the UK and internationally.

Jacqueline Sirota MSc BACP Senior Registered Practitioner UKRC

Jacqueline is an independent psychodynamic counsellor and organisational consultant. She gained her MSc at the University of the West of England, Bristol studying Group Relations and Society, the psychodynamics of groups and organisations. She is an experienced Social Dreaming Host and has employed this methodology in research projects. This has included a series of social dreaming matrix events during the 'Breaking the Chains' exhibition commemorating the abolition of the transatlantic slave trade in Bristol. With Dr Julian Manley, she co-wrote and presented a paper on this research to the ISPSO Annual Meeting in Toledo, Spain.

She has worked with colleagues from the Tavistock Institute facilitating Social Dreaming Events at 'Occupy', Finsbury Square Tent City and St. Paul's as a peripatetic researcher. She is an associate of the Tavistock Consultancy Service, a member of ISPSO, the International Society for the Psychoanalytic Study of Organisations, an associate member of OPUS, Organisation for the Promotion of Understanding of Society. She was, until relocating to Kent, chair of the Bridge Consultancy Group and Director/Trustee of Avon Psychotherapy Service.

Laurie Slade

Laurie is a UKCP registered analytical psychotherapist, in private practice in West London. He is a member of the Guild of Psychotherapists, the Confederation for Analytical Psychology, and the International Neuropsychoanalysis Association. He is an Associate of the Gordon Lawrence Foundation for the Promotion of Social Dreaming, and has been actively involved in social dreaming since 2001, hosting sessions in a variety of settings, in the UK and internationally. He helped devise the first programme for professional development of social dreaming hosts in 2007. He is co-founder of the Queer Social Dreaming Matrix, running since 2016, a monthly open access meeting in London for sexual minorities. His published papers on social dreaming include Social Dreaming for a Queer Culture (*Self & Society*, 2005), and Image to Gesture – Social Dreaming with Student Theatre Directors (in *The Creativity of Social Dreaming*, Karnac, 2010).

Artist note about the cover:

In this project, Borough's Cut Up method is applied. This procedure exactly corresponds with Sigmund Freud's interpretation of the human dream.

PREFACE

Jonathan Gosling

In Candy Neubert's novel *Big Low Tide* (2012 p. 92) Brenda prepares for a difficult conversation with her self-absorbed lover. She wakes before him so that "when he is fully awake but with the pockets of his mind still empty from the night, she will sense her moment and slip into it."

Those moments between sleep and wake, when "the pockets of the mind" are not yet filled, carry the faintest vibrations of a different kind of knowing. This book is concerned with this knowing, apprehended in dreams but which so often slips out of the pockets of the mind as we wake. The central chapters chart many attempts to re-capture dreams and to understand the kind of knowing they represent. Part 1 offers a comprehensive theory of this kind of knowing, and how it is realised in the particular context of a social dreaming matrix.

As the editors point out, it is important to realise that the kind of knowing available to us at night, in our dreaming states, is not the same kind of knowing as we habitually exercise in relation to waking sense-data or conceptual thinking. The objects of knowledge – what we perceive, how we perceive it, and how we represent those perceptions to ourselves – are something apart from reason and conceptualisation.

Naturally people have always theorised about dreams (in Chapter 1 of this volume, Susan Long offers a comprehensive review), and most modern theories recognise the significance of the context in which dreams are recovered, told, heard and thought about. Indeed, modern theorising can be defined by this acknowledgement that the purposes, methods and context in which we examine phenomena (including dreams) are choices that determine the meaning and significance we find in them; and even the ontological status we ascribe to them. As McLuhan said, "the medium is the message" (1964 p. 9).

Most contexts for examining dreams involve two or more people contemplating the narrated images of a dream, and wondering what they might mean. In social contexts, this tips towards "what the dream might mean for us, collectively" (rather than what it suggests about the dreamer's psychological state). So while dreams have forever been shared and interpreted in social situations, the Social Dreaming Matrix is thoroughly modern in *choosing* to construe dreams and dreamers in this way.

The underlying assertion of this book is that there is much value to be gained by accessing this different knowledge, and that social dreaming is a technique suited to elaborating some possible meanings in ways that will be useful for other purposes. The book therefore locates social dreaming within the instrumentalism of social science – it is valuable because it helps us do other things such as (*inter alia*) articulate shared anxieties and prejudices, predict likely responses, enhance cultural surveys, inform managerial policies and embody community affiliation. (This instrumentalism might be contrasted with social dreaming as participatory art, such as the weekend of "motel dreaming" in a Tasmanian motel, organised by David Patman in 2014: www.moteldreaming.com).

However, if social dreaming is to become a social science method, it requires a coherent epistemology, related to but distinguished from theories of knowledge that apply to other forms of knowing. This is the first significant contribution of the book. Two substantive philosophical essays by the editors explore how a theory of dream-knowledge might be derived from the work of Pierce (Long) and Deleuze (Manley). These two essays are crucial in establishing the distinctive but de-centred and elusive field we are drawing on here. As Long has shown in earlier work, Pierce's concept of abductive logic recognises the emergence of distinct ideas from the unconscious, rendering the idea or way-of-seeing into a handy object that can be adopted as a working hypothesis. Social dreaming is thus located as a method for working with emergent ideas.

Secondly, Manley invokes Deleuze's metaphor of the rhizome to describe the way that dream-material spreads and crops up all over the place, connecting apparently separate ideas, and generating fragments that sometimes grow and extend unexpectedly.

By describing dreams as emergent and rhizomatic, social dreaming becomes allied to contemporary theory in other fields. For example, in *Strategy Without Design* Chia and Holt (2011) define strategy as a process of learning characterised by an attitude of alertness and readiness for associative thinking because individual agency is limited, conditional and dependent. They argue that conscious intention is an inadequate explanation of strategy, which is better understood as collective responsiveness to emergent awareness.

Social dreaming is thus in tune with other non-rational aspects of future imaginings and responsive actions.

Another key element is doubt in the ability of individual or even collective *conscious intent* to explore the potential for a future that remains relatively obscure – an obscurity that becomes more intense as we consider climate change (bio-diversity loss, air pollution, etc) may induce a "tipping point" into unpredictable instability. Ecological collapse is not the only conceivable catastrophe – colonial invasions have always wreaked this havoc, and many cultures have been utterly obliterated as a result. In the more colloquial world of business, firms collapse or are absorbed ruthlessly into others, dissolving ties to community, location and national identity; and social institutions that appeared to be fixed parts of the cultural landscape – such as the welfare state or NHS in the UK – are dismembered before our eyes and beneath our hospital beds.

Such frailty, such treacherous inconstancy, such self-destructiveness is inherent to what Marx called the bourgeois era:

> *All fixed, fast-frozen relations, with their train of ancient and venerable prejudices and opinions, are swept away, all new-formed ones become antiquated before they can ossify. All that is solid melts into air, all that is holy is profaned, and man is at last compelled to face with sober senses his real conditions of life, and his relations with his kind.*
>
> *(Marx, 1888 p. 45)*

As Jonathan Lear (2006) points out, cultures do not routinely educate their populations or prepare them for the possibility of catastrophic collapse. It is effectively a "blind spot" of any culture:

> By and large a culture will not teach its young: 'These are ways in which you can succeed, and these are ways in which you will fail; these are dangers you might face and here are opportunities; these acts are shameful, and these are worthy of honor – and, oh yes, one more thing, this entire structure of evaluating the world might cease to make sense.'
>
> *(2006 p. 83)*

As I have suggested elsewhere in bringing social dreaming to bear upon such questions,

> *these are educational priorities which we should be considering as we face the prospect of deepening ecocrisis and its likely bio-physical and socio-economic consequences. In effect, we need to find ways of imagining cultural catastrophe now if the worst excesses of what may be in prospect for western civilization – and those peoples and species also implicated by western-induced ecocrisis - are to be mitigated.*
>
> *(Gosling & Case, 2013 p. 709)*

Social dreaming might be a means for engaging this possibility, because devastation, collapse and failure are perfectly conceivable in dreams.

This book provides several examples of social dreaming used for such "prescience" to discern coming events; but it may be that its relevance is at least as much in its ritual function, because by lifting the veil to the unconscious, social dreaming symbolically enacts a contemporary concern with apocalypse ('apocalypse' in Greek is ἀποκάλυψις *apokálypsis*; "lifting of the veil" or "revelation"). In other words, as catastrophic predictions fill more of our conscious awareness, practices that rehearse the unreason and fantasy become more comprehensible and perhaps necessary. As Norman Cohn (1957) suggested in relation to medieval experience of epidemic plague, when catastrophe strikes, destroying the order that we have become used to and by which we define ourselves, the apocalypse appears more potent, present and real.

This construes social dreaming as an intervention in social wellbeing, rather than simply a means for gathering and analyzing data from dreams. Most of the applied chapters in Part 2 of this book take this interventionist stance, showing how specific groups of people can benefit from participating in the collective emergence of the social dreaming matrix. Social science becomes a therapeutic and revelatory practice, as well as an information-gathering and processing method for research.

Nonetheless, the editors insist on analytical attention to dreams and social dreaming. The term "analysis" is inextricably linked to work with the unconscious for good reason. *Ana-Lysis* comes directly from the Greek "loosen up", because it eases the tightly-bound coherence of the accounts we are given, to reveal constituent elements and dynamic forces that could perhaps be put together in other ways. A financial analyst "undoes" the reports and accounts put out by a company to try to find out how they have been put together, under what assumptions and to serve which interests; and then puts them back together in a new rendering. So, social dreaming may be an analytic method in which the undone threads of dreams can be examined and re-connected to inform and enlarge the perspectives of particular communities. The chapters of this book also present social dreaming as analytical deconstruction and re-construction of social life.

I commend it to the reader.

References

Chia, R.C. and Holt, R. (2011) *Strategy Without Design*. New York: Cambridge University Press.

Cohn, N. (1957) *The Pursuit of the Millennium: Revolutionary Millenarians and Mystical Anarchists of the Middle Ages*. Oxford: Oxford University Press.

Gosling, J. and Case, P. (2013) 'Social dreaming and ecocentric ethics: sources of non-rational insight in the face of climate change catastrophe'. *Organization*, 20(5) 705–721.

Marx, K. and Engels, F. (1888) *The Communist Manifesto*. Moscow: Progress Publishers (1952 edition).

McLuhan, M. (1964) *Understanding Media: The Extensions of Man*. New York: Mentor.

Neubert, C. (2012) *Big Low Tide*. Bridgend, Wales: Seren (the Poetry Press).

INTRODUCTION

Susan Long and Julian Manley

This book provides a continuation to, and a development of the series of books published by Karnac on social dreaming. Here we extend and deepen an understanding of the theory and method of social dreaming within the tradition begun by W. Gordon Lawrence with Patricia Daniels in 1982 at the Tavistock Institute in London (Lawrence 1998). Daniels appears not to have continued working with Lawrence after this initial experiment, and social dreaming has since come to be identified with Lawrence. In an article following Lawrence's passing in 2013, Manley points out that Lawrence's brilliantly creative mind was able to posit tantalising ideas or working hypotheses, as he liked to call them, about social dreaming, but provided us with "little analytical understanding of social dreaming in scientific terms" (Manley 2014, p. 325). It is this "analytical understanding" that this book begins addressing.

Lawrence's first book of essays on social dreaming featured an introductory section by David Armstrong. We regard this volume, nineteen years later, this time with a preface by Jonathan Gosling, as another new beginning; the closing of a cycle and the emergence of another. In his first book, Lawrence, with his customary frankness, stated that he did not "fully understand what [he was] doing" (Lawrence 1998, p. 12). We do not claim that we necessarily understand social dreaming either, but we hope that this edition marks a significant milestone towards an understanding.

Since its early beginnings, the sharing of dreams and associations within a social dreaming matrix has been used by organisational consultants, psychotherapists and other practitioners in many countries worldwide. It is sometimes described as a "democratic" forum (Lawrence 2005, p. 38), where participants have the same opportunity to contribute with dreams that each have equal value. In it, the dreams speak rather than the dreamers. Any personal meanings a dream may have for the individual dreamer are subdued in favour of a meaning that is shared and developed by the participants in the matrix as a whole. The matrix participants are the vehicles through which the dreams become connected and developed through associations that throw light on the conscious and unconscious knowledge that is shared in the groups and societies where they live and work.

The practice of social dreaming as we know it emerged almost by chance, while Lawrence was struggling to understand how to deal with dreams in the context of his group work at the Tavistock (Lawrence 1998), however, the sharing of dreams has its roots in ancient practice. Dreams have long been regarded as carrying important information: from the gods, from nature and, in the age of psychoanalysis, from the unconscious. Sometimes they were interpreted as messages which warned of dangers or presaged the future. They have been understood to guide individual and collective decisions or to make sense of intuitive and emotional insights. Many cultures have wondered at dreams, sharing them and attempting to decode the messages that they hold.

Gordon Lawrence was influenced by such traditions, by scholars, psychoanalysis and the dynamics of groups. But it was through reading the work of Hannah Beradt (1968), who collected the dreams of patients during the Nazi regime, deciphering them to reveal the culture of those times rather than their individual meanings, that led him towards the exploration of the social meanings of dreams through the social dreaming matrix.

There have been many books and some articles written about social dreaming, the majority edited by Lawrence (1998; 2003; 2005; 2007; 2010; Clare & Zarbafi 2009). We won't repeat the descriptions of social dreaming from those editions here. We do say, however, that although the social dreaming method has grown and diversified since its initial inception, it stays true to its main purpose: to enable the dreams to speak to us about the worlds we live in that may be unconsciously experienced but not readily accessible in our day to day conscious living. It is a shared experience that social dreaming can access and that we can glimpse in the work of the matrix.

We wish to stress in this introduction that social dreaming is about the dreams, not the personalities of the individual dreamers. The matrix is a setting where dreams can be expressed, heard, expanded, associated to and linked to the experiences of the social groupings that are in the matrix. Despite the use of social dreaming in groups, organisations and communities, there has been little work published on investigating the method or the philosophy of science that underpins it – with the exception of Lawrence and Long (2010) who explore the theory behind the creative frame of mind required in social dreaming; Manley, who provided an overview of the philosophical background to psycho-social studies as part of his work on social dreaming (2010), and a theoretical overview of social dreaming following Lawrence's death in 2013 (2014); Long and Harney (2013) who propose and describe the associative unconscious along with the philosopher Charles Peirce's concept of abductive reasoning, as basic to social dreaming and other socioanalytic methods; and Long (2016) who writes on the history of the concept of the unconscious. As Manley has pointed out in an article summarising the current state of social dreaming and the need for developments in theory (2014), Lawrence's passing has highlighted the necessity for further thought on the philosophy and ideas that are behind the method as a practice. It is this further development that our book aims to cover.

This book, then, has four aims, these being:

1. to develop the epistemological and ontological roots of social dreaming in the tradition pioneered by Lawrence for over twenty-five years;
2. to reflect upon and extend the theory and philosophy behind the method;
3. to present and discuss research in social dreaming; and,
4. to present and discuss current social dreaming practice and related methods from diverse localities.

The authors have been invited to write towards these aims. We summarise their chapters below.

Section 1

Towards a philosophy of science in support of social dreaming

This section presents two papers that approach a philosophy of science and research in support of social dreaming and related methods for accessing the unconscious at a social/collective level, together with theory about the method of social dreaming. It gives a substantive scientific underpinning to the practice of social dreaming.

In Chapter 1, Susan Long examines the ways in which we discover meaning in dreams. She examines dreams as signs in a social context. In becoming signs, meaning is discovered or uncovered. The chapter also examines some of the psychological and social processes of dreaming. Importantly, a distinction is drawn between the complex mental processes that create dreams and the outcome of those processes that we call a dream. The "dream" as experienced and the "dream" as recounted, shared and finally given meaning in a social dreaming matrix is a semiotic process subject to influences from the most personal of histories and desires and the broadest of social and cultural content.

In the second chapter in this section, Julian Manley begins by locating social dreaming ontologically in the world of embodied cognitive processes, and in doing so suggests that an understanding of social dreaming must situate itself in a holistic universe that gives primacy to qualities of affect in the context of Deleuzian rhizomatic structures of cognition rather than understandings emanating from thought conclusions in the context of Cartesian structures of linear thinking. Key to this understanding of social dreaming is "associative thinking" that leads to understandings through the shifting interconnectivities between the dreams and associations of the matrix. The meanings of a social dreaming matrix, then, are never definitive. They are constantly developing according to the process of the continuously fluctuating affect of the matrix.

Section 2

The nature and processes of social dreaming: Theory and research

This section provides chapter contributions from scholars and practitioners who are interested in beginning a process of reflection into the nature and processes of social dreaming. This begins to establish a corpus of research into social dreaming.

In Chapter 3 Richard Morgan-Jones explores a hypothesis that:

> *the social dreaming matrix, its prequels and derivatives, embodies the yearning to belong to a society bigger than one's own body to facilitate facing contradictory painful and joyful truths about human emotional living in a wider human world, which need to be dreamt to be realised.*

He examines the contention that the body dreams what the mind may not have thought and reports research from neurology, dream research and social dreaming matrices.

Chapter 4 by Laurie Slade claims that "the resources of the dreaming mind seem inexhaustible. Social dreaming is one way of accessing those riches, but its effectiveness depends on the context – on whether or not it is accepted that sharing dreams can be an authentic and creative form of dialogue – a way of thinking in community." The chapter argues for dreams as an important resource for a community that can access and use this resource.

Rose Mersky provides, in Chapter 5, a theoretical background to dreams. This is a theory of production and practice. It encompasses not just how dreams are produced from the unconscious, but the particular ways with which they are worked. Together, the theory and practice guides researchers and practitioners and provides a solid grounding in working with dreams and making them an essential resource for organizations, groups and individuals.

An action research approach to dream-sharing as a socially-constituted practice forms the basis of Chapter 6. Here Ruth Balogh shows how action research can be deployed to explore the practice of social dreaming. She argues that action research offers a way into "more openly collaborative communicative spaces, [where] inquiry becomes possible into how collective meaning-making could become more fully available to participants themselves."

In Chapter 7, the work focusses on the application of social dreaming to anthropological studies and group processes. Domenico Agresta, proposes that the social dreaming matrix is a device that helps the researcher to find social and mental structures as a way to connect identity, history and anthropological places. It does this, he argues, by providing information about the constitution of the ego-identity of the community under investigation.

Francesca La Nave describes, in Chapter 8, a development of the social dreaming method, involving the use of art-making to extend and amplify the material emerging from a social dreaming matrix. Taking art therapy methodology as her starting point, her work uses art-making as a way of externalising and processing transpersonal phenomena, held within the unconscious-conscious continuum of the dreams' narrative. She argues that this use of image-making can provide a non-verbal and sensual context where themes, feelings and ideas can be both amplified and framed, supporting the social dreaming task.

Section 3

Social dreaming practice

Appearing in this section are chapter contributions from practitioners using social dreaming with the idea that social dreaming is a method in itself for exploring groups and society. The social dreaming ventures described come from different countries and contexts.

In Chapter 9, Hanni Biran, Judith Ezra, Or Netanely, and Hanan Sabah-Teicher describe a series of gatherings open to a community in Tel Aviv, Israel. The authors use a social dreaming matrix to loosen up concrete ways of looking at society. New ideas and conceptualizations were experienced, through the invitation to contribute dreams and associations. In a socially oriented sense-making process, participants examined uncanny, obscure and emergent experiences that were left opaque at the individual level. As a result, stereotypical symbols of utopian peace, catastrophic violence, and challenging otherness are explored, turned on their heads, and trans-formed. The result is a complex set of symbols and concepts which could serve as a basis for a fresh dialogue in the split Israeli society.

Moving from Israel to the UK, in Chapter 10, the authors, Nuala Flynn and Ruth E. Jones trace a five-year open access social dreaming process. Emerging as the London Hub, this matrix seemed to assert a primary urge to exist, and subsequently has con-tinued to make its identity felt. This has challenged a core of committed hosts to sustain and make sense of this evolving nature. The chapter maps the increasing authority of the matrix as its focus shifted away from social dreaming as an instrument for constellating new thinking, towards a form of radical practice at the personal and collective levels attending to emergent processes sometimes forming new thinking. By serving the social dreaming matrix over time, the authors have come to perceive the task of social dreaming as one of attending and providing hospitality to "London Dreaming" as a new form of cultural activism and renewal.

Chapter 11, by Mannie Sher, describes the adventures of running social dreaming matrices in a variety of bounded and unbounded social spaces and the exciting opportunities of experiencing social dreaming through which people can make links and find connections between their dreams and the social. The paper builds on the experiences of many practitioners who have utilised social dreaming matrices in dif-ferent environments, making social dreaming available to diverse groups of people around the world. The experience of such diversity enables the study of the nature of dream content and its relationship to the social milieu in which the matrices take place.

Jacqueline Sirota, through the prism of social dreaming, in Chapter 12, traces a per-sonal journey exploring and giving voice to the dreams and associations arising from the

Occupy London protest tent-city in St. Paul's Square, London 2011/12. She describes the genesis of this endeavour and explains her thinking and the preparations she made prior to going solo in her explorations. She then presents the dreams and associations noted over the five days whilst endeavouring to contextualise each day's work.

Franca Fubini's contribution in Chapter 13, explores the contribution of social dreaming to organisational consulting. She does this through looking at three inter-related areas, each essential to the unfolding of an organizational consultation: First, space considered in terms of its quality of emptiness, in touch with the unknown where new thinking can emerge, Second, space thought of as landscapes, mainly built ones, creating the environment, the background stage for the diverse phenomena of the life of an organization and of life in general; and Third, the place of social dreaming, dreams and myths as the container – and the propeller – of culture and identity-formation. A clinical case will illustrate the interplay of the three.

End

Finally, in Chapter 14 Julian Manley and Susan Long, editors of this volume, explore some of their thinking about where social dreaming might go in the future.

We believe that this book is a much-needed addition to the social dreaming literature and we are grateful to the authors for their varied and rigorous contributions. The method has been proven useful to many: to organisational consultants, health professionals, social scientists, students and communities. We hope that with this book, social dreaming can find its place amongst other research methods as a rigorous and well-established way of accessing the social and associative unconscious.

References

Beradt, C. (1968) *The Third Reich of Dreams*. Chicago, IL: Quadrangle Books.

Clare, J. and Zarbafi, A. (2009) *Social Dreaming in the 21st Century*. London: Karnac.

Lawrence, W.G. (Ed.) (1998) *Social Dreaming @ Work*. London: Karnac.

Lawrence, W.G. (Ed.) (2003) *Experiences in Social Dreaming*. London: Karnac.

Lawrence, W.G. (2005) *Introduction to Social Dreaming. Transforming Thinking*. London: Karnac.

Lawrence, W.G. (Ed.) (2007) *Infinite Possibilities of Social Dreaming*. London: Karnac.

Lawrence, W.G. (Ed.) (2010) *The Creativity of Social Dreaming*. London: Karnac.

Lawrence, W.G. and Long, S.D. (2010) 'The Creative Frame of Mind' in *The Creativity of Social Dreaming* edited by W.G. Lawrence. London: Karnac.

Long, S.D. (2016) 'The Transforming Experience Framework and Unconscious Processes: A brief journey through the history of the concept of the unconscious as applied to person, system and context with an exploratory hypothesis of unconscious as source' in *Transforming Experience in Organisations* edited by S.D. Long. Karnac: London.

Long, S.D. and Harney, M. (2013) 'The Associative Unconscious' in *Socioanalytic Methods* edited by S.D. Long. London: Karnac.

Manley, J. (2010) 'From Cause and Effect to Effectual Causes: Can we talk of a philosophical background to psycho-social studies?' *Journal of Psycho-Social Studies* Vol 4/June 2010.

Manley, J. (2014) 'Gordon Lawrence's Social Dreaming Matrix: background, origins, history and developments'. *Organisational and Social Dynamics* Vol 14/2014.

SECTION I

Towards a philosophy of science in support of social dreaming

1

DREAMS AND DREAMING

A socioanalytic and semiotic perspective

Susan Long

What are dreams and what do they mean?[1] This is a question asked throughout human history. Dreams provide a mystery. They visit us while we are asleep and we appear to have little control over them despite the phenomenon of lucid dreaming. They can be fragmentary and fleeting or may appear as long narratives. Some people say they dream in colour; others in black and white. Many dreams are disturbing nightmares, while others provide pleasant and comforting experiences. Contemporary dream research shows them as a product of the brain during the particular stage of sleep called REM sleep; named after the rapid eye movements that appear, as if the sleeper were tracking the progress of their dreams. But their occurrence during particular brain activity tells us no more about their meaning than does the knowledge that left brain hemisphere activity tends to accompany linguistic logic. This is a correlative not a causative answer. Meaning can only be found in understanding the human symbols involved. Discovering meaning resides at a different logical level to that of correlative occurrence.

This chapter will examine the ways in which we discover meaning in dreams. It will examine dreams as signs in a social context. In becoming signs, meaning is discovered or uncovered. The chapter will also examine some of the psychological and social processes of dreaming. Importantly, a distinction must be drawn between the complex mental processes that create dreams and the outcome of those processes that we call a dream. A further distinction must be drawn between the 'dream' as experienced and the 'dream' as recounted, shared and finally given meaning. Such a meaning may be understood to be discovered rather than attributed, because in its long journey of creation the dream is subject to influences from the most personal of histories and desires and the broadest of social and cultural content.

Some of the meanings attributed to dreams

Discovering and creating meaning, especially group and cultural meaning is essential to human growth and creativity. Anomie and lack of meaning is part of depression. When there seems to be no meaning, humans seek it out; at times creating strange meanings to justify beliefs, feelings and observations. At other times, the search for meaning confronts us with deeply spiritual challenges.

There have been many beliefs and theories about the meaning of dreams. Many ancient civilizations believed that dreams were direct messages from the gods; messages that aid people in their searches for answers to problems and conundrums. Hailes (2011) says:

> Dreams have been seen as holding wisdom and knowledge to guide leaders in decisions that relate to their communities. One of the underlying beliefs is that dreams provide a direct pathway to the supernatural in the form of gods who can provide enlightenment for human problems.

Dreams were seen as a medium for discourse with the spirits in animistic beliefs (Wax 2004); and have been regarded as experiences of the spirit during sleep. (www.dreamresearch.ca/pdf/cultural.pdf). Linked to the idea that dreams are messages from the gods is belief in the predictive power of dreams. Joseph's interpretation of Pharaoh's dream (Gen. 41:14–24) as a prediction of future destabilization of the country, and the dream warning Mary and Joseph to flee from Herod are but two examples of many provided in the scriptures. Modern day Quakers also believe that dreams are messages from God and they use them communally to seek spiritual guidance (Tarter 2007).

In many communities, dreams have been used for guidance in matters of state as well as in everyday decisions:

> Kings in the ancient Near East had their dreams interpreted in the royal courts (Oppenheim, 1956 cited in Bulkeley 1994, p.8). High ranked officials in fourteenth-century China were obliged to spend their first night in a walled city in a temple so as to receive instructions from the City God. Judges struggling over a difficult point of law also spent the night in the temple to seek enlightenment from God (Laufer, 1931 cited in Bulkeley 1994, p. 11).
>
> Hailes (2011)

Anthropologist Brody (2013) describes the ways in which the Inuits of British Columbia use dreams to inform their understanding of their territories and hunting expeditions.

Throughout history, there have been beliefs in the healing powers of dreams. Many native tribes in the Americas had and still have cultures that rely on dreams for major decisions and for their healing powers. For example, Black Elk, the famous Sioux Indian elder born in the mid 1800s used dreams to predict the disasters that would visit his tribe. He also used them to develop ceremonies of healing for the community. Jung was influenced by his understanding of the Pueblo Indians reading of dream symbols. Garnering twentieth century science, Garfield (1992) describes how dreams can indicate health problems through their connectedness with the dreamer's body.

Perhaps the most recent influential Western tradition of understanding dreams comes through twentieth century psychoanalysis which puts dreams at the centre of access to the unconscious and its processes. Freud (1900) and Grotstein (2000) provide two publications that span the century. The former sets out a theory of dreams that draws on their ability to transform and disguise the desires of the dreamer, while at the same time expressing those desires. This dynamic, that is, the capacity for a thought, an image and even an emotion to represent both a desire and its opposite is a hallmark of psychoanalytic thinking: a capacity found in language where some words equally denote opposite meanings (contronyms). For example, "cleave" can mean either "sever apart" or "bind together"; or "bolt" can mean "lock up" or "escape". Moreover, it represents the creative capacity of the dream, albeit a capacity also to hide and dissimulate.

At the end of the twentieth century, Grotstein (2000) takes up this idea, describing the dream as a dramatic narrative presented by a dreamer – the unconscious unknown to us and a dreamer who also is audience to the dream.

> *Dreams are dramatic narrations written, directed, and produced by a composite dreamer who is unknown to us, who employs narrative as the instrument of phantasy and myth and uses neurophysiological perception-namely, visualization-to organize the chaotic, fragmented accretions of mental pain left over as residues of yet one more day of existence. What we commonly call a dream is the visual transformation of a never-ending pageant of events in the internal world .... we never stop dreaming .... There is a dream audience who anticipates the dream and requisitions it from the dream producer in order to recognize its own problems and resonate with its own hostaged self ..., which is forged in the smithy of dream work by the Dreamer Who Dreams the Dream .... In the rhythmic concordance between the dream actor and the dream audience, the preliminary certification of one's emerging authenticity occurs preparatory to a real certification through experience in the real world .... The Dreamer Who Understands the Dream is the audience that verifies the passion of the dreamer .... it is also the barrier that contains the dream .... the background that compels the foreground hypothesis to remain in the foreground until it has become sufficiently defined.*
>
> *(Grotstein 2000, pp. 10–12)*

For Grotstein, the dream is a sign to the dreamer from his or her unconscious. The psychoanalytic view has influenced twentieth century sensibilities and is used extensively in psychotherapy, counselling, life coaching and executive coaching, alongside every-day parlance.

Further developments in psychoanalysis either extend upon or differ from Freud's views with regard to dreams. Roheim (1952) developed a theory of dreams as a defence against regression during sleep; a regression due to extended human dependency during infancy and fear of separation; a return to the womb. He saw dreams also as a source of myths and hence of culture. Langs (1988) sees dreams as responses to current traumas and as attempts to adapt to change. Dreams, he claims are "*an expression of human adaptation to an emotionally charged situation*" (Langs 1988, p. 4). Hartmann (2008) argues that dreams focus on a central image that represents an emotion and the dream has an adaptive function; making new connections for the dreamer. These perspectives resonate with the theories of Finnish neuroscientist Revonsuo (2000) who, following analysis of normative dream content, suggests that dreams have a biological function to simulate threatening events that allow the dreamer to rehearse threat perception and threat avoidance; and Barrett (1993) who gathers evidence to support the idea that dreams are involved in problem-solving. Although current neuroscientific research may be as yet inconclusive, it does challenge those who claim that dreaming is a simple, meaningless bi-product of brain activity.

As can be seen from these various ideas, the context of the dreaming is important to the meaning attributed, whether it be a religious message, an intuition of things to come, a sign of illness or a creative activity. The process of dreaming is common across all cultures and it seems is not limited just to our species (MIT News 2001). Dreams, while experienced by a sleeping individual person, have always been discussed and shared and meanings have been created through this sharing. Wax (2004) for instance, notes that small hunter gatherer communities commonly shared dreams. This dream sharing expands the meaning of the dream from the individual to the group. Tedlock (1987) says of the native American dreams she studied: "Dreams that begin as personal entities shift during dream telling or performing to provide a cosmic doorway into another dimension of reality" (p. 183). Her approach within what is called "the communicative approach to dreaming" considers the creation and psychodynamics of the narration of the dream, and the interpretative framework of the culture of the community of dreamers, as a magnification of the manifest content of the dream.

For the Quakers (Friends) dreams are messages from God and Quakers have historically recorded their dreams in journals for spiritual and every-day purposes. Gerona (in Michele Lise Tarter 2007) provides an account of how dreams were used in the new American transatlantic colonies. She describes how initially dreams were regarded as prophetic and their meanings used to further the ideals of the Quakers, often in dramatic pronouncements and political accusations. Later dreams were used as "powerful narrative tools" (Tarter 2007, p. 302) for the community and effective "platforms" for influence. The belief in their prophetic nature persists as a way of approaching spiritual guidance and growth.

The God who gives dreams to the Quaker is not an external God delivering messages from on high, but a God that dwells within and provides an "inner teacher". In many ways, the messages in the dreams might be regarded by psychoanalysts as messages from the unconscious to the dreamer. But beyond the personal message is the communal one. Sharing and working with dreams is always important for Quaker societies. Sharing dreams is a way of making private realisations public, of discovering new ways to interpret the messages and enrich their meanings, and, ways of building and seeking advice for the community.

In this tradition of dream sharing, Gordon Lawrence has developed a theory and method of *Social Dreaming* practised in order to understand the social content of dreams, and their links and associations within interacting communities.

Social dreaming

*Social Dreaming is a way of working with dreams where the focus is on the **dream** and not the dreamer, where dreams are shared amongst people who come together solely for this purpose. With Social Dreaming, the meaning of a dream is about the broader world in which one lives. In a Social Dreaming event, participants are invited to offer their dreams and, through association, explore the possible social meanings contained within them.*

(Gordon Lawrence Foundation www.socialdreaming.com)

Social dreaming is a current expression of dream sharing with the intent to formulate or discover new hypotheses about the community. Lawrence was familiar with dreams as they are used in psychoanalysis. He was also aware of the other ways in which dreams are used in a variety of cultures. Amongst the influences on him was a work by Hannah Beradt entitled *The Third Reich of Dreams*. Beradt had collected the dreams of hundreds of Germans between 1933 and 1939. As a set, they appeared to have "rehearsed, presented and foreshadowed political events" (Armstrong 1998, p. xviii). Lawrence thought that sharing dreams with a focus on their social content could aid in creatively thinking about and addressing issues in the social systems to which dreamers belonged. His link was between the content of dreams and the nature of the social systems of dreamers. The dreams are shared in a "matrix" where dreamers are encouraged to make associations and connections to all dreams presented. The work of the matrix differs from that of a group insofar as the focus is not on interactions between the members but on the dreams and the associations and connections arising.

The emergent free associations and connections give access to the "associative unconscious" (Long and Harney 2013) which is a mental network of thoughts, images, symbols and signs shared by an interacting community but not accessible in its entirety to any one individual or sub-system. The focus on the dream shifts the emphasis in social dreaming away from the psychology of the individual (which Lawrence tags as "Oedipus") to the semiotic field of the community ("Sphinx"). In social dreaming, the focus is on the dream not the dreamer. Just as Hartmann (2008) argues, the dream itself enlarges the associations and connections available; in social dreaming, the availability is for the community.

Dreams as signs

Whether messages from the gods as in antiquity; a message from the unconscious to a dreamer as in psychoanalysis; rehearsing, presenting and foreshadowing political events as in the work of Beradt; simulating traumas or solving problems as shown by neuroscience; or, accessing hidden social meaning as in social dreaming; it seems that dreams are understood as signs in many theories of dreaming.

This takes us to the nature of signs. There are many definitions of a sign: dictionaries usually state that a sign indicates some occurrence or object including possible future events or occurrences. In this chapter, the semiotic work of philosopher Charles Peirce will be used (see also Long and Harney 2013).

According to Peirce a sign is:

> something which stands to somebody for something on some respect or capacity. It addresses somebody, that is, creates in the mind of that person an equivalent sign, or perhaps a more developed sign.
>
> (Peirce 1984, p. 99)

It is the practice of social dreaming that recognises that dreams are not only signs from a personal unconscious to the dreamer – as in the psychoanalytic meaning of dreams – but are shared signs between people, as in Peirce's description: that is, they create equivalent or more developed signs in the social domain. This does not negate the psychoanalytic aspect of dreams; the somebody who is addressed by the dream may well be the dreamer as indicated by Grotstein. But dreams are not restricted by this because they emerge as much from the associative unconscious as the individual repressed unconscious. Just as Freud's discovery of free association in the individual led to a deeper understanding of the repressed unconscious; associative links between people tap into the shared associative unconscious of a social system. As Grotstein indicates "There is a dream audience who anticipates the dream and requisitions it from the dream producer in order to recognize its own problems and resonate with its own hostaged self" (2000, p. 11). Social dreaming takes Grotstein's idea further by recognising that the audience may also be the social dreaming matrix (standing for a community), and through the associative unconscious may call forth dreams through its members that resonate with an underlying social reality.

Peirce's semiotic theory

To understand dreams as signs, we need to explore more fully the nature of signs. Charles Peirce developed a wide ranging semiotic theory (theory of signs) as "an account of signification, representation, reference and meaning." (Stanford Encyclopedia of Philosophy). Although Peirce did not develop his semiotics in relation to dreams, some basic ideas within this theory shall be discussed as background to their use in understanding dreams.

The basic form of a sign consists of a triadic unity of "sign-vehicle", an "object" and an "interpretant". For Peirce, the sign is constituted of all these three together, not just the sign-vehicle. They are tri-dependent and not reducible to any pair. Peirce's sign-vehicle is what we might normally think of as a sign; for example, a word; a gesture; a logo; smoke (as a sign of fire). An object in this schema is an aspect or phenomenon associated with the sign-vehicle. For instance, a closed door might be a sign-vehicle for the fact that the room's occupant wants privacy.

For Peirce, an object determines the sign in the sense that the object puts constraints on the capacity of the sign to signify or create meaning. The fact that the occupant of the room closed the door constrains the ability of the closed door to signify its meaning. In our example, the *possibility* of a wish for privacy by the occupant of the room, constrains the meaning of the closed door. The door of course might be closed because the occupant is out or asleep. In this case the sign would not operate as a sign that the occupant wanted privacy. It wouldn't be *that* sign. A different sign-vehicle might occur (hence a different sign). The sign-vehicle might be a closed door with a note on it that says the occupant is out. This brings us to the third part of a sign: the interpretant. Basically, the interpretant is the meaning generated by the sign about the relation of the sign-vehicle to its object. There are many elements to a closed door. Its size and colour; its age, history and patina. But it is the element of closure that enables it to operate as a sign for the particular object of the possibility of the occupant's wish for privacy. The interpretant is the meaning generated – in this case, the meaning that the room's occupant wants privacy. The interpretant can then become a sign for another process of semiosis or sign generation.

Semiotics does not just address the social. For example, a tropism in a plant such as growth towards the light demonstrates the presence of a sign. The sign-vehicle is the sunlight, the object is the plant's movement and the interpretant is the biological makeup of the plant that turns it toward the light. No thinking is involved. It is a Peircean example of thirdness, Signs are natural phenomena and for Peirce the social/nature distinction is artificial. The "social" is really a part of nature. This may link to dreams felt directly in the soma prior to any symbolisation (see Chapter 3 in this book).

Peirce's theory articulates signs in three major forms: iconic, indexical and symbolic.

An icon resembles what it stands for. Many road signs are iconic. A picture of a kangaroo means that there are kangaroos in the area. A hand held high with palm out means stop. The form of a woman on a door indicates female toilets.

An indexical sign relates to its object causally or existentially. For instance, smoke has a causal relation to fire. A smell may indicate a particular animal to another animal. The smell (sign-vehicle) and the animal (object) are existentially linked. Indexical signs may be known instinctually or they may be learned. In essence, there is a correlation within the sign between the sign-vehicle and the object.

Symbols are related to their objects by convention. Generally, words are learned links to something – an object, an emotion, another word. So, words are true symbols; as are coins or mathematical signs. The symbol arbitrarily stands for the signified.

How might we then understand dreams as signs in the Peircean sense? The following two dreams were reported on-line to a closed list following the Paris bombings of 2015.

Dream 1

I dreamt I was on a bus sitting next to a proud father holding a baby. When I looked closely the baby girl's body was repeated upside down. Whichever way you held her there was another head at the other end of the body. She seemed quite content, but I worried how she would survive or grow with 2 heads opposite each other.

*I went into the university and saw a large hall spread with blankets and many stu-
dents watching. In the middle was a naked man with brown hair. Then the rest of the
blankets were covered with body-parts, fingers, hands, arms, feet, all there to demonstrate
the variety of genetic links between people. I knew the baby was going to be part of the
display and I was worried that the proud father would be ashamed at being part of a
laboratory demonstration.*

Dream 2

*I am making, or reconstituting, a bomb. I tie it with transparent nylon thread,
securely knot the thread, and prepare to lower the bomb out of the window. I realise my
fingerprints are all over it, and that if it goes off, my DNA will be on the fragments and
so enable the police to identify me. I think 'I should have worn gloves,' but then I feel
that even with gloves on I could not have eliminated every trace of my DNA from every
fragment.*

The images in these dreams might include those regarded as iconic, indexical
and symbolic, depending on how one interprets them. For example, a proud father
holding a baby might be seen as a sign-vehicle for the object of paternal love.
Shame as a result of a demonstration of body parts might be indexical; and DNA,
being everywhere, and being a linguistic convention, might be seen as symbolic of
biological connections between humans. Of course, each of these images might be,
and probably are representative of all three – icons, indexes or symbols – such is
the complexity of signs discovered in dreams – and any interpretation can only be
at best a hypothesis. In social dreaming meaning is not achieved through a singular
interpretation, but through the multiple associations that access the associative
unconscious and allow the group or community to make conscious connections.

I collected several dreams from people on the above-mentioned list involved in
the week following the Paris bombings.

- Just over half of the dreams contained family members, often with anxieties
  about them (12).
- Many dreams had anxieties about babies and children (6).
- There is violence in many of the dreams – threats, dismemberment, dangers of
  things falling or crashing.
- There are dreams of people helping others (6).
- There are other dreams where people can't find help.

What might be made of this mini exploration? Clearly the bombings made
people anxious, particularly for the welfare of their nearest and dearest. The dreams
might have been attempts to deal with the trauma as suggested by Langs (1988)
and Revonusou (2000). They may also have used the trauma as a vehicle for the
symbolisation of other unconscious fears or desires as suggested by Freud. But an
association made by one of the dreamers made a connection to the idea of the
dreams as presented and discussed together as signifying shared trauma, the possibility of hope and a healing connection for the community of dreamers.

I listened to a radio program about a man who over sixty years ago survived a shipwreck off the coast of Tasmania. After a horrendous trip in a life raft they finally arrived at a shore. They collapsed on the shore and were amazed the next morning that they had all had the same dream. It was of helicopters rescuing the group. In the midst of trauma – even then two of them died before being found – the dream connected them.

As described, a sign includes an interpretant which mediates and gives meaning to the relation between the sign-vehicle and its object. I said that the dream contains many signs – icons, indexes and symbols – but in a more holistic sense it is the dream as a whole that may be a sign; its object being discovered through the associations and connections of the social dreaming matrix and the associative unconscious. It is the dream as remembered, articulated, associated to or interpreted that is the sign. The parts of that sign are: the sign-vehicle (the dream as reported); the sign object being the pattern of associations and connections; the interpretant mediates the dreams with the associations and connections and gives rise to the meaning that emerges. So, in these terms, I see the matrix as the interpretant. Social dreaming is a method for discovering the social meaning of dreams.

Meaning, experience and the nature of thinking

Signs create meaning. While in everyday life we are most interested in the meanings created because they form the basis of our communications, beliefs, values, decisions and actions, it is the process of thinking and meaning formation that is of greater interest to philosophers and scientists. Peirce, as philosopher is interested in the creation of meaning. While Peirce's semiotic work has been examined from a psychoanalytic stance (see for example, Muller and Brent 2000; Colapietro 2006) the relation of his thinking to that of Wilfred Bion (from whom Gordon Lawrence derived much of his inspiration) has been attempted only sporadically. Muller and Brent's book primarily uses a Freudian perspective and as Rothschild (2003) points out the unconscious of Freud is very different from the unconscious of Peirce. But the more "cosmic unconscious" of Peirce is much closer to the infinite unconscious of Wilfred Bion and Gordon Lawrence than the unconscious of Freud.

For Bion, thought is a transformation of emotion. Raw emotional data – beta elements – are transformed through alpha function into dream thoughts and alpha elements and the distinction between conscious and unconscious is made possible (Bion 1962a). This transformation is at the basis of the capacity to think (Bion 1962b). In this theory, dreaming is not just a night-time activity but occurs unconsciously throughout the day. It is the continuous process of alpha function, allowing some thoughts, emotional experiences and sensory impressions – the day residue, desires, fears and thoughts about the future – to be processed unconsciously. Alpha function is a hypothetical as yet unknown process (Bion 1962a). It is different to "day-dreaming" which is a form of conscious fantasy. The dream process is the process of the alpha function. Night dreams are alpha process experienced as bodily sensations, primarily visual images. Although current neuroscientists describe some cognitive, motivational and affective processes outside of awareness (Berlin 2011), these are most likely the products of alpha function, just as are dream thoughts, pre-conceptions and conceptions. The narrative of the dream is a sense-making activity, perhaps even retrospectively formed upon waking.

Bion sees raw emotional experience as a potentiality. Some of this potentiality does not readily reach consciousness. Beta elements are those emotional experiences that are unable to be processed by alpha function and remain inchoate in the unconscious. They gain some partial form of consciousness only through hallucina-tion or those parapraxes and Freudian slips that see unconscious elements leak into consciousness. Alpha function enables the production of alpha elements, able to be brought into consciousness and developed through a meeting of pre-conceptions with reality and from there to more sophisticated forms of thinking. The process of dreaming then is fundamental and necessary for thinking.

As indicated earlier, a distinction must be drawn between the dream process and the dream that is remembered and recounted. For Freud (1900), the dream work consists of the condensation and displacement of unconscious thoughts. This work produces the manifest dream – the one that is remembered. This may again be transformed in its recounting, as words must be found to describe the dream, usually experienced as ephemeral, shifting and often rapidly disappearing from conscious attention. Often, we try to find a dream narrative, as if the dream is telling a story. Just as often we can recall only fragments. Sometimes, the dream is stark and raw; vivid in memory. The dream that is eventually described is the end product of a complex mental process. Dreaming is an ongoing process that produces dreams.

For Bion, dreaming is not yet thinking. Thinking is the process whereby "thoughts" can be "thought about". In his epistemology, he discerns a level of experience which can only be described as ineffable, unknown and infinite. He calls this "O" – ultimate reality; the godhead. Grotstein (2007) argues that "O" is the source of thoughts: "thoughts without thinkers" (Bion 1965) and that the experience in O (at-one-ment in O) is the experience of a mental activity that transcends what we normally consider to be thinking. This harks back to Schel-ling's eighteenth-century ideas about the unconscious as "unground" or God as infinite (Schelling 1942). It is, perhaps, the source of the associative unconscious in its potentiality. If our minds are able, thoughts may be entertained. They come from "O" and surprise us. We are able to work with the surprise if our mind can tolerate its newness. A mind able to do this, according to Bion, must be in a state without memory, desire or irritable reaching after understanding. What is termed negative capability.

Thinking, for Bion is not just a conscious intentional activity. A thought is rea-lised in its finite form by what he refers to as the mating of a pre-conception with a realisation. A pre-conception is a kind of nascent thought, perhaps experienced as a dream thought, perhaps a bodily sensation. Pre-conceptions are akin to Plato's perfect forms or Kant's "a priori" ideas. When the pre-conception finds a realisa-tion – when the dreaming of a touch meets the reality of a touch – a thought of the touch occurs. Following his Kleinian background, Bion talks of the infant having a pre-conception of the breast which when the breast is presented, allows the infant the thought of a breast. The infant may then be able to think that thought and have access to that thought on other occasions. It is as if the pre-conception anticipates its future; what Bion calls a memoir of the future.

In terms of Bion's theory, the practice of social dreaming is where meaning is made of reported dreams and their emotion. The images, emotions and narratives expressed, even after the secondary work done by the dreamer and whatever the personal associations of the dreamer, have connections for the matrix: the network of the associative unconscious.

Hence, there are four points in the dreaming process that we can discern:

1.   the primary or "raw" dream (Freud's "latent" content);
2.   the dream that is remembered (Freud's "manifest" content);
3.   the dream that is reported;
4.   the dream that is extended through associations and connections in the matrix: the dream extended through the associative unconscious of the interacting community.

These four points in the continuum of dream formation will be discussed more fully below. By considering Bion and social dreaming, these four "dreams" can be discerned. There may, naturally be many more dreams or versions of those dreams within the ongoing process of dream creation.

Social Dreaming as the creation of signs

If dreams are more than random disturbances of the brain or "dustbins" removing unwanted neural connections (such as proposed by Crick and Michison 1983), but are signs (natural or symbolic) then how then are these signs created? What are the sign-vehicles, objects and interpretants that make them signs?

I have argued in this chapter for the dreaming process to be considered as a continuum with four major points. I will elaborate these:

1.   What I am calling the "raw dream" begins the process. Different theorists give different explanations of this raw dream which may be a bodily sensation, an emotion (Hartmann 2008; Bion 1962b), a repressed or simple wish (Freud 1900); even a desire for solutions to problems (Barrett 1993) or for trauma relief (Langs 1988; Revonsuo 2000). This is the initial "dream"; not yet a thought, nor even necessarily an image, but perhaps a kind of natural sign stimulating what Bion calls the alpha process of dreaming. Freud named this the latent content of the dream. In the case of the raw dream, the sign-vehicle is the initial unconscious form of the dream, unknowable to the conscious mind; the object would be the sensation, emotion or desire; the interpretant would be the alpha process of transformation.

2. The formation of the dream "as experienced" is complex. Freud claims that the day residue – thoughts, images or emotions left over from the day, join with the wish and thus create dream images. The dream as experienced is what he terms the manifest content. For Bion, dream thoughts are communicated as images which are the manifest content of the dream. In waking life, pre-conceptions waiting, as it were, to become thoughts, concretised in reality, are based upon such dream thoughts. The sign-vehicle is the dream as experienced; the object would be the sensation, emotion or desire; the interpretant would be the dream narrative or the particular pattern of images produced, including words, numbers, sensations or even music. This interpretant is influenced by the personal history of the dreamer, the social context and the thoughts, symbols and narratives available from the culture of the dreamer.

3. The dream "as reported" is another part of the continuum of dream development. For Freud, the work of secondary revision changes the dream from the moment we start to recall it. In the report that the dreamer gives him or herself, thoughts and images unacceptable to consciousness are repressed or defensively transformed. Due to the social unconscious described by Fromm (1962) and Hopper (2003) some thoughts that are unacceptable to the group may be repressed. In the report given to others, some elements of the dream may be consciously discarded or changed for a variety of reasons including shame, guilt, social sensitivities and political reasons. But the dream as reported is now in a consciously accessible form. The dream as reported becomes the sign-vehicle, the object is the expressed dream meaning and the interpretant is the network of possible meanings available and accessible to the dreamer/reporter for whom the dream is a sign. It should be noted that the social unconscious as described by Fromm and Hopper is different from the associative unconscious insofar as it, the former, is the unconscious formulation and operation of social rules and mores that become instituted and hence affect behaviour through constraint and motivation; while the latter is a broad semiotic field shared by an interacting community. The social unconscious may restrict or allow associations; the associative unconscious exists as a potential and actual semiotic field.

4. The dream, extended in the social context, brings yet further transformations. The dream moves from being an experience of the dreamer to becoming a representation or sign of something for the community in the social dreaming matrix, or whatever form a community might have for sharing dreams, and from them to the broader community. Social dreaming is a method whereby dreams can be presented to a matrix of people from an interacting community. In the matrix, dreams are reported and matrix members associate to the dreams and make connections between them. The matrix is basically a container or place for things to grow. In the social dreaming matrix, social meaning is grown. The dreams as they evolve are the sign-vehicles, the object is the unconscious of the dreaming community and the interpretant is the

matrix. This is despite there being many people in the matrix – perhaps each with their own "interpretations" or ways of making meaning - in social dreaming it is the matrix as a whole with its thinking and emergent meaning that is the Peircean interpretant.

5. Essentially, the matrix is formed from the associative unconscious of the represented community. This associative unconscious, as previously described, is a network of all signs and symbols available to that community. In the case of the social dreaming matrix, these signs and symbols are drawn upon – through the process of free association – in order to find new connections and associations; to extend the dreams, to discover new meanings and to use these new meanings for better understanding society. In the matrix, the restrictions on free association are the usual ones: repression; suppression; thoughts disallowed through social pressure and influence, limitations due to technologies as yet uncreated and biological limitations. The dream thus extended in the matrix becomes a sign for the community. Out of this meaning emerges.

Social Dreaming and creativity

In this section, I expand upon the idea of the associative unconscious and its links to creativity. Dreaming is a way into the associative unconscious: "a mental network of thoughts, signs, symbols and signifiers able to give rise to feelings, impulses and images" (Long and Harney 2013, p. 30). It is a network shared by any interacting community through their shared language, history, myths, emotions and experiences, and, as Jung argues in his concept of the collective unconscious, runs across all cultures at some deeply unconscious levels. Unlike Jung's collective unconscious though, the associative unconscious is not so much biologically determined and identical in all individuals as culturally built; each individual holding only a part of it – albeit an overlapping part with others. We each contain aspects of our culture and need to collaborate with one another to overcome many obstacles in order to access the whole.

> *The associative unconscious is the infinite of human thought in all its possibilities. For individuals, their capacities and histories may cause repression of that portion of the associative unconscious which they may have initially gained access to but are now unable to tolerate. At times, a psychotic function or process may deny access or alternatively swamp the individual or group in the network such that normal thinking is precluded. For many, the constraints of particular cultures such as national, corporate, gender or familial cultures pose barriers to access. However, because of the associative unconscious (that which is implicate but not yet conscious) new thoughts and new combinations of thought are possible. Hence, the associative unconscious is the crucible of creativity.*
>
> (Long and Harney 2013, pp. 31–2)

The associative unconscious as accessed is not, of course complete (the complete of all potentiality is perhaps impossible to access – Bion's "O"), and the gaps that are covered over and that are accompanied by existential angst (Freud 1900; Boxer 2014) are certainly part of the idea of the associative unconscious and its links to the repressed unconscious of psychoanalysis. But the idea of completion is an ideal form – a potentiality for all thought across all time: a possibility to be yearned for at a more spiritual than psychological level. Any one community or organisation has only its incomplete pictures, its gaps and its yearnings.

Just as Freud (1900) sees dreams as the "royal road" to the repressed or dynamic unconscious of the individual, so when shared and associations are made, dreams become the passage to the associative unconscious with its possibilities of new combinations and connections.

How then does social dreaming give access to new ideas? Here we return to Peirce and his ideas of abductive logic. Abduction generates possibilities and hypotheses beginning with a surprising fact. In simple terms, something is noticed (attended to) that is surprising or unusual. We then guess at why this unusual occurrence, event or "thing" has come about. If the guess is a reasonable explanation insofar as if our guess were true then the occurrence, event or "thing" would not be surprising, then we may accept it.

> *A surprising fact, C, is observed.*
> *But if H were true, then C would be a matter of course*
> *So, … (hypothetically) … H is true.*
>
> *(Peirce 1984: CP 5.189)*

Of course, there may be alternative hypotheses and they may have to be tested. That is the work of normal science. But the creative start to any new discovery is the initial abduction. Take, for example, the surprise that came to Fleming that led to the discovery of penicillin.

> *Returning from holiday on September 3, 1928, Fleming began to sort through petri dishes containing colonies of Staphylococcus, bacteria that cause boils, sore throats and abscesses. He noticed something unusual on one dish. It was dotted with colonies, save for one area where a blob of mould was growing. The zone immediately around the mould –later identified as a rare strain of Penicillium notatum –was clear, as if the mould had secreted something that inhibited bacterial growth.*
>
> *(American Chemical Society 2016)*

This observation and the thoughts that came with it surprised Fleming. His mind was able to receive and think the new thought that the mould was secreting something that upon later investigation became known as penicillin. His reasoning was a case of abduction. His receptive mind came from both his experience as a scientist, his close observation and his readiness to be open to new ideas.

This description bears similarities to Bion's idea, described earlier, that "thoughts" (without thinkers) may surprise us and that in order to accept and think these thoughts our minds must be in a state of receptivity: in a state of negative capability. It is this state of negative capability that prepares the mind for the creative leap toward the new idea. Whereas the scientist can be open to new thoughts from close observation of and receptivity toward the "surprises" in nature; and the psychoanalyst can be open to new thoughts from close observation of and receptivity toward the internal world of the analytic pair (what Bion refers to as non-sensory intuition), it is the leap of intuition from the surprise to the hypothesis that is the basis of creativity. So too the social dreamer can be open to new thoughts from close observation of and receptivity toward the surprises in the dreams; and, in essence, dreams are always surprising. The social dreaming matrix is designed to facilitate such a receptive state of mind in its participants, through its physical distribution of chairs so that participants are not facing one another, and more importantly through its injunction to free associate.

Closing

As this chapter has shown, dreams are variously regarded as signs of the future, intimations of immortality, signs of guidance or warning to the dreamer, signs for the community and connections to the natural world. I would like then to put forward a hypothesis using Peirce's abductive logic formulation. If our minds share in a transcendental state of pre-conceptions, nomina, a priori thoughts waiting to find a receptacle where they can be realized, and if dreams are directly related to such a state, then dreams may also be memoirs of the future for our dreaming communities. Following Peircan abductive logic:

> Let C = the surprising new thoughts prompted by sharing of dreams in a matrix.
> H = dreams are signs from a mental activity that transcends what we normally consider to be "thinking".
> And, if H is true then C (i.e., the idea that sharing of dreams in a matrix prompts new thoughts about an interacting community) would be a matter of course.

So hypothetically H is true. Dreams are signs from a mental activity that transcends what we normally consider to be "thinking". They can give us access to new ways of thinking about and apprehending our futures.

Note

1 I sometimes refer to meaning being discovered and sometimes to meaning being created. This is the curious paradox of 'meaning' because it is both discovered and created simultaneously. I relate this to Donald Winnicott's ideas of the transitional object and transitional space. Moreover, 'Meaning' is found in the social. As with language, it belongs to the social system and is appropriated by the individual.

References

American Chemical Society www.acs.org/content/acs/en/education/whatischemistry/la ndmarks/flemingpenicillin.html.

Armstrong, D. (1998). In W.G. Lawrence (ed.) *Social Dreaming @ Work*. London: Karnac Books.

Barrett, D. (1993). "The 'Commitment of Sleep': A study of dream incubation for problem solving" *Dreaming* 3(2) www.ncbi.nlm.nih.gov/pubmed/11515147 (recovered 20/11/2016).

Berlin, H. (2011). "The Neural Basis of the Dynamic Unconscious" *Neuropsychoanalysis* 13 (1) pp. 5–71.

Bion, W.R. (1962a). *Learning from Experience*. London: Heinemann Medical Books.

Bion, W.R. (1962b). "A Theory of Thinking" in *Second Thoughts: Selected papers on psycho-analysis*. London: Heinemann, 110–119.

Bion, W.R. (1965). *Transformations*. London: Heinemann (Reprinted London: Karnac 1984).

Boxer, P. (2014). "What Makes an Economy a 'Libidinal' Economy" *Lacanticles*www.laca nticles.com/category/identification/.

Brody, H. (2013). *Maps and Dreams*. BC: Douglas and McIntyre.

Colapietro, V. (2006). "Pragmatism and Psychoanalysis – C.S. Peirce as a mediating figure" *Cognitio* 7(2) pp. 189–205.

Crick, F. and Michison, G. (1983). "The Function of Dream Sleep" *Nature* 30(4) pp. 111–114.

Freud, S. (1900). *The Interpretation of Dreams*. London: Hogarth Press and the Institute of Psychoanalysis.

Fromm, E. (1962). *Beyond the Chains of Illusion: My encounter with Marx and Freud*. New York: Simon & Schuster.

Grotstein, J.S. (2000). *Who is the Dreamer Who Dreams the Dream: A study of psychic presences*. Hillsdale, NJ: Analytic Press.

Grotstein, J.S. (2007). *A Beam of Intense Darkness: Wilfred Bion's legacy to psychoanalysis*. London: Karnac.

Hailes, J. Unpublished PhD thesis RMIT University Library, Melbourne Australia.

Hartmann, E. (2008). "The Nature and Functions of Dreaming" in D. Barrett (ed.) *The New Science of Dreaming III*. New York: Praeger Publishing, 171–192.

Hopper, E. (2003). *The Social Unconscious. International library of group analysis 22*. London: Jessica Kingsley Publishers.

Langs, R. (1988). *Decoding Your Dreams: A revolutionary technique for understanding your dreams*. New York: Henry Holt and Company.

Long, S.D. and Harney, M. (2013) 'The Associative Unconscious" in S.D. Long (ed.) *Socioanalytic Methods*. London: Karnac.

MIT News (2001). http://news.mit.edu/2001/dreaming.

Muller, J. and Brent, J. (2000). (eds.) *Peirce, Semiotics and Psychoanalysis*. Baltimore: John Hopkins University Press.

Peirce, C.S. (1984). *Writings of Charles S. Peirce 1867–1871: A chronological edition volume 2*. Bloomington: Indiana University Press.

Revonsuo, A. (2000). 'The Reinterpretation of Dreams: An evolutionary hypothesis of the function of dreaming' *Behavioural Brain Science* 23(6) pp. 904–1121.

Roheim, G. (1952). *The Gates of the Dream*. International University Press. Rothschild, L. (2003). "Peirce, Semiotics and Psychoanalysis (Book Review)" *Psychoanalysis*. New York: American Psychological Association.

Schelling, F.W.J. (1942). *The Ages of the World*. F. de Wolfe Bowman Jnr. (Trans.) New York: Columbia University Press.

Tarter, M.L. (2007). "Gerona's 'Night Journeys: The power of dreams in transatlantic Quaker culture' – book review" *Quaker Studies* 11(2) Article 12. Available at: http://digitalcommons.georgefox.edu/quakerstudies/vol11/iss2/12.

Tedlock, B. (1987). "Dreaming and Dream Research" in B. Tedlock (ed.) *Dreaming: Anthropological and psychological interpretations*. Cambridge: Cambridge University Press.

Wax, M.L. (2004). "Dream Sharing as Social Practice" *Dreaming* 14(2–3) pp. 83–93. http://dx.doi.org/10.1037/1053-0797.14.2-3.83.

2

ASSOCIATIVE THINKING

A Deleuzian perspective on social dreaming

Julian Manley

Introduction

Social dreaming is a way of thinking. As soon as we accept this from the beginning we can work towards creating a theory of the phenomena of social dreaming which takes us away from the distraction of the idea of the dream as being in some sense a mystifying and/or mystical abstract representation of something which is so ineffable and confusing that it might as well be nothing. The purpose of this chapter is to reassess the nature and validity of the thoughts emerging in dreams that are shared in the context or container of a social dreaming matrix, and in doing so create a theory of social dreaming, or at least to make a start in this direction. Long (in this volume) and Long and Harney (2013), focus on a semiotic approach that takes as its basis the philosophy of Charles Peirce applied to social dreaming, including his theories of abductive reasoning, and sign-vehicles. However, in this chapter I want to concentrate on the use and meaning of the term "association" in the context of social dream-ing. Long and Harney (ibid) have also noted the importance of associative thinking to social dreaming and have coined the useful term "associative unconscious" to describe a key feature of the thinking process in psychosocial thinking or socioanalysis. The theory of social dreaming that I wish to pursue in this chapter concentrates on this aspect of social dreaming, not so much on the dreams themselves within the matrix as individual objects or signs to be shared by the participants in social dreaming, but the gaps in between, the links, connections and relationships that are developed through associative thinking that lead to the transformation of the dreams from single objects into living processes that constitute thinking: moving fragments of thought in con-stant flows of never-ending incompletion.

Thought as process

One of the difficulties of understanding and using social dreaming lies in our attitude towards what constitutes a valid or "objective" thought. The reductionism associated with many traditional forms of scientific enquiry, with their roots in Cartesian approaches to thinking, renders the thought processes of social dreaming unusable due to the impossibility of paring away the meaning from the multiple possibilities that dreams contain both within themselves as individual dreams and, even more so, as a complex collage of inter-connected and multi-faceted dream images. The meaning of a dream is notoriously difficult to be certain about. The very nature of dreams, through what Freud dubbed "condensation" (Freud 1953, pp. 279–305) is opposed to the thought process that would wish to slice away superfluous material and eliminate ambiguity to reach for clarity of meaning: to be able to say "this means that" in a manner of thinking that closely resembles Cartesian patterns of cause and effect. A contrary process governs the meaning of the collected dreams in a social dreaming matrix. Understanding is embedded within the accumulated contents of the dreams and associations as they are shared in the matrix. Its sense reveals itself periodically in spontaneous moments of affective intensity and in conjunction with other meanings within the same matrix by the ways each participant in a matrix perceives or rather intuits the developing collage of associations that form as the matrix proceeds. And once formed, such meanings may dissolve in order to create further or other meanings, which may then dissolve or remain or mutate into further thoughts and feelings as the process of accumulation of dreams continues in the matrix. As a process, the meanings are therefore never static but always on the move.

When the matrix is over, the multitude of meanings are still in flux, even if they are stilled temporarily by a different process, that of the "Dream Reflection Dialogue", or another more cognitive reflection that might take place after the matrix. In the Dream Reflection Dialogue, the "reverie" (Bion 1970) of the matrix is replaced with a more conscious state of reflection that brings us back into a mode of thinking that we are more used to in our day-to-day activities. In this second stage process, the matrix becomes a group that begins an inter-pretative process by sharing and contrasting personal sense-making with other people's experiences of the dreams in the matrix. In this stage of thinking, the multifarious thoughts, images and feelings of the matrix are, to a certain extent at least, distilled, channelled and categorised into thoughts that can be taken away and used. In Bion's language (ibid), the Beta elements of unprocessed thoughts of the matrix are being transformed into Alpha elements which can then become part of the stuff of daily life. Due to the inherent complexity of the dreams, associations and the way these are weaved together in the matrix, some Beta elements will remain, and yet more will be in limbo as thoughts that are both emerging and yet to emerge. There is never a completely rounded and definitive solution to the problems raised in the matrix. There are only ways forward and new insights that can be taken away and applied to each individual's relationship with and understanding of her social environment.

Understanding meaning as process rather than an end is, therefore, an essential element of this theory. This is not necessarily an easy way of considering thought, since it challenges a scientific way of thinking that prizes logic and rationality above all other thought. However, neither is this attitude completely new. Wittgenstein famously concluded that words were limited in their expression and sometimes became "language games" when they reached the limits of the rational. In discussing "language games", Wittgenstein emphasised the special "game" of dreaming; how dreams bring us to the limits of language and reasoning through language by presenting impossibilities or absurdities together in images:

> *What this language primarily describes is a picture. What is to be done with the picture, how it is to be used is still obscure. Quite clearly, however, it must be explained if we want to understand the sense of what we are saying. But the picture seems to spare us this work: it already points to a particular use. This is how it takes us in.*
> *(Wittgenstein 1953, p. 157)*

Susan Langer's seminal work, *Philosophy in a New Key* (1948), also pointed to the special "meanings" that could only be transmitted through the arts:

> *Really new ideas have their own modes of appearance in the unpredictable creative mind.*
> *(p. 164)*

These "really new ideas", do not, according to Langer, emerge from the use of language, which is the instrument of reason:

> *Language, in its literal capacity, is a stiff and conventional medium, unadapted to the expression of genuinely new ideas, which usually have to break in upon the mind through some great and bewildering metaphor.*
> *(p. 164)*

The clue that links this to social dreaming is the idea of new ideas emerging from metaphor. There is no sense to much of the social dreaming matrix except through a poetic sensitivity to metaphor or figurative language in general, for the dream is better understood in this way. For Langer, it is not language but music, in its non-representational expression that brings the individual closer to emotion. Indeed, there is a certain musicality to the expression of dreams in the matrix. Just as music is understood through the interconnectivities between the notes, so too do the dreams make sense through the way the social dreaming matrix allows for interconnectivity between them. In music, we may not be able to give meaning to the notes (with some exceptions, as for example programme music, there is no clear meaning to music) but we nevertheless react and respond and gain an affective understanding of sorts; so too in social dreaming. We have therefore alternative ways of approaching knowledge, as long as we understand that the use of language in the matrix is figurative in nature and affective in quality. In other words, although we inhabit a world of knowledge-making in social dreaming, it is a form of cognition that is not subject to the rules of language in its "literal capacity".

This alternative way to knowledge has been the subject of other thinkers' pre-occupations in recent years, not related to social dreaming but nevertheless relevant. Some have sought to demonstrate how cognition needs to be understood as more than what emerges from the rational brain (LeDoux 1999; Damasio 2000); that cognition should include information that is harnessed through its embodiment in the being, including the nervous system (Varela et al 1993; Nuñez & Freeman 1999); through sensitivity to understanding through affect (Damasio 2003); and even through a sense of our inter-relationality with our environment. (Roszak, Gomes & Kanner 1995) Even some branches of post-modern continental philosophy, especially in the work of Gilles Deleuze, question the primacy of logic and elevate the value of creativity. For Deleuze, a primary function of the philosopher is the creation of new concepts, which is why his philosophical works often seem to border on the metaphorical or creative (Deleuze & Guattari 1994). Similarly, Deleuze's world of created concepts consists largely of a panorama – or in his words a "rhizome" on a "plateau" – of affect that moves thinking away from cognition and towards intensities of affectivity in a Spinozian sense of the word (Deleuze & Guattari 1988; Deleuze 1988). It is these kinds of processes that make up the collage of multi-layered meanings that are embedded in the images of the social dreaming process, meanings that are communicated through what I have previously dubbed "image-affects" (Manley 2009).

If, then, the language of social dreaming – its dreams and associations – is indeed that of created thoughts and figurative language, embodiment and affect, our approach and attitude towards the knowledge within the social dreaming experience cannot be that of the habitual and rational. It is at this point, therefore, that I return to an approach based on the understanding that associative thinking can bring to social dreaming.

Associative thinking

The use of free association in dream work comes, of course, from Freud's dictum to his patients that:

> *We therefore tell him that the success of the psychoanalysis depends on his noticing and reporting whatever comes into his head and not be misled, for instance, into suppressing an idea because it strikes him as unimportant or irrelevant or because it seems to him meaningless.*
> *(Freud 1953 p. 100)*

A version of this process is in play in the social dreaming matrix. Instead of interpreting the meaning of a dream, a participant in the matrix will either offer another dream that seems somehow (inexplicably perhaps) related, or offer a spontaneous association to another's dream, where the connection might be as implicit as explicit. This is done without attention to rational or logical thought, and with no desire for overt meaning making. The connection between this mode of proceeding – which, in

Freud's case, was about unearthing the repressions that prevent a patient from leading a healthy life – and the creation of new thoughts first emerged in André Breton's artistic circle of surrealists in the early twentieth century. Instead of focussing on the dyadic relationship between analyst and analysand and the clinical repression of the latter, Breton's group would use associative techniques such as "automatic writing" and the "automatic message" in an attempt to avoid what they understood as being strictures of standard thought and to allow creativity to freely emerge into new patterns of expression. The "automatic messages" included illustrations, while "automatic writing" concentrated on words, and the combination shows the emphasis this technique placed on the visual (Breton 1933 [1997]; Breton and Soupault 1920 [1997]), just as dreams may begin as a narrative but often end up being remembered for their visual impact. The results of automatic writing can often sound like dreams:

> *I leave the halls of Dolo with grandfather very early in the morning. The kid would like a surprise. Those halfpenny cornets have not failed to have a great influence on my life. The innkeeper's name is Tyrant. I often find myself in this beautiful room with the volume measurements. The coloured reproduction on the wall is a reverie that always makes a reappearance…*
>
> *(Opening to "Seasons" in Breton and Soupault ibid, p. 67)*

A similar process of associative thinking in the social dreaming matrix is what creates new thoughts, these being one of the stated objectives of the matrix. There is a link, therefore between associations and creative thinking. Because these associations exist in the context of *social* dreaming, there is also a link between the social and associative thinking. For some social scientists, this link is what brings them to question the very nature of the social. In the case of Bruno Latour, for example, the word "social" needs to be reconfigured as "association". In trying to redefine sociology, Latour struggles with terms such as "sociology of associations" and wishes he could use the term "associology" (Latour 2005, p. 9). What Latour is attempting is a new, contemporary and more valid understanding of the word "social" as being equivalent to or better expressed as a network of associations that, like the associations in social dreaming, are in a constant state of flux. For Latour, the word "social" has outlived its usefulness. It has been transformed into a restricted object that is used to define a thing that does not really exist:

> *What is called "social explanation" has become a counter-productive way to interrupt the movement of associations instead of resuming it.*
>
> *(ibid p. 8)*

In a way that reminds me of social dreaming, Latour suggests that the rigidity of "explanation" actually removes the flowing, multi-faceted layers of meaning that come with the "movement of associations". In social dreaming, this would be the way that interpretation would interrupt the movement of images, thoughts and feelings of the dreams and associations by giving meaning or explanation which would foreclose further meaning-making by reducing its sense to a particular moment in the matrix. By doing so, the potential for the dream or association to influence the development of meaning after the foreclosure of interpretation is stymied and the very nature of this process of knowledge creation is curtailed. This is why an experienced host (the word for "facilitator" in social dreaming) in a social dreaming matrix will do everything in her power to provide working hypotheses, (as opposed to hypotheses to be tested and proved), instead of interpretations. As has been explained elsewhere – see Lawrence (2005, pp. 35–37) for an initial definition; Long and Harney (2013) for a discussion informed by Peirce – the working hypothesis opens out a sense of fluid mean-making that constitutes the very essence of the social dreaming process. Another way of understanding the function of the working hypothesis is through associative thinking. That is to say, the reason the hypothesis is a working one that has no intention of being proved is because it recognises that a particular collage of associations of a given moment – the one of the hypothesis – is only the prevalent sense of the matrix at a particular time that also recognises the shifting nature of these associations in a future time of the matrix process.

It should be pointed out that Latour's ideas in this regard are not completely new. He supports his "associology" with thoughts from the work of semi-forgotten philosopher Gabriel Tarde, pointing out the vital importance of inter-relationality and movement in Tarde's work. For Tarde, the social "was not a special domain of reality but a principle of connections … sociology was in effect a kind of inter-psychology" and was even described as "circulating fluid" (Latour 2005, p. 13). In social dreaming, the dreams and associations can also usefully be described as a circulating fluid, and their associative strength is partly based on the maintenance of this fluidity. A working hypothesis that might be offered by a host in the social dreaming matrix facilitates fluidity by emphasising the links and connections of the flow of associations rather than stemming them through a series of interpretations. To offer interpretations would be like constructing a series of dams or weirs in a flowing stream.

A heterotopian collage of image-affects

The image of the flowing stream is not, however, complete as a description of the flow of association in the social dreaming matrix. Returning to Tarde, we are reminded that the fluidity is circulating. This in turn reminds us of another feature of the associative thinking in the matrix, that of the tendency of the associations to become linked through randomly created connections between the dreams and associations. The associations are not inter-connected solely through a sense of a linear passing of time, and the result is not merely a straightforward sequence of ideas. It is *un*like a flowing stream. Instead, such associations are often created spontaneously as a result of the many multilayers of imagery that exist within each dream. Associations then begin to emerge and become relevant in unexpected ways in the course of the matrix as a whole. An image from a dream may be more relevant to another dream or association that might occur at any point in the matrix including a point that is far removed from its immediate sequentiality. The following example, taken from Karolia and Manley (2018) illustrates this. In this social dreaming matrix, hosted in the context of the Muslim community in England, my colleague and I were seeking to understand how British Muslims felt about their Muslim and British identities in the wake of terrorist attacks in Europe. Each intervention is signalled by a dash. The line numbers of the transcript indicate the sequences and the jumps:

9   - *I had another dream, we were at the train station, and then I got lost and*
10   *then some old lady came and she goes are you alright and then and then I was*
11   *ducking away from the cops and I found my sister.*
12   - *I had a dream that I bought a really expensive pair of shoes and they got*
13   *stolen, before I could even wear them.*
14   - *I had a dream, that I was in jail, and then I smashed the wall and I escaped. I*
15   *passed out and then they put me back in jail.*

★★★

38   - *I had a dream, my father's a cop. He was in the police car, and he was*
39   *driving around shooting people. I was watching a movie before I went to sleep.*
40   *And then the people turned into zombies.*
41   - *That reminds me of when people who are terrorists they think they're*
42   *going to be in heaven, they're like zombies*
42   - *I had a dream that Donald Trump became president, scared the hell out of me.*

A working hypothesis from these two extracts might be that for British Muslims the police embody fear, persecution and lack of certainty about the fairness of authority, as indicated by "ducking from the cops" and the impossibility of escaping from jail. Later in the matrix this is picked up again in the dream of the father as a cop, which adds a twist to the first dreams of persecution and authority, since in the latter example the cop is the dreamer's father. When the figure of authority is both a murderous cop and a father, the fear and persecution become embodied in the figure of Donald Trump, the fearful authority of the "free" world. This dream was offered before Trump's election to the Presidency.

There may be other elements that could be suggested and deduced from the dreams to add to this working hypothesis, but the point I want to emphasise is that the hypothesis has been created by a collage of associations that is not immediately sequential. In order to get there, we have had to go from a sequential block of lines 9–15 to lines 38–42. In our minds, then, these blocks are extracted from the logic of the time sequence of their expression (which at its most rational proceeds from line to line) and respond instead to another pattern of thought. Such a pattern then resembles more a collage of associations that is the fruit of associative thinking that emerges from the associative unconscious than to a rational, linear train of thought. It is up to the participants in the matrix to create these patterns since they are not explicit or given; they are not the result of language in its literal capacity.

The ensuing patterns resemble a collage of associations that has been created from the space of the social dreaming matrix. The creation of this collage of associations between the image-affects of the matrix is like a Foucauldian heterotopia, where disparate elements find form and meaning through the links and connections made by the participants of the matrix. It is a space of knowledge that Foucault would describe as an "archaeology", that is to say an epistemology that does not rely on sequences of logic. Instead of this, "archaeology" addresses itself "to the general space of knowledge, to its configurations, and to the mode of being of the things that appear in it (Foucault 2002, p. xxv). This is what Foucault called "the pure experience of order and its modes of being" (ibid, p. xxiii), where disparate elements are given sense by the creative will of the mind. In the social dreaming matrix this is the creative and shared mindset of the participants, an example of heterotopias which

> secretly undermine language, because they make it impossible to name this and that, because they shatter or tangle common names, because they destroy 'syntax' in advance and not only the syntax with which we construct sentences, but also that less apparent syntax which causes words and things (next to and also opposite to one another) to 'hold together'.
>
> *(ibid, p. xix)*

Foucault indicates the link between such heterotopias and a surrealist way of thinking by using as an example a painting by the surrealist, Salvador Dalí, which is in line with the example mentioned above of Breton's efforts at automatic writing. The painting in question, (*Sewing Machine with Umbrellas in a Surrealist Landscape*, (1941)), depicts an unlikely combination of a sewing machine and an umbrella where, "for an instant, perhaps forever, the umbrella encounters the sewing machine." (ibid, p. xix) Such unlikely combinations resonate with the way the dreams and associations in social dreaming weave, interconnect and make sense within the created space of the social dreaming matrix.

A rhizome of associative thinking

By moving away from a linear concept of expression towards the heterotopian space of the social dreaming matrix, we are able to replace linearity with what Deleuze called a "rhizome". That is to say a randomly self-selecting set of interconnected image-affects that pulse in intensity at a given moment of perception. Instead of lines of thought, Deleuze and Guattari posited the concept of the rhizome to describe a "circulation of states" (Deleuze & Guattari 1988, p. 21) that have no predestined direction, no centre, no hierarchy or guidance from any authority. This describes well both the structure of the collage of associations of the social dreaming matrix and the way it is created, i.e., through the unfettered, unguided expression of dreams and associations of the participants in the matrix, a space devoid of the authority of a leader (the host for example), who deliberately plays down any leadership role that might be expected of her in another configuration, for example that of a group. Instead, the dreams and associations are self-organising and create their own collages of potential meaning, a meaning that is constantly shifting, nevertheless, through connections that are intuitively made through a sense of their relative intensities of affect. That is to say, the language of social dreaming is predominantly visual; embedded in the images of the dreams is a condensation of affect that becomes significant to the speakers and listeners of the matrix according to how intensely they are felt. In the example quoted above, therefore, the first dream is clearly not primarily a story about escaping the police, but rather an expression of complex affect: the fear that is felt in a situation that should be designed for its opposite, the reduction and control or containment of fear, (what cops should do). The intensity of this fear is increased due to the sensation of the joining of opposites through the image in the dream: the cop produces fear. For Deleuze, these moments of intensity of affect are both rhizomatic in the way they are connected and also in a state of constant flux.

Following Spinoza, Deleuze conceived of affect as being an experience of moving emotions, shifting from greater to lesser according to the different configurations in the rhizome. Therefore, although the dream images and associations exist in the open once they have been expressed, they are never static expressions that are completed through that expression. Instead, they fluctuate or pulsate in intensity. In the example above, the most intense moment of affect comes in the dream of Donald Trump. Here, the image is not only intense in its own right; its intensity is maximised through the connections to deviant authority expressed in the dreams and images that resonate with it. It is as if the dreams of the cops, the father cop, the jail and Donald Trump all pulsate together in a moment of intensity that connects them as a single pattern despite not being connected sequentially.

The role of the host in social dreaming is to support this associative thinking, contain the associative unconscious, and create a space of absolute freedom of movement of thoughts and feelings through minimum intervention in the process. This freedom of thought that allows for the self-organisation of affect is the same as the space Deleuze called "smooth space". Deleuze distinguished this smooth space from what he called "striated space", with the former allowing a complete freedom of thought, feeling and expression, while the latter denotes a channelled and restricted, linear mode of thought (Deleuze & Guattari 1988). Finally, this movement of affect through the smooth space of the matrix becomes what Deleuze termed "nomadic". That is to say, the dreams and association of the matrix can be compared to the movement of the nomad: spontaneous, guided by the way and environment, living with uncertainty, embracing chance encounters. The dreams and associations of the matrix are thus expressed according to the feeling of when the moment is right. There is no turn taking, no guidance, no obligation to speak: things happen.

Nomads of the matrix

Taking her cue in part from Deleuze, Rosi Braidotti (2011) has centred her work on "nomadic theory". In her writings, she emphasises the positive and affirmative aspects of nomadic theory and contrasts this with the negative feel of dealing with Freudian repression as part of a psychoanalytical approach to knowledge. This echoes Gordon Lawrence's refusal to interpret dreams in the social dreaming matrix. For Lawrence, like Bion, the unconscious was so much more than a store of potential repressions. Lawrence emphasised positive outcomes that emerged from the matrix that he described as the "infinite", influenced by Bion and used as an alternative to the unconscious. Very often, then, the feeling of a social dreaming matrix is not one of negativity and angst, but rather a joy in infinite possibility, even when the content of the dreams and associations is dark or gloomy. This is close to Braidotti's concept of nomadic thinking:

> *Nomadic thought rejects the psychoanalytic idea of repressions and the negative definition of desire as lack … It borrows instead from Spinoza a positive notion of desire as an ontological force of becoming. This achieves an important goal: it makes all thinking into an affirmative activity that aims at the production of concepts, precepts, and affects in the relational motion of approaching multiple others.*
>
> (Braidotti 2011, p. 2)

An aspect of how this is achieved is undoubtedly the shared nature of the matrix, where one is able to approach multiple others. In the case of a social dreaming matrix, these multiple others constitute the whole of the matrix, the space where dreams are offered and once offered no longer belong to the dreamer. Such offerings immediately transfer to the heterotopian space of the matrix. As is well known in social dreaming circles, social dreamers are interested in the dream and not the dreamer and this is due to the shared nature of the matrix, which is unlike the expression of a personal dream in a clinical context. Within the matrix, dreams and associations are offered nomadically; the dreams are given as a response to the landscape created at any particular moment in the matrix.

As part of this nomadic process, the participants in the matrix find themselves in states of what Braidotti, following Deleuze, calls "becoming". That is to say, the image-affects of the social dreaming matrix are not interpreted cognitively but are approached intuitively and affectively through a sense of empathy and attraction that can become so intense that each participant may feel as if she is becoming a dream or a dream state or embodying the affect that is contained therein. This in part explains the sensation that many participants in social dreaming express of surprise at not only finding other people's dreams interesting but actually believing that those dreams, or the image-affects within them, actually feel like their own.

I have previously given examples of the process and effects of "becoming" in social dreaming in Manley and Trustram (2016), where in a discussion of social dreaming in the context of a museum exhibition about the abolition of the slave trade, various "becoming animals" – a crocodile, then a whale – created a feeling of empathy and understanding for the participants of what it might have been like to be a slave in the hold of a slave ship. In doing so, the participants in the matrix were able to use the collage of dreams to create combinations that together made meanings through a sense of becoming the dreams that would otherwise – in a literal capacity – have been difficult to comprehend: "becoming slave".

Conclusion

In this brief and incomplete theory of social dreaming I have intended to demonstrate how there is a need to begin with the basics of thought, the premises of what can be agreed is appropriate to call thinking. For this reason, I began by locating social dreaming ontologically in the world of embodied cognitive processes that contrast with a prevalent understanding of cognition as a Cartesian brain. If we are agreed that this mode of thinking is acceptable, then the task of understanding the nature and quality of the knowledge imparted in the process of social dreaming becomes clearer and more useful as a means of acquiring a more rounded, holistic view of the thinking process. This could lead to a richer understanding of the complexities of real life situations and consequently more effective decision-making in the context of the social dreaming matrix.

As an essential part of what this different perspective of thinking entails, I have introduced the term "associative thinking" to describe how the emergence of thoughts is created in social dreaming through the links and connections between the image-affects of the matrix rather than through interpretations of the meanings of the dreams. Instead of interpretations, I have emphasised the importance of the working hypothesis, that hints and opens out possibilities of meaning without ever foreclosing the potential of a dream or association to contribute to the accumulation of meaning that may come from making further connections with other image-affects that are expressed through further dreams in the matrix.

The process of associative thinking of the social dreaming matrix takes place in what I suggest is a space of creativity that can usefully be described, following Foucault as a heterotopia, that is to say a space where unusual connections can be made between the image-affects of dreams which make sense in the creativity of that space by making connections that would otherwise seem absurd or illogical. The connections are between expressions of affect in a Deleuzian/Spinozian sense rather than between ideas, and they are formed in what Deleuze and Guattari termed a rhizome: a non-hierarchical, self-organising, collage of interconnections between different intensities of affect transmitted through the dream images. The journeys of these image-affects into meaning emerge as a result of a freedom of movement which is facilitated by the nature of the social dreaming matrix as a "smooth space". That is to say a space of unrestricted movement, which is nomad-like in the sense that it guides itself intuitively and according to context and the creativity of the participants in the matrix. Like nomads, we travel.

References

Bion, W.R. (1970). *Attention and Interpretation*. London: Karnac.
Braidotti, R. (2011). *Nomadic Theory*. New York: Columbia University Press.
Breton, A. (1933 [1997]). *The Automatic Message*. London: Atlas.
Breton, A. and Soupault, P. (1920 [1997]). *The Magnetic Fields*. London: Atlas.
Damasio, A. (2000). *The Feeling of What Happens*. London: Vintage.
Damasio, A. (2003). *Looking for Spinoza*. London: William Heinemann.

Deleuze, G. (1988). *Spinoza. Practical Philosophy*. San Francisco: City Light Books.

Deleuze, G. and Guattari, F. (1988). *A Thousand Plateaus*. London: Continuum.

Deleuze, G. and Guattari, F. (1994). *What is Philosophy?* London: Verso.

Foucault, M. (2002). *The Order of Things*. London: Routledge.

Freud, S. (1953). (ed. J. Strachey) *S.E. Volume IV (1900): The Interpretation of Dreams (First Part)*. London: The Hogarth Press.

Karolia, I. and Manley, J. (2018). "'1 in '5 Brit Muslims' Sympathy for Jihadis': An insight into the Lived Experience of UK Muslims following the Terror Attacks in Paris." In J. Adlam, J. Gilligan, T. Kluttig and B.X. Lee (eds) *Creative States: Overcoming Violence*. Vol.1, Part 3, Ch.4. London: Jessica Kingsley, pp. 161–177.

Langer, S.K. (1948 [1942]). *Philosophy in a New Key: A Study in the Symbolism of Reason, Rite, and Art*. New York: NAL Mentor.

Latour, B. (2005). *Reassembling the Social*. Oxford: Oxford University Press.

Lawrence, W.G. (2005). *Introduction to Social Dreaming. Transforming Thinking*. London: Karnac.

LeDoux, J. (1999). *The Emotional Brain*. London: Phoenix.

Long, S. and Harney, M. (2013). "The Associative Unconscious." In S. Long (ed.) *Socio-analytic Methods*. London: Karnac.

Manley, J. (2009). "When Words are not Enough." In S. Clarke and P. Hoggett (eds) *Researching Beneath the Surface*. London: Karnac.

Manley, J. and Trustram, M. (2016). "Such endings that are not over": The slave trade, Social Dreaming and Affect in a Museum. In *Psychoanalysis, Culture and Society*. doi:10.1057/s41282-016-0032-x

Nuñez, R. and Freeman, W.J. (eds) (1999). *Reclaiming Cognition. The Primacy of Action, Intention and Emotion*. Thorvertone: Imprint Academic.

Roszak, T., Gomes, M.E., and Kanner, A.D. (1995). *Ecopsychology. Restoring the earth, healing the mind*. San Francisco:Sierra Club.

Varela, F.J., Thompson, E., and Rosch, E. (1993). *The Embodied Mind*. London: MIT.

Wittgenstein, L. (1953). *Philosophical Investigations*. Oxford: Blackwell.

The nature and processes of social dreaming: Theory and research

3

THE DREAMING BODY YEARNING TO BELONG TO A LARGER SOCIAL BODY

Richard Morgan-Jones with Angela Eden

Introduction

This chapter seeks to follow the theme of this book to "extend and deepen an understanding of the theory and practice of social dreaming" (Introduction). I begin with the overlap between neurology and psychoanalysis to affirm how it is the body that dreams, followed by an account of developments in clinical psychoanalytic work with dreams. This seeks meaning in what the body may have lived, but the mind has not experienced, so it has not become available for repression although it is unconsciously stored, unrepressed, in the somatic sensations of the body. These two developments have paralleled Gordon Lawrence's creation of Social Dreaming Matrices and yet have been little inter-related. I next move to earlier experiments that drew upon right-brained imaginative access to dreaming in a group. One elaborates dreams through poetry, while the other encourages dream-like experiencing gazing at a cathedral window. Finally, I turn to the subject of this book in a report of my first experience of being a host for a social dreaming matrix. My fundamental hypothesis being tested is this:

That the social dreaming matrix embodies the yearning to belong to a social body bigger than one's own body and mind, to facilitate contradictory painful and joyful truths of hitherto unlived human experience in a wider human world, which need to be dreamt to be realised.

The body that dreams

Neuro-psychoanalyst Allan Schore (2017, p. 73) argues that, "After a century of disconnection, psychoanalysis is returning to its psychological and biological sources, and this reintegration is generating a palpable surge of energy and revitalisation of the field." Key in this development is the idea that the brain to the neurologist, like the mind for the psychoanalyst, is divided. The emphasis on left-brained cognitive and behavioural function, beloved of academic psychology and western intellectual discourse, has risked ignoring right-brained access to implicit knowledge and models of the mind, essential to both conceptual development, and daily problem solving (McGilchrist, 2009).

For centuries, it has been observed that dogs chase in their dreams. Their muted actions in sleep are as clear as those of humans. As neurologist Hobson conjectures, rather than the Cartesian "I think, therefore I am", it might be more accurate to state: "I move, therefore I am." This in turn reveals the idea that *thinking is virtual movement* (Hobson, 2015, p. 19). However, we could also reverse this perspective to describe *feeling moved emotionally* by internal or external experience as the other side of where body meets mind. These two sides of the brain can be linked by working with dream experience.

Psychoanalytic developments in working with dreams

Freud's approach to what he described as the "Royal Road to the unconscious mind" was to treat dreams as disguises for painful truths which could not be faced and were repressed (Freud, 1900). He analyses four defence mechanisms, condensation, displacement, altered representability and secondary revision. Such defences repress anxiety filled emotions behind a contact barrier which is a semi-permeable membrane, like a skin (Morgan-Jones, 2017). Through this skin a dream narrative draws upon experiences, characters and contexts from daily life, and truths about motives that the conscious mind represses. This suggests a function for the contact barrier that is in one way, protecting the conscious mind from its unconscious motives.

Freud's purpose was to draw attention to the way dreaming protected sleep so that the body and mind could recover through the skin of dreaming, while Bion (1962) took Freud's idea of a contact barrier further. He suggests that the unconscious mind is being protected from the realities of conscious and external experience that could also be overwhelming. Pathology, the repeating cycles of suffering, self-destructive behaviour and the experience of relating, could be explored in the failure of the contact barrier to manage the spacing between what was conscious and unconscious in the mind. Waking anxiety signifies failure to protect the mind from the overwhelming demand both internal and external experience. When this overwhelm occurs before a child develops a sense of their own mind emerging from their own bodily identity, Winnicott (1965) described this as "premature impingement from a failing family environment". Further, dreaming and waking dream-like thinking is a way of working across the contact barrier and establishing communication linkages through which the mind could grow to be able to dream up life encompassing both an imaginative and a cognitive aspect (Ogden, 2017). Developing a skin for dreaming could be one way to describe not just social dreaming but the range of methodologies described as "socioanalytic methods" (Long, 2013).

For psychoanalyst Ogden (2001), the key to dream work is to develop a capacity to dream in a way that allows for freeing the movement between conscious and unconscious experience. Madness for Ogden (2005), following Bion, is the incapacity to sleep and to dream and the incapacity to wake up and experience reality. This painful world of the unborn, unlived life is captured in the poem "Invisible Dreams" by Toi Derricote in which she describes her eyes as blind to herself in the state of being neither able to sleep, nor quite wake up (Derricotte, 2017).

Through "Dreaming Undreamt Dreams and interrupted cries" (Ogden, 2005 title page), the analyst enters into the world not of the repressed unconscious, but of the unrepressed unconscious. In other words, into the world that has never been lived because the person/child was not present in mind for lived experience, through either being undeveloped or dissociated. Such overwhelmed, un-present, unrepressed experience is communicated often through bodily presentation rather than being articulated through words. Such non-experience seeks to belong to a body and mind larger than one's own in order to borrow a skin within which dreaming up experience becomes possible. If this is the task in clinical psychoanalytic work with early trauma and developmental loss, then it is also a task within organisations. This is particularly relevant to institutions whose emotionally containing skin is blind to the human risks it imposes upon its work force both consciously and unconsciously whose workers suffer such risks (Morgan-Jones, 2009; 2010). Here too we are on the edge of the boundary with economic, societal and political systems, whose leaders may be similarly imposing upon their citizens (Morgan-Jones, 2011a; 2011b; 2013).

This is a possible role for the social dreaming matrix. Susan Long and Maurita Harney have postulated a rich vein for exploration of the links between the psychoanalytic and socioanalytic unconscious through the idea of an "associative unconscious" (Long & Harney 2013; Long 2016 and this volume). This chapter seeks by contrast to explore how a skin for dreaming may be enhanced in order to address the dissociated unconscious experiences.

Awakening contemplative intuitive thinking, encouraged by associations in social dreaming matrices, the space between left and right brained thinking may be bridged. For Bion, it is the impression of sensory experience that is at once, confusingly, bodily and emotional, that begins experience. This "protomental" emerging experience of "becoming" he described as the transformation of beta-elements through alpha function of an internalised maternal reverie, into emotion, which then becomes available for thought (Bion, 1962).

Piecing together the narrative for such experience demands speaking about what is not yet known. Psychoanalyst Antonino Ferro (2002) proposes that along the path towards alpha function, what is produced are icons, symbol elements, shapes of experiences, even characters in dreams, that become playthings, like toys. For him this involves the investigation of the *force field* created not by the patient, nor by the analyst, but by the interaction between them. This is the heart of *Post-Bion Field Theory,* a new trans-theoretical development in psychoanalysis. Ogden describes this dimension as "the analytic third". The development of icons and symbol elements is the attempt to arrive at exploring the unrepressed unconscious and the discovery of implicit memory that has not been repressed because there was no sufficiently developed ego to digest the experience or because the person was absent from being able to experience an event through traumatic impingement or dissociation, described by Shore and others (see Craparo & Mucci, 2017). These sensations, icons, characters and narratives, become the building blocks for what Gordon Lawrence described as the potential of social dreaming matrices to be a vehicle for "thinking new thoughts" (Lawrence, 1999).

Yet deep within both early traumatised patients as well as in better adapted people there are encapsulated pockets of unlived experience seeking recognition. Such encapsulated pockets demand dreaming, narrative and myth in order for the mind to do the work to transform inner terrors, hopes and joys. The desire to belong to a body bigger than one's own is the precondition for such dimensions of unconscious human experience becoming available through the shared social context of words and language. The analytic pair is the social context which embodies the wider field of the analytic third that makes uses of socially constructed meanings in language to reach for transcending truths and manage the enormity of becoming real to emotionally charged experiencing.

Inspired by Bion's thinking, Donald Meltzer describes "the task of the analyst hearing the dream is no longer to receive it for analysis, but rather to allow the patient's dream to intuitively evoke your own, which might put you in a position to *light a candle in the dark that might enlighten his dream*" (Meltzer, 1984: personal communication). This is parallel to thinking that has been key in social dreaming although the two fields have not always connected.

Here we can make a further connection to British psychoanalyst Winnicott's notion of *transitional space*, where imagination and reality meet as they do in dreams (Winnicott, 1971). What is significant in his work is that long before the possibility of symbolic interpretative work, the psychoanalyst's task is to facilitate experience through a second mind. This provides both maternal attentive listening, reverie (Bion, 1962) and a playful, safe and facilitating environment (Winnicott, 1965).

This takes us towards Bion's description of the mind's attempts to find knowledge (K) or truth about reality from within the depths of experience. He suggests that this could only ever be provisional or limited in the face of further experience that would always transcend limited knowledge and understanding. To describe this transcendence, he deploys language drawn from spiritual traditions and inspired by philosophical and mystical experience. So "the ultimate reality", "things as they are in themselves", and the spiritual traditions of the yearning for a god described by John of the Cross in the "Dark Night of the Soul" and Julian of Norwich in her "Cloud of Unknowing" become the phrases he uses to describe the yearning he points towards under the sign "O" (Bion, 1977/1989). The work of the Grubb Institute the use of "yearning" to describe the longing of the person for deeper and wider transcendent meanings, including relating to the wider purpose of the social system (Long, 2016).

> *What the absolute facts of a (psychoanalytic) session are cannot ever be known, and these I denote by the sign O.*
>
> *(Bion, 1965, pp. 16–17).*

In relation to the conscious and unconscious mind, O represents that potentially overwhelming aspect of the truth or facts about emerging experience that seek expression and yet avoids it. O contains both sensation of undigested experience and bodily impact, as well deeper or higher truths that are too bright for the eyes to dare to open themselves towards. O and protomentality/beta-elements interpenetrate. This chapter attempts to make a link between these two concepts. As Grotstein puts it: "The fundamental anxieties that underlie the basic assumption group resistances were originally thought of as *proto-mental phenomena* (Bion, 1961, p. 101). These would be the forerunners of Bion's later concept of beta-elements and O" (Grotstein, 2007, p.192).

Yearning

By using the word "yearning" in the title of this chapter, I have sought to represent the feeling of deep desire representing bodily need acknowledged, yet transcended. This takes us beyond the satisfaction of a wish that establishes equilibrium in the biological way that Freud conceived of the narcissism of the pleasure principle. It borders into Lacan's version of desire. Lacan's idea of desire is reached for when it is described as "the difference that results from the subtraction of the appetite from the demand of love" (Cléro, 2002, p. 24 *author's trans.*).

For Lacan, desire appears as a reality, impossible to fully grasp. It is ineffable, unknowable and revealed only through what is unconscious and transcendent. It is characterised by what has been lacking in a life as an experience. It is here that need and want, having done their job as shapers of the experience of desire, then get left behind. They become transformed, having been "lent upon", through the experience of what has gone missing in individual and collective lives. Such transcendence reveals that desire can be survived without the regressive pull of the wants and needs of the body, whose urges have given birth to it. Here I argue that the desire for a social context or group that will facilitate the courage to face unsatisfiable desire is an ever-present yearning. It is also worth noting the choice of the term "yearning" by staff at the Grubb Institute and Guild who, in their work with organisations and society, have sought to conceptualise the experience of the person reaching for transcendent meanings to their work engagement with others (Long, 2016).

The word *yearning* seeks to describe the feeling, that is at once in touch with primitive bodily based wants, like the hunger to be filled and to find an object to remove feelings of loneliness. Yet at the same time such a feeling transcends itself by searching for an internalised sense of self and continuity that evokes the capacity to live through such *dark nights of the soul* into more fulfilled and courageous living. But where does such a sense come from? Where is developed the capacity for patience that Bion described the man of experience and the *language of achievement*, embodied in Keats phrase *negative capability:* "that is when man is capable of being in uncertainties, Mysteries, doubts without any irritable reaching after fact & reason…" (Keats, 1958, p. 193).

Perhaps the quasi mystical language of Anglo-American poet T.S. Eliot (1969, p. 180) also might point in this direction when in the Four Quartets he commands his soul to be still and to wait with no vision of either hope or love. For Eliot faith, hope and love are to be found in waiting and echoed in a blindness that brings light and a stillness that brings the movement of dance.

The yearning to belong to a body bigger than your own

Elsewhere I have tried to show how the overwhelmed experience for which the person was absent creates a desire to belong to a body larger than one's own and that this in turn creates a yearning desire for a group with a specific emotional patterning outlined in Bion's shared basic assumption theory of group dynamics (Morgan-Jones, 2009; 2014; 2017). This echoes Bion's idea of valency described well by Richard Billow, who argues that individuals who have conflicted emotional experiences of love, hate and curiosity are drawn to belong to groups or careers shaped by each of Bion's basic assumptions, dependency, fight-flight and pairing respectively (Billow, 2003). It is the wider context of the social dreaming matrix that seeks to explore such experiences of belonging that can embody social sense making and new thinking for all participants. Thus, the matrix becomes a larger, longed-for social body where primitive right-brained experience can grow.

So, yearning becomes endurable and transformed through the internalised experience of being both satisfied and yet weaned by a maternal body larger than one's own into a wider environment. Nuno Torres has extended Freud's *Id* not just an object seeking drive, but also a social seeking drive (Torres, 2010). Joining the group that can use socially constructed language for dreaming experience provides dreamers with the environment for realised living and new thoughtfulness. Here I want to go further in exploring the longing to be able to enjoy experience in a social context.

The Dream Poet (A prequel to social dreaming)

The link between the artistic form of poetry and dreaming was opened up by Richard M. Jones in book entitled "The Dream Poet" (1980). Jones describes a dream seminar whose task is elaborating dreams in a group through poetry. His procedure goes like this:

1. Students give copies of their dream to group members.
2. The author reads the dream aloud along with their reflections. Others are encouraged to respond internally with their own imagery to enter into the dream.
3. Students then offer questions, hypotheses, hunches, with the understanding that it is for the dream author to judge what is helpful. (30–120 minutes)
4. The dream author then reflects and summarises privately on what is useful while the rest of the group write a poem or prose appreciation, a story, play or draft paper related to the week's course prescribed reading. (120 minutes)

5.   Returning to the seminar each person reads what they have written and the group reflects further. Along the way, the group is encouraged to reference authors they have been reading. (Jones, 1980, pp. 58f)

Jones notes that it is in this last stage that a step change in group creativity and energy is released as one dream releases others.

One example of this experience in a dream poetry workshop I conducted with a group involved the dream of one member, afraid of drowning by falling off a sailing boat that had capsized, and that the boat that would leave him behind. His associations to the dream included that he had just become a father for the first time and was both excited but also overwhelmed by a sense of responsibility for his vulnerable new baby that he was not sure he could live up to. He was also overwhelmed by his feelings of fascination for this addition to his life that he had helped bring into the world. His own father had been impatient with his growing up, revealed in bad moods and rages. He was not sure he could deal with both the horror and the wonder at what he was now part of, namely, the uncertainty of the anxious attachment to his own parents which had hardly prepared him for transition to the role of father.

After creative individual time, one of the group brought back to the session the following short poem that spoke for itself:

"*For the child is father to the man*". (A Nod to Freud.) (Anonymous author, reprinted with permission)
Calming wind ripples the coming tide
As my beach-filled, play-fuelled youth vanishes without permission,
Under the auspices of desire for new life beyond my own.

Comes the wind, comes the storm.
You can't sleep now.
Change the sails.
Point the boat to the gale's
eye before the swamping capsize.

Thus the urgent remedy for the wind shaking a sailor's core,
Again, the threatened flooded hull of his universe,
As he journeys onwards with new lives protected,
not just his own.

Without his knowing it,
his child then became the wind that brought him knowing -
How to be the father he had not had.
No more the rage-filled terrorising gale could capsize his life in fear.

Thus saving the world from engulfment of both man and child
Could save them both
For the child could become father to the man.

So the dream's gale through the group teems,
While all grew in its turbulent waters.
And our shared dreams became
Playful children who fathered our cause.

The beauty of this poem is that it speaks directly to the dreamer beyond *the frontier of dreaming* (Ogden, 2001). It speaks towards the desire for transformation of situations in life that demand dream work from the *yearned-for* society of the group.

From the work of neurological advances that inform clinical psychoanalytic experiences and the dream poetry seminar, we now move to a different form of evocative expression through the world of the visual arts.

Art and wonder: the vastness of gazing and the particular experience shared in a large group

Coventry Cathedral was bombed in 1940 in the first fire-storm raid of the second world war and a new cathedral has been built tangential to the ruins of the old. This building attempts to architecturally represent Christian beliefs in the capacity to revive and live after death and destruction. In addition to being a sacred space for worship, its modern and often non-representational art work provides for group visits. In a sense, the art work itself is an object to gaze at, experience and use for reflection. Part of my job on the education team, was to organise a guided tour for the large groups of different ages who arrived at the Cathedral each year.

Reversing the traditional role of an "explaining tour guide", I re-conceive, with a team of volunteers, an approach where a group of up to eighty young people were divided into teams to visit and gaze at different corners of the cathedral and then to return to the large group, take them to where they had been in turn and describe their feelings and questions about what they had found and what it might mean.

In an alternative approach, I would sit down a large group on the cathedral floor and spend time gazing at the huge transparent Cathedral screen decorated with angels, or at the huge tapestry behind the main altar. Most vibrant and evocative is the John Piper designed Baptistery window composed of nearly two hundred rectangles of primary coloured stained glass interspersed with stone. The arc shape of this wall of colour, the vivid dark colours towards the edges and the almost blinding glare of golden light in the centre are hugely evocative.

In leading reflections on the window, my approach, with any age group was the same. Look for shapes. Look for colours. See what moods they evoke. Search for images that can describe what you feel inside about them. Then look at a section of light and colour and where there is a contrast between different colours or shades. Think of words that might describe how parts make you feel or think. Finally, I asked the group to associate to feelings or experiences evoked by the window, its whole or its parts. Responses varied, some individual, some stimulated by others in the group. Here are some of the responses:

Sort of dark, like going to sleep in deep winter; waking up on a cold frosty morning; summer holidays, beach, sand; something horrid happening, like being bullied; a trip or treat in the holidays; a warm coal fire at home and the smell of fish and chips; something new every time I look; too much, I have to look away; fireworks; I want to get really close up and touch; some colours feel hot, some cold; I can see a shoe; ... and a stone; ... and waves on the sea; and crumbling rocks falling;... and part of school on fire.

Some responses seemed to go deeper as the beauty and maybe terror of the window evoked half lost sensation-based life memories:

Hearing my Gran had died and crying; laughing with my friend and not being able to stop; winning a football match; finding a friend to play with in the school play-ground; Dad having to go away to work all week; dreaming and waking up and you don't know if it's real or if you're still dreaming; Mum in tears and not knowing why; smoking behind the sheds; blushing and feeling bad for what I had done; hating my sister for being mean to me...

and so they went on.

It was as if each of these experiences, distinct, heard by the speaker in their mouth, told to the group, held the quality of each of the rectangles of coloured light that make up the window. John Piper who designed the window wrote that "A blaze of light, framed and islanded in colour, seemed a possible solution and it was this blaze of light ... that remained the motive of the whole design."

Such activity in a large group in an even larger space naturally attracted attention and other visitors came to join the experience listening quietly to the children's moments of revelation as each spoke their increasingly emotional truth. Many years later, I have come to realise that what we were doing was in fact a version of social dreaming, set in an open space that opened up the matrix to transcendent experiences to nourish the soul of both individuals and the whole group or indeed anyone who might be listening to children growing up to their truth in such a freeing manner. It was an embodiment of the divine in a social context that legitimised imaginative intuition. Perhaps we could suggest that the horror of destruction of war and the beauty of the art that contained hope and despair, hatred and love all had a place in opening young hearts to growing experiences. The working hypothesis is that the window, as a work of beauty, would inspire new feeling and thinking, and like the panes of differently coloured glass represent rather precisely how feeling and thought are born of distinct sensations, icons of images and glimpses of half-remembered experiences, just like dreams.

With such an introduction, a logical extension of such work might be to hold a social dreaming matrix in an art gallery, the members having had the chance to visit a themed and curated exhibition.

Near Dark: A social dreaming experience at the Towner Art Gallery, Eastbourne, UK

My local art gallery has curated exhibitions that I believed could be highly evocative for social dreaming. Wishing to host such a matrix, I turned to my colleague, Angela Eden, who I knew developed training role workshops with Gordon Lawrence and is authorised by the Gordon Lawrence Foundation for Social Dreaming in the role of trainer for social dreaming hosts (Eden, 2010). She worked with me in designing and hosting this event, as well as adding her experience of being an artist.

Our chosen exhibition was curated by Swedish film maker John Skoog and entitled "Near Dark". The invitation to the event was introduced as follows:

> John Skoog's curated exhibition 'explores the space between night and day ... and where every being becomes his own shadow.' This is the moment of dreams.
>
> The experience of art evokes barely conscious memories, images, associations and emotion, as does the experience of dreaming. New perspectives about the dream can offer new doorways to awareness, new ways of seeing and new creativity.

The programme was framed by an introduction to social dreaming, two social dreaming matrices and a *social dream dialogue* in a room adjacent to the gallery, although it might have been done in one of the exhibition rooms. A coffee break was built in for people to re-visit the exhibition as they had been encouraged to do before and after the event.

The introduction

I began the introduction using John Skoog's words, that had been posted at the entrance to the first gallery. I suggested that where he uses the word "story", the word "dream" could equally make sense.

> A story (dream) is never alone, it demands your company. It only works when someone experiences it, like watching a film or walking through the galleries at the Towner. The story (dream) only lives when it is read.
>
> The story (dream) is full of clues, hints, and dead ends: narratives are begun and left in suspension. We zoom in and out, persons appear and re-appear, places travel from the frame of one picture to the next, some landscapes are quickly sketched out, others are laboriously painted, and in the end, there is a film.

The first four dreams in the first **social dreaming matrix** spoke of experiences of regression in entering more primitive and survival experiences with language closely linked to bodily sensations: an independent little girl, awaking with a dream, an insurance that needed renewal and a familiar courtyard with a child's chair where there was risk of flooding. The texture of these images was connected to the gallery film image of harvest being wrapped, against experience that might flood. The next three dreams became more menacing with impersonal messy industrial landscape being linked to the scream of foreboding at the film's imagined suicide risk, overwhelming by the sea and gravestones covering a football field. The stormy dream weather and associations seemed then to pass as the screamer was seen to smile at a cathartic opportunity drowned by the noise of the passing train, a bus being carried by a truck. This shaped the emerging theme that if our journey broke down, it would be supported by the matrix. This last dream then opened up a string of associations, many from the exhibition: its movement of light towards near dark as you moved through galleries; initial disappointment with the pictures on first viewing, changing with this exchange seeing through others' eyes; the car with headlights driving around the corner as a searching for a future. This pointed towards the unconscious desire to belong to a dreaming body larger than one's own that would carry into the future.

The **second dream matrix** began with a chain of elephants connected by trunks and tails with an individual small contented elephant unconnected to the chain, but without a trunk. Associations to India's disabled, to what was missing or a void, "wonderful in its nothingness", and the pencilled lighthouse on an otherwise painted canvas invited or forced the looker to "dream it up". This chain of dreams and associations suggested absent presences and the experience of not being quite there until dream work could transform the dissociation. Like some of the images from the first matrix, experience was either partly absent or too much. This represented a sensory contact barrier or skin that was either overwhelmed or too insulated. The galleries were also likened to being in a fast train getting fleeting glimpses of passing landscape indicating experience to be had as it passes. A further dream revealed a pool with edges covered by water and something sexual indicating spillage and how dreams are never a gentle flow running along, they are glimpses like the drawing of the disembodied arm.

The social dream dialogue session focussed on possible social meanings as well as a chance to reflect on the experiences. People talked about the newness and pleasure in a busy world in having a deep sense of re-creation, of looking at the world in a new way, of becoming inter-connected with others through sharing dreams. The atmosphere of equality was evoked by the image of a dream in which sandbags had to be filled equally like sharing between siblings. Relief was felt at being carefree rather than feeling squeezed into evidence-based accountability at work. It was as if the matrix had provided a surprising series of opportunities for social relating that was so lacking in current hectic living. This was a hitherto rare glimpse of something people seemed not to have articulated for themselves before as it could only be perceived in the meeting of the need. The gallery image of a curtain (c.f. contact barrier) reflected respect for privacy in the face of work organisation insanity by intrusive demands. There also followed a discussion of the advantages and safety of the closed sessions and yet also the possibility and wisdom of one session of such an experience being conducted in the gallery as a sort of installation with seats for visitors to listen and join in.

Hosts' reflections

Richard Morgan-Jones writes:

One afterthought was how social dream experience might be used to shape a curated exhibition, as maybe that is what curating does. It curates a dream born from a dialogue through a societal context, between a curator, the artists and the imagined public, itself a social matrix. The overlap of John Skoog's vision and surprises with familiar materials evoked so easily dream experience and enabled shared social meeting with minds with new openings. A key one was to linked this social dreaming material to psychoanalytic approaches to dreaming and the links between undreamed experience and the dissociated unconscious.

Angela Eden writes:

The experience of hosting a social dreaming event, in an art gallery, was profoundly moving. It tapped into a visual vocabulary, that is intrinsic to art. It deepened the body metaphor to include our eyes and the how we described what we saw. In this chapter, we see "rare glimpse"; we use "reflection" as we gaze at the paintings and re-visual the dream.

Whilst hearing dreams, I often notice the strong visual links, as the dreamer tries to convey the world they were in during the dream. Usually dreams are reported in a clear, even naive way; yet here in the middle of an art space, the participants came with a fresh experience of visual connections. Even more interesting was how the visual response became visceral, as Richard infers, embodied by the dream. In other social dreaming experiences, I remember bright green parrots, a huge white box on a green hillside; a red stain seeping across a landscape. The images from this exhibition, "glimpses of landscapes", the "passing train", "the football field" were described. as were the more surreal images of a blue Ganesh which excited more visual associations.

In conclusion, I can only infer that the stimulus of being in a space dedicated to the visual, was another layer of the body and eyes of the dream. For the American poet Langston Hughes, life without dreams is like a wounded bird who cannot fly or like a field under snow defying growth of any kind. (Hughes, 1967)

Conclusion

In this chapter, I have tried to explore two experiences of quasi-social dreaming that for me pre-dated the introduction to becoming a host of a social dreaming matrix. The learning experience afforded through Richard Jones' dream poetry seminar and gazing at a cathedral window served as a prelude to introducing myself and others to new frontiers in exploring the overlap between social dream and clinical psycho-analysis. Each experience expresses a surprised yearning for a social group, where such "right-brained" and more primitive intuitions could be explored in community.

The chapter began with neurological and psychoanalytic advances which position practitioners to be able to open up rhyme and reason for our ventures into embodied right-brained experience. These blend imaginative sense-based fantasy with realities that, akin to dreaming, awaken the yearning desire to belong to a social body larger than one's own. Theoretically this chapter seeks to make links between Bion's early understanding of group dynamics founded in the protomental matrix with his later approaches to dreaming and thinking that have shaped *Post-Bion Field Theory*. Within the matrix offered by social dreaming, Gordon Lawrence and others have fleshed out a facilitating environment for what Ogden describes vividly as: "Conversations at the frontier of dreaming" (Ogden, 2001). It is for this vision that I have entitled this chapter: *The dreaming body yearning to belong to a larger social body*. My working hypothesis is:

> *That the social dreaming matrix embodies the yearning to belong to a social body bigger than one's own body and mind, to facilitate contradictory painful and joyful truths of hitherto unlived human experience in a wider human world, which need to be dreamt to be realised.*

References

Billow, R.M. (2003). *Relational Group Psychotherapy: From Basic Assumptions to Passion.* London: Jessica Kingsley.

Bion, W.R. (1961). *Experiences in Groups.* London: Karnac.

Bion, W.R. (1962). *Learning from Experience.* London: Karnac.

Bion, W.R. (1965/1991). *Elements of Psychoanalysis.* London: Karnac.

Bion, W.R. (1970/1988). *Attention and Interpretation.* London: Karnac.

Bion, W.R. (1977/1989). *Two Papers: The Grid and Caesura.* London: Karnac.

Cléro, J.-P. (2002). *Le vocabulaire de Lacan. (The Vocabulary of Lacan).* Ellipses: Aubin.

Craparo, G. & Mucci, C. (2017). *Unrepressed Unconscious, Implicit Memory, and Clinical Work.* London: Karnac.

Derricotte, T. (2017). *Invisible Dreams.* Accessed 12/01/2017 at: www.poetryfounda tion/poems-and-poets/poems/detail/48753.

Eden, A. (2010). "Learning to host a Social Dreaming Matrix." Ch. 6 in W.G. Lawrence (2010) (ed.) *The Creativity of Social Dreaming.* London: Karnac.

Eliot, T.S. (1969). *The Complete Poems and Plays of T.S. Eliot.* London: Faber.

Ferro, A. (2002). *Seeds of Illness, Seeds of Recovery.* London: Routledge.

Ferro, A. (ed.) (2018). *Contemporary Bionian Theory and Technique in Psychoanalysis.* London: Routledge.

Freud, S. (1900). *The Interpretation of Dreams.* S.E. Vol IV. London: Hogarth.

Grotstein, J. (Ed.) (1991). *Do I Dare Disturb the Universe?* Beverly Hills, CA: Caesura Press.

Grotstein, J. (2007). *A Beam of Intense Darkness. Wilfred Bion's Legacy to Psychoanalysis.* London: Karnac.

Hobson, A. (2015). *Psychodynamic Neurology: Dreams, Consciousness, and Virtual Reality.* Fl: CRC Press/Taylor Francis Group.

Hughes, L. (1967). *The Collected Poems of Langston Hughes.* New York: Alfred A. Knopf/ Vintage. Accessed from www.poets.org, 11/06/2018. and YouTube.com, 11/06/2018.

Jones, R.M. (1980). *The Dream Poet.* Cambridge, MA: Schenkman.

Keats, J. (1958). *The Letters of John Keats. 2 vols.* (Edited by H.E. Rollings) Cambridge, MA: Harvard University Press.

Lawrence, W.G. (1999). *Social Dreaming @ Work*. London: Karnac.

Long, S. (2013). (Ed.) *Socioanalytic Methods*. London: Karnac.

Long, S. (2016). (Ed.) *Transforming Experience in Organisations: A Framework for Organisational Research and Consultancy*. London: Karnac.

Long, S.D. & Harney, M. (2013). "The associative unconscious" in S. Long *Socioanalytic Methods*. London: Karnac.

McGilchrist, I. (2009). *The Master and his Emissary*. Yale: YUP.

Meltzer, D. (1984). *Dream-Life: A Re-examination of the Psycho-analytical Theory and Technique*. London: Clunie Press for Roland Harris Trust Library.

Morgan-Jones, R.J. (2009). "The body speaks: Bion's protomental system at work", *British Journal of Psychotherapy* 25(4): 456–476.

Morgan-Jones, R.J. (2010). *The Body of the Organisation and its Health*. London: Karnac.

Morgan-Jones, R.J. (2014). "The invaded Skin: From humiliation trauma through humbling to recovery". Unpublished paper given in Oct. 2014 to "Poland on the Couch" conference organized by Ratsow Clinic, Polish group Analytic Society and Centre for Special Education, Warsaw, Poland.

Morgan-Jones, R.J. (2011a). "The attempted murder of money and time: Addressing the Global Systemic Banking Crisis". In S. Long and B. Sievers (eds) *Towards a Socioanalysis of Money, Finance and Capitalism: Beneath the Surface of the Financial Industry*. London: Routledge.

Morgan-Jones, R.J. (2011b). "What are we celebrating in the celebrities?" in H. Brunning (ed.) *Psychoanalytic Reflections on a Modern World*. London: Karnac.

Morgan-Jones, R.J. (2013). "The vulnerability of the European nation state and its citizens in a time of humbling". In H. Brunning (ed.) *Psychoanalytic Essays on Power and Vulnerability*. London: Karnac.

Morgan-Jones, R.J. (2017). "The Language of the group skin" in *Gruppo: omogeneità e differenze, rivista annuale*, www.argo-onlus.it/la-rivista/. Special edition edited by T.H. Ringer, "Thinking about Groups and Teams."

Ogden, T.H. (2001). *Conversations at the Frontier of Dreaming*. London: Karnac.

Ogden, T.H. (2005). *This Art of Psychoanalysis: Dreaming Undreamt Dreams and Interrupted Cries*. London: Karnac.

Ogden, T.H. (2017). "On Talking-as-dreaming". In Reiner, A. (ed.) (2017) *Of Things Invisible to Mortal Sight – Celebrating the Work of James S. Grotstein*. London: Karnac.

Schore, A. (2017). Allan Schore on the Neurobiology of Secure Attachment. Accessed at: https://kindredmedia.org/2017/01/allan-schore-neurobiology-secure-attachment/.

Torres, N. (2010). "Social stress related epidemic diseases: Failures in emotional containment". Ch. 6 in R.J. Morgan-Jones (ed.). *The Body of the Organisation and its Health*. London: Karnac.

Winnicott, D.W. (1965). *The Maturational Process and the Facilitating Environment: Studies in the Theory of Emotional Development*. London: Hogarth Press & The Institute of Psycho-Analysis.

Winnicott, D.W. (1971). *Playing and Reality*. London: Tavistock.

4

'RENEWING THE LAND'

The dreaming mind in community

Laurie Slade

I have been involved with social dreaming since 2001. In the first matrix that I attended, at a Jungian congress in Cambridge, an Israeli therapist shared a dream of attempting to pilot a plane with no landing gear, and a Mexican therapist shared a dream of ironing clothes while watching a volcanic eruption. One month later we were hit by 9/11 – the twin towers of the World Trade Centre were burning. A friend left me a voice-mail with the news, ending: 'Norma says we still have to eat'.

I thought of planes which could not land, and of deadly infernos. In the Cambridge matrix, associations to the Mexican therapist's dream had suggested that doing the ironing while a volcano erupted was a norm of survival: we must maintain basic functioning in a time of crisis. In the wake of 9/11, Norma was re-stating this. I felt my experience in the Cambridge matrix had prepared me for the trauma we were now facing, by giving me meaningful images with which to think about it. The capacity to think in a crisis is another aspect of survival functioning.

But these were not *my* dreams. They had come to me through the generosity of the matrix. After this, how could I not take social dreaming seriously?

First steps

Further experiences of social dreaming reinforced my enthusiasm and fascination with the process. I shared this with colleagues in my professional organisation, the Guild of Psychotherapists. Within six months I was invited to host a matrix at the Guild's annual Summer Conference.

I invited Jan Lee, a friend from the Guild, to co-host with me. Jan had been at the Cambridge matrix, and was equally affected. We discussed how we would approach the function of hosting, and agreed to share our dreams as well as conscious thoughts in preparation:

> *I did dream last night. Not very clear images, but a clear message – 'The land will be renewed', or 'The land will renew itself', I'm not quite sure which …* (28.1.2002)
>
>   *I too had a dream on the same night you did and 'the land' featured in mine as well! I spoke to a beautiful, young Hispanic girl and saw a Spanish word meaning maiden. I saw the same word on a map of a foreign land showing a mountain range with this word written across it. The implication was that this was exciting new territory to be explored. The girl was complaining that England was too wet for her, her country was warm and beautiful …* (1.2.2002)

The synchronicity in our dreams suggested we were tuning-in to each other and to matrix thinking. This was 'new territory' for us, as well as for the Guild. Thanks to the Hispanic girl, it seemed welcoming.

When we came to it, the first Guild matrix was remarkable. Sixteen dreams were shared in the space of an hour – nine of them in the first fifteen minutes. It felt like a sudden release of energy.

The specificity of social dreaming

Since those first steps, I have hosted many matrices, in the UK and internationally, in many different settings, ranging from self-development groups, work with sexual minorities (Slade 2005) and drama students (Slade 2010), and at conferences on a wide range of themes, where the matrix provides a refreshing complement to the predominantly left-brain activity of plenary sessions. Social dreaming, it seems, can 'renew the land' – facilitate emergent thinking – in whatever context it takes place.

But sharing dreams is nothing unusual. Our species has been doing it for millennia. What is distinctive about social dreaming? I suggest it is the specific nature of the task we engage in, when we meet in the matrix.

The first formulation of this task came from Gordon Lawrence and Patricia Daniel, when they arranged an experimental series of matrices at the Tavistock Institute in the early 1980s. Lawrence later described their developing thoughts as to what these sessions would involve. Initially, they defined their task as:

> *to interpret and associate to the potential social content and meaning of the participant's dreams.*
> *(Lawrence 1989)*

Lawrence noted that there was then a crucial shift of emphasis:

> *On further reflection and before the venture began the two verbs were transposed because we felt that association must come before interpretation.*
>
> *(ibid)*

That brief paragraph defines what has become an essential aspect – if not *the* essential aspect – of social dreaming: it is an associative process, not an interpretative one.

Formulations of the task in social dreaming have varied through the years, and continue to vary with individual practitioners (see Slade 2010, p. 28 for discussion). The formulation I prefer is as concise and functional as possible:

> Our task in the matrix is to share dreams and share our associations to each other's dreams, making connections where possible.

But in this one respect nothing has changed. There is implied, and often explicitly stated, a taboo against interpreting dreams in the matrix in terms of what they signify for the dreamer. Instead, there is an invitation for each of us to respond to the dreams in terms of how they affect *us* – whether they arouse a sensation, prompt an image, trigger a memory, or evoke another dream.

For those with experience of psychoanalysis, this sounds familiar. In his *Introductory Lectures*, Freud summarised the 'fundamental rule' of free association:

> We instruct the patient to put himself into a state of quiet, unreflecting self-observation, and to report to us whatever internal observations he is able to make – feelings, thoughts, memories – in the order in which they occur to him …
>
> *(Freud 1916–17, p. 286)*

Lawrence shared with Freud this belief in the value of a free association method. But sometimes we define ourselves in terms of what we are not, and for Lawrence the Other, that which social dreaming essentially is not, was psychoanalysis.

Oedipus and Sphinx

Lawrence talked in terms of Oedipus and Sphinx. The Sphinx he had in mind was a mythical creature from ancient Greece, which caused havoc for the citizens of Thebes. It asked anyone who was passing an impossible question, and throttled all who gave the wrong answer. Oedipus successfully solved the riddle of the Sphinx, inspiring an immortal play by Sophocles – and psychoanalytic history.

Lawrence maintained that psychoanalysis is about Oedipus – endeavouring to understand the psychology and psychopathology of the individual – while social dreaming is about Sphinx – endeavouring to understand how a group as a whole is trying to make sense of its life. (Lawrence 1998, p. 5).

Oedipus needs answers. Sphinx asks questions. Oedipus makes the *dreamer* central, emphasizing the individual, the past, the finite. Sphinx makes the *dream* central, emphasizing the social, the future, the infinite. For Oedipus, life is a personal story, however painful. For Sphinx, life is a tragedy in which we all participate. Therapeutic dream-work and social dreaming may be complementary, but are essentially distinct. (Lawrence & Biran 2002).

I have certainly met analysts who will not accept that dreams can signify beyond the personal, whether inside or outside their consulting rooms. But the psycho-analytic model which Lawrence invoked in comparison with social dreaming was in my view too circumscribed – perhaps rooted in the culture of the Tavistock in the early 80s, perhaps rooted in Lawrence's own experience of psycho-analysis. For example, he showed relatively little appreciation of the increasing emphasis on the relational and inter-subjective in psychoanalytic practice, reflected in the work of Stephen Mitchell and others (see Mitchell 2000), or of the concept of the psychoanalytic field, which Antonino Ferro and Giuseppe Civitarese have developed (see Ferro & Civitarese 2015, and earlier references cited there).

I suggest there is much in contemporary psychoanalytic practice that engages with the Sphinx as well as Oedipus. Lawrence himself regularly spiced his writing with lengthy quotes from Bion, acknowledging that his thinking about the antithesis between Oedipus and the Sphinx itself derived from Bion's classic text, *Experiences in Groups* (Lawrence 1998, p. 5).

Bion's thinking was essentially 'binocular' and process orientated, embracing the dynamic tension we have to negotiate between the polarities of what is conscious or unconscious, known or unknowable, finite or infinite. Social dreaming seems to me to be more allied with than opposed to this approach. Indeed, one major effect social dreaming has had on my practice as a therapist is to deepen my under-standing of these developments in psychoanalytic thinking.

A client in individual therapy recently shared this thought about a session that was ending:

> *It's like looking through a telescope at the starry sky, knowing I will never fully understand it. And I love it.*

We had been wrestling with some messy Oedipal stuff, and to that we would have to return, but when we later revisited my client's remark, it was clear he had had a glimpse of Sphinx – the infinite constellations of meaning that form and dissolve during a therapy session – as they do in a matrix.

So in my view, Lawrence's insistence that psychoanalysis and social dreaming are mutually exclusive was primarily because this served a purpose. It enabled him to define what social dreaming was about for him.

But Lawrence did not seek to create an orthodoxy for social dreaming. He left the rest of us to find our own way with it. In the process of identifying what social dreaming means for me, I have found it helpful to consider the strands of thought which came together for Lawrence and inspired him when he conceived the social dreaming project – seeing where that takes me:

1 The multi-dimensionality of dreams

At the Tavistock, Lawrence was involved in facilitating experiential groups. Increasingly he felt that dreams were being shared which did not merely signify for the dreamer. They illuminated and connected individual dreamers with the unfolding life of the group (Lawrence 1989). He wanted to engage with this wider dimension of the dreams he was encountering, this sense that my dreams come through me but may not be exclusively about me.

Lawrence's reference to the connection between the individual and the group highlights a central aspect of social dreaming. As he observed, in social dreaming:

> *Once a dream is offered, there can be as many associations as there are people in the room – and that's a lot of associations.*
>
> *(Lawrence 1998, p. 31)*

Each individual voice is respected within the matrix. Through social dreaming I suggest, we have an experience of community, and it is a very democratic community (an observation also made by Szekacs 2003, p. 251). No particular response to a dream is privileged, and there is no attempt in the matrix to arrive at a consensus or group-think on the significance of the dreams we share.

At the same time, our dreams do not cease to have personal significance through being shared in the matrix. The social aspect of a dream is what we engage with there, but when I had my first taste of social dreaming I was still in analysis. I continued to talk to my analyst about my dreams, and I found their significance for me was enriched through their being picked up, elaborated, and associated to in a matrix.

Consequently, one lesson I have learnt through my experience of social dreaming is that the dreaming mind is multi-dimensional. Whether we are concerned with our own dreams or those of our companions or colleagues or clients, whether we engage with these dreams at a personal or social or trans-personal or at any other level whatever, we have to accept that there is always more to a dream than we can engage with consciously in any particular context. The dreaming mind is bigger than we are.

Such thoughts feel Jungian, as was Lawrence's second source of inspiration: Jung's insight into the transpersonal dimension of his dreams.

2 The social unconscious

In *Memories, Dreams and Reflections*, Jung described how he was bombarded by apocalyptic dreams and visions during the summer of 1914. When World War I broke out, Jung felt there was a connection:

> *Now my task was clear: I had to understand what had happened and to what extent my own experience coincided with mankind in general.*
>
> *(Jung 1964, p. 170)*

Lawrence observed:

> *If any justification is needed for listening to the messages of one's visions and dreams, it is there in Jung's experiences.*
>
> *(Lawrence 1998, p. 15)*

I suggest Jung was alluding here to two aspects of the transpersonal, both of which find expression through dreams. One is the aspect so often dwelt on in Jungian psychology, the archetypal collective unconscious, representing the accumulated history of our species, ethnicity and culture, predating us as individuals, in which we are inevitably rooted.

But what determines whether an archetypal pattern manifests in a particular time and place? Jung's insight was not simply into the historic propensity of mankind for war. The archetypal unconscious has a complementary and more immediate aspect, a collective in the here and now, whether in the family, group, community, state or indeed our common humanity – a collective represented in any gathering in which we find ourselves – what S. H. Foulkes identified as the 'social unconscious' (Foulkes 1964, p. 52).

I suggest Jung's imperative can be paraphrased for each of us: I have to understand how my experience coincides with that of others around me, and the social realities of the wider world in which we now live.

Social dreaming came as Lawrence's response to the urgency of Jung's agenda. The measure of his contribution in this respect is reflected in comments from Kevin Power – a group-psychotherapist – after a matrix I hosted at a conference in 2006:

> *What social dreaming reveals is that we probably do not dream alone, but instead dream as part of a social matrix… The unconscious is not an individual's possession, rather the repository of dynamic, unconscious processes, and social dreaming is a way to explore what is there.*
>
> *(Power 2006)*

But this social matrix, and the ways in which dream-sharing can reveal it, were recognised long before Jung's premonitions of World War I and the late 20th century emergence of social dreaming.

3 The pervasiveness of social dream-sharing

A third inspiration for Lawrence came from comparison with other cultures. Since I became interested in social dreaming, I have found countless examples of dream-sharing as a community based activity, with the dreams of individuals regarded as having meanings or implications for the community as a whole. What seems novel to us nowadays was once commonplace in our part of the world – and still is, elsewhere.

Two examples stand out:

(a) The Crow Nation

In *Working through the end of civilization*, Jonathan Lear described how the Crow Nation – an Indian Tribe of the Northwestern Plains – used dreams and dream-sharing to prepare for and negotiate the changes they experienced through the advent of the white man (Lear 2007).

In the mid-19th Century, a nine-year old Crow boy had a dream-vision in which the buffalo disappeared down a hole in the ground, while strange spotted bulls and cows emerged. A terrible storm was on its way, which would devastate the forest, leaving only one tree standing – the tree of a bird-person called the chickadee (a North American species of tit). The chickadee was seen to be unobtrusive, observant, adaptable. In his dream, the boy was told to be like the chickadee.

He reported his dream to the elders. It was interpreted as meaning that the buffalo would be replaced by the white man's cattle and the Crow's traditional way of life was ending. The chickadee would become a role model for them, in their uncertain future.

Civilisation as they knew it did end for the Crow – and for the other Indian Nations – when they were moved onto the reservations. But the Crow have survived, in changed circumstances – creating new meanings for themselves as a people. It is more than 150 years since that boy shared his dream with the elders, but mothers and grandmothers still teach young Crow that they must follow the example of the chickadee (ibid, p. 303).

In psychoanalytic terms, the young boy metabolised the unconscious anxieties of his tribe in a dream narrative – which the elders were then able to engage with and use, making those anxieties conscious and formulating strategies to address them (ibid, p. 300). This only worked because the whole community accepted – as social dreaming does – that dreams have a social valency.

(b) The Kukatja people

On the opposite side of the globe, in Australia's Western Desert, Sylvie Poirier observed dream-sharing practices among the Kukatja people. For the Kukatja, dreaming of the land is literally a way to renew it – relating to the land in a caring way, with the expectation of a positive response. Poirier's informant, Napangarti, could say:

> This is good country. We are good dreamers.
>
> (Poirier 2003, p. 113)

Poirier commented on the way in which the Kukatja shared their dreams:

> When a dream is narrated, for example around the camp in the morning hours, people will listen to the story but will not necessarily attempt to decipher it or confirm its import …
>
> The dreamer, or somebody else, might make a few comments, or someone might carry on with another story (either a dream, an anecdote, a mythical sequence or a past event) often suggested by the first one …
>
> The dream does not belong to the dreamer to the extent that it is seldom seen as being addressed solely to the dreamer, who considers him or herself rather as a messenger or witness of something that, as it is being shared, is liable to become meaningful or relevant to others …
>
> What seems at first to be a lack of interest in dream interpretation reveals, on closer examination, another local reality, one that became quite evident during my research: the primacy of the activity of dreaming over the dream content …
>
> (ibid, pp. 116–8)

In Lawrence's terms, this is Sphinx, not Oedipus. An anthropologist watching a social dreaming matrix in progress might make very similar observations.

4 Dreams in a context of social trauma

Finally, in the inspirations which Lawrence acknowledged, he discovered *The Third Reich of Dreams*, by Charlotte Beradt - a study of the dreams of ordinary people living in Nazi Germany between 1933 and 1939. Beradt suggested that the dreams she collected could be taken together, and would then be seen as presenting and foreshadowing political events, and peoples' response to and construction of those events.

Here again, as if wanting to verify for myself Lawrence's sources, I have kept an eye open for comparable material on dreams in a context of social trauma. I found it in a study by Irina Paperno of dreams during the Stalinist terror in the late 1930s (Paperno 2009).

These dreams came to light through archives created in the Glasnost era in Soviet society. Paperno did not simply show – as Beradt did – how the dreams of individuals in isolation might express the prevailing social reality when viewed collectively. She also showed how:

> The circulation of dreams served as an instrument of myth-making and community building. Here I highlight the social function of soviet dreams.
>
> *(ibid, p. 187)*

What Paperno described was an informal practice among a group of soviet writers, the most celebrated of whom was the poet Anna Akhmatova. This group shared their dreams in correspondence with each other, and responded to each other's dreams, through associations and by making imaginative connections. Paperno's conclusion was:

> Sharing their dreams (and discovering that they dreamed similar dreams, or dreamed of one another), these people gained a sense of connection, intimacy, and significance that served as protection, however precarious, from the social environment that threatened them with annihilation.
>
> *(ibid, p. 193)*

I have had personal experience of how sharing dreams can provide containment in traumatic circumstances. My most striking example comes from a matrix at the Guild of Psychotherapists, held a fortnight after the London bombings of 7/7 in 2005, only days after the failed attempts at further bombing on 21/7.

Those of us in the zone at the time of the London bombings will remember the impact they had. A client of mine lived in the area where the bombs exploded. He said it was like walking around in a dream he could not wake up from. In a world gone mad, the distinction between our waking and our dreamt realities can become scarily blurred.

By 2005, social dreaming had become a regular practice at the Guild's summer conferences. On the first day of the conference, the London bombings were barely mentioned. They seemed unspeakable. On the second day, we had our social dreaming matrix.

In previous years, the dreams had come tumbling out. On this occasion, in the wake of the London bombings, we were stuck. We had a few dreams, then a long gap, with fragmented conversational exchanges.

Such inhibition can occur when a matrix takes place in the context of collective trauma. I had a similar experience in a matrix after the Second Iraq invasion in 2003 – 'shock and awe' stunned us all – and again after the Paris terrorist attacks in 2015. Similar observations were made by other social dreaming practitioners after 9/11, in 2001 (see Szekacs 2003, p. 251; Clare & Zarbafi 2009, p. 40). I am curious about the source of this inhibition.

One of the only disagreements I had with Lawrence concerned the negative effects of anxiety in the matrix. His approach – as I understood it – was fairly bullish: the task of the matrix is clear and participants need to get on with it. In my view, it is understandable that there may be anxieties around which inhibit the sharing of dreams, ranging from hesitation due to the novelty of the activity, to a commonly felt concern that the dreams will prove overwhelming once we open ourselves up to them, to the sometimes disturbing content of the dreams themselves, or – as with the traumatic events of 7/7 – the context in which a matrix takes place. In these circumstances, I suggest, some facilitation may be needed, to contain the anxiety and free up the flow of dreams.

At the Guild matrix, one participant eventually said:

> Last night we were walking to a restaurant. I saw a broken green bottle. Piercing shards. I didn't know what to do with it. Afraid it might damage someone.

I felt this image might be articulating our stuckness in the matrix. Judit Szekacs has suggested that in social dreaming, transference is to the dreams, not to the group or individuals in the matrix (Szekacs 2003, p. 248). With this helpful insight in mind, I said:

> I'm wondering whether there's a dream here that someone is afraid to share, for fear it might hurt us.

Immediately, this dream was offered:

> I had a dream that I was in a room – like an art gallery. There was an installation of body parts – torso, arm, hand. They were mounted round the room. One was a face. As I looked at it, it started sniffing. I looked around. All these body parts were alive.

In Lawrence's terms, this dream spoke to the life of the group. It was all we needed. As the associations began to accumulate in the matrix, a connection was made with the mangled bodies of those destroyed or injured in the bombings. Suddenly we were talking about the horror of it, the different ways in which we had experienced that horror, interweaving those details with other images and associations. Sharing this traumatic dream made a conversation about our collective trauma possible. In Paperno's words, 'connection, intimacy and significance' were the result.

More recently, I have been hosting with George Taxidis a series of Queer Social Dreaming matrices at the London Friend, a support centre for sexual minorities. Our third meeting took place in July 2016, shortly after the homophobic massacre at a gay bar in Orlando, the shooting of MP Jo Cox, and the shock result of the Brexit referendum. A Spanish participant later posted a touching article on what the matrix had offered, describing it as:

> a huge oasis… a common space that somehow we will always be able to go back to, looking for relief, suggesting answers or simply lighting the way for future meetings which, with different topics, will in my opinion, help us resist the dictatorship of totalitarian thinking which lies ahead, that so subtle and wickedly, conditions our daily life depriving us of nocturnal peace.
>
> (Diaz 2016)[1]

I am left wondering what difference it would have made, if there had been a similar 'oasis' – an equally safe space – for Beradt's dreamers to share their dreams.

Conclusions and assumptions

Lawrence died in 2013. At his memorial service, I was privileged to read Caliban's speech from *The Tempest* (Shakespeare 1916), describing life on Prospero's island:

> And then, in dreaming,
> The clouds methought would open and show riches
> Ready to drop upon me, that when I wak'd
> I cried to dream again. (Act III, Sc.ii)

Retracing Lawrence's footsteps, as he felt his way towards the social dreaming project, I have been taken in different directions, arriving at some conclusions. The resources of the dreaming mind seem inexhaustible. Social dreaming is one way of accessing those riches, but its effectiveness depends on the context – on whether or not it is accepted that sharing dreams can be an authentic and creative form of dialogue – a way of thinking in community.

That in turn requires a communal commitment to hold a space for social dreaming in the face of the other pressures of 21st Century living – not always easy to find. Traditional cultures like the Kukatja seem enviable in their capacity to integrate social dream-sharing into the rhythms of their daily lives.

More fundamentally, social dreaming requires a readiness to accept that engaging with dreams on any basis can be a meaningful and rewarding activity. Such a proposition does not necessarily have general acceptance in our time and culture. I work as a psychoanalytic psychotherapist, and prior to that I had many years of analysis, so for me the value of working with dreams is a given, and my concern in any context is how I do it.

I came to social dreaming when I was newly-qualified through the Guild, and my exploration of the matrix has run in tandem with the development of my practice as a therapist. I have already touched on the interplay for me between social dreaming and psychoanalytic thinking. The impact of Sphinx on Oedipus has been particularly noticeable when I consider the implications for my therapeutic work of social dreaming's taboo against interpreting a dream for the dreamer.

Perhaps it's Freud's fault. He called his masterpiece *The Interpretation of Dreams*. This led me to believe initially that interpreting dreams is the cleverest thing we can do with them. Even while training, I began to realise it is not so simple. Robert Wallerstein's *The Talking Cures* highlighted the divisive debate which has continued since the early days of psychoanalysis, as to whether it is the analytic interpretation or the affective relationship that is mutative – that facilitates change. (Wallerstein 1995, p. 267). Daniel Stern offered me a bridge across this divide, in *The Present Moment in Psychotherapy and Everyday Life* (Stern 2004), with his emphasis on dyadic process in therapy. As he put it, two minds are working together in the consulting room to maximize coherence. Any meaning that emerges is cocreated or coadjusted, 'each move and moment creating the context for the one that follows.' (Stern 2004, p. 158).

In other words, an interpretation is never an event in isolation. It is only one link in a chain of interactions. Stern suggested it is where the links take us which is crucial. So, working with dreams in therapy has become for me more of a mutual exploration with my clients. We associate to the dreams, and explore the affects they arouse, making connections where possible – as we would in a matrix. Occasionally a pattern may emerge, and identifying that is a form of interpretation. Beyond that – through social dreaming I have experienced how dreams which are not interpreted or treated as an object of investigation can become a vehicle – taking us in unexpected directions. In sessions with clients I now tend to postpone any interpretive act as long as possible, and wait to see where we end up – often talking about something we had not talked about before, or not in that way – like that conversation about the London bombings in the Guild matrix.

I could illustrate this with a clinical vignette, but in the context of social dreaming, I feel I should draw on my own experience. Here is a dream from 30 years ago – my early days in analysis – which I have re-visited in the light of what I am saying.

I dreamed of a box with 4 heart shaped chocolates covered in red foil, a gift for mother.
(1984)

Oedipal interpretations spring readily to mind, as possible solutions to the riddle of this Sphinx, and no doubt I explored them at the time with Rosemary, my analyst, along with the transference implications.

Mother-love? It's classic. And this was my second analysis, as my first analyst – William – had died suddenly a few months earlier. My father had also recently died. These deaths would confirm an oedipal view – the death of father times two left me with no rival in my incestuous desire for mother times two – which gives us four chocolates! Great! We're getting somewhere! Or are we? Fortunately, Rosemary had too much respect for Sphinx to be fixated on simplistic oedipal interpretations of this kind. Working with her on dreams was usually a very rewarding experience.

But my point is – I do not remember any of the interpretative work I did with my analyst on this particular dream. I am not saying it was irrelevant, but it has left no conscious trace. What I do remember is what happened after I had talked about the dream in analysis. On my own, I began playing with the dream in visual terms – engaging in what Jung called 'active imagination.' I sketched the box of chocolates. I abstracted the outlines of the chocolates, and arranged them in a circle, like a gothic rose window, with the heart-shapes as panes of crimson glass.

Then I saw through that window, in the sense that it mutated into something else. The next image was more like a flower, with the heart-shapes forming petals in the centre – or a flower embedded in a stem, as the surrounding border was in shades of green. I remembered lines from a poem by Dylan Thomas, 'The force that through the green fuse drives the flower' (Thomas 1934). In the wake of two major bereavements, and with the benefit of some analytical parenting, my dream had brought me to a transcendant image of on-going life, and a poem celebrating inescapable but ecstatic mortality.

Looking at this image 30 years on, I can still relive that moment of transformation – a moment beyond any previous act of interpretation. Of course, the previous work with my analyst fed into that outcome, and that outcome itself would have been open to interpretation – but any further interpretation was after the event. In my view, now, the interpretation of dreams – what we do with them – is secondary to our experience of the dreaming mind as process – what it does with us.

Freud himself acknowledged that interpretation has its limits. I was reminded of this recently, when I encountered an enigmatic image in a rock shelter in the Cederberg mountains of South Africa: an ethereal figure painted in red ochre floats around a circular hole – a hole like a navel in the rock face. What this image signified for its creator centuries or millennia ago remains a mystery. But there is no doubt it was meaningful rather than decorative. According to David Lewis-Williams, it would have reflected trance experience – been a manifestation of the dreaming mind – and creating it was a social act – this image spoke not merely for the artist but to the life of a group (Lewis-Williams 1990). Here is my association – what that image said to me – and what Freud said to us:

> There is at least one spot in every dream at which it is unplumbable – a navel, as it were, that is its point of contact with the unknown.

> (Freud 1900, p. 111 n.1)

This paper is based on a presentation *The Dreaming Mind in Community*, given at the conference *Working with the Dreaming Mind – Perspectives from Contemporary Psychotherapeutic Practice,* presented by Confer at the Tavistock Centre, London on 30.1.2016.

Note

1 'un immense oasis… un espacio commún al que de alguna forma pudiésemos retornar buscando alivios, sugiriendo respuestas o, simplemente, iluminado el camino para future reunions las cuales, tratando otras temas, servirán en, mi opinión, para resistir la dictadura del pensiamento totalitario que se nos avecina y que, tan sutil y maliciosamente, condiciona nuestra vida diaria privándonos de la paz noturna.'

References

Beradt, C. (1968). *The Third Reich of Dreams*. Chicago: Quadrangle Books.

Bion, W. (1961). *Experiences in Groups*. London: Tavistock Publications.

Clare, J. and Zarbafi, A. (2009). *Social Dreaming in the 21st Century*. London: Karnac.

Diaz, N. (2016). *Sueños lúcidos de una noche de verano*. Politica Local, Madrid – http://politica local.es/558634/suenos-lucidos-una-noche-verano.

Ferro, A. and Civitarese, G. (2015). *The Analytic Field and Its Transformations*. London: Karnac.

Foulkes, S. H. (1964). *Therapeutic Group Analysis*. London: George Allen & Unwin.

Freud, S. (1900). *The Interpretation of Dreams*. Standard Edition, 4. (transl. 1953) London: Hogarth Press.

FreudS. (1916–17). *Introductory Lectures on Psycho-Analysis – Part III*. Standard Edition, 16.

Jung, C. G. (1964). *Memories, Dreams, Reflections*. London: Collins and Routledge & Kegan Paul.

Lawrence, W. G. (1989). *Ventures in Social Dreaming*. Author's copy – text published in *Changes* 7:3.

Lawrence, W. G. (Ed.) (1998). *Social Dreaming @ Work*. London: Karnac.

Lawrence, W. G. and Biran, H. (2002). The Complementarity of Social Dreaming and Therapeutic Dreaming. In Friedman, R. et al (Eds) *Dreams in Group Psychotherapy: Theory and Technique*. London: Jessica Kingsley, International Library of Group Analysis.

Lear, J. (2007). *Working Through the End of Civilization*. In *International Journal of Psychoanalysis*, Vol. 88 Part 2, pp. 291–308.

Lewis-Williams, J. D. (1990). *Discovering South African Rock Art*. Cape Town and Johannesburg: David Philip.

Mitchell, S. A. (2000). *Relationality – From Attachment to Intersubjectivity*. New Jersey: Analytic Press.

Paperno, I. (2009) *Stories of the Soviet Experience*. Ithaca and London: Cornell University Press.

Poirier, S. (2003). 'This Is Good Country. We Are Good Dreamers.' Dreams and Dreaming in the Australian Western Desert. In Lohman, R. I. (Ed.) *Dream Travelers – Sleep Experiences and Culture in the Western Pacific*. New York: Palgrave Macmillan.

Power, K. (2006). 'Social Dreaming.' From 'Reflections on UKCP/EAP Congress' (Cambridge 2006) in '*The Psychotherapist*' – Issue 32 – Autumn/Winter 2006.

Szekacs, J. (2003). Social Dreaming: A Paradox Accepted (a psychoanalyst's condensed thoughts on social dreaming). In Lawrence, W. G. (Ed) *Experiences in Social Dreaming*. London: Karnac.

Shakespeare, W. (1916). *The Complete Works of William Shakespeare*. Edited by Craig, W. J.. Oxford: Oxford University Press.

Slade, L. (2005). Social Dreaming for a Queer Culture. In *Self & Society*, Vol. 33, No. 3, pp. 32–40.

Slade, L. (2010). Image to Gesture – Social Dreaming with Student Theatre Directors. In Lawrence, W. G. (Ed.): *The Creativity of Social Dreaming*. London: Karnac.

Stern, D. N. (2004). *The Present Moment in Psychotherapy and Everyday Life*. New York: W.W.Norton & Co.

Thomas, D. (1934). '*The Force That Through The Green Fuse Drives The Flower*.' From '*18 Poems*'. London: Fortune Press.

Wallerstein, R. S. (1995). *The Talking Cures – the Psychoanalyses and the Psychotherapies*. New Haven: Yale University Press.

5

AN INTEGRATIVE THEORY OF DREAMING UNDERLYING SOCIAL DREAMING

Rose Redding Mersky

Since being discovered and developed by Gordon Lawrence, social dreaming events have been held worldwide, as parts of professional development programs, group relations conferences, organisational interventions, stand-alone community events and in other creative and important ways. But, what, in fact, is the theory of dreaming that underlies this praxis? And how is this theory actualised in the course of a social dreaming event?

The purpose of this chapter is to offer an integrative theory of dreaming that grounds social dreaming practice. The theory presented in this chapter encompasses not just how dreams are produced from the unconscious, but the particular way in which they are worked with in practice. This is a theory of production and practice. Together, this guides researchers and practitioners and provides a solid grounding in working with dreams. Since being discovered and developed by Gordon Lawrence, social dreaming events have been held worldwide, as parts of professional development programs, group relations conferences, organisational interventions, stand-alone community events and in other creative and important ways. But, what, in fact, is the theory of dreaming that underlies this praxis? And how is this theory actualised in making them an essential resource for organizations, groups and individuals.

This theory of dreaming is derived from a combination of many theoretical sources and the work of many great thinkers, which, taken in combination, resonate with this methodology. I developed this theory as part of my doctoral work in developing and researching "Social Dream-Drawing", a socioanalytic methodology based on social dreaming.

I have divided this discussion into four different areas:

- Dreams belonging to the whole; where I discuss the way that in social dreaming dreams can be regarded as belonging to the system of interconnected dreamers.

- The unconscious; where I compare Freud and Jung's notions of the unconscious and how one's notion of the nature of the unconscious influences how one takes up the role of social dreaming host.
- Dream formation, production and access; where I examine theories of where dreams come from and the processes by which they are produced along with the specific theories behind free association and amplification.
- Dreaming as thinking; where I summarize the ideas of Wilfred Bion (1962) and suggest how social dreaming events can make use of the thinking from the dreams.

Dreams belonging to the whole

Social dreaming is based on the core concept that, while one person may produce the dream, the material relates, in fact, to the social unconscious field of which the dreamer is a part. The dreams presented in the social dreaming matrix reveal its "associative unconscious … a network and a process of unconscious thinking that belongs to the system and its context, rather than to the individual person" (Long 2016 p. 93). It is composed of "a matrix of thought that links members of a community at an unconscious level" (Long 2010).

For centuries dreams have been taken seriously by cultures from around the world and have been an important element of cultural and societal interest. In some cultures, for example, someone was chosen as the dreamer for the community and some were even elevated to a special status because of this function. One example comes from the Crow Nation, a North American Indian tribe, in the late 19th and early 20th century. This tribe was faced with imminent destruction by white settlers and soldiers, who were crowding them out of their native lands and killing off their beloved buffaloes. They sent out identified members, usually young men or boys, who were called dream-seekers, to the wilderness. Their task was to "plead for the Great Spirit to grant a dream" (Gosling & Case 2013 p. 711). After a dream came, the young man would share it with the elders, who would interpret it, according to their own "cosmology of dreams" (ibid.) in relation to whatever the collective issue was, in this case, their survival following the loss of their hunting grounds.

C.G. Jung coined the term "collective unconscious". What was collective to him was the history that all humans share in the same way and that "represent the life and essence of a non-individual psyche" (Jung quoted in Coxhead & Hiller 1976 p. 16). This notion of "identical psychic structures common to all men" (ibid.), which is composed of images that were inherited generation after generation, built a growing stock of unconscious visual references over time, what Edgar (1999 p. 199) describes as "a common and universal storehouse of psychic contents."

His concept stands in contrast to the socioanalytic notion of the associative unconscious, in two significant ways. First, at the level of the associative unconscious, all members of the collective do not hold the exact same images. In fact, individuals hold only a part of the collective whole in their unconscious, which makes the case for accessing all parts, in order to have a better sense of the whole. Second, the associative unconscious does not hold fixed images, but instead contains a world of infinite mental images. Jung's collective unconscious may be regarded as one part of the larger, infinite associative unconscious.

Jung differentiates personal dreams, dealing with the daily lives of the dreamers, from what he called dreams from the collective unconscious. This is an idea taken up by Lawrence in social dreaming. For Jung, "Personal dreams are limited to the affairs of everyday life and one's personal process, offering information and guidance pertaining to what is going on in our current lives. These are the everyday dreams, the 'bread and butter' of the dream world" (1930 [2009] p. 10). The collective dreams have a much broader meaning.

Linked to this notion of the collective nature of dreaming, is Lawrence's concept of the matrix, where this collective meaning begins to be revealed in the free associations, amplifications and further hypothesising by the hosts and members of the matrix. The work in the matrix is the engine that not only allows the unconscious thinking from the dream to emerge, but is the cushion and the holding system for the work to take place. The dream is seen as an expression of the group's unconscious and is worked with in this way and under this assumption. Perhaps this is comparable to the deliberations of the elders of the Crow nation.

In terms of the practice of social dreaming, this cultural history and the concept of the associative unconscious orients the hosts to developing and sharing hypotheses that relate to the matrix as a whole, rather than to individual dreamers in the matrix. This is similar to the work of large and small group consultants in group relations practice, whose work is to offer hypotheses relating to group-as-a whole dynamics.

The social dreaming matrix is not a group, even though the group may be present. By offering hypotheses linking dream material, hosts seek to illuminate the collective unconscious of the matrix, which may either prompt new dream material or free associations and amplifications connected to these hypotheses. This is described in the host's opening statement, e.g., "Our role, as hosts, is to develop hypotheses that link the dream material, in order to deepen our general learning". Additionally, participants are reminded that in the matrix, we work with the dream and not the individual dreamer.

Dreaming as thinking

Before explaining more about the unconscious and dreaming, in this section, I explore the key epistemological assumption that dreaming is a form of thinking. Bion offers the notion that thinking comes from unconscious processes (1962) and that, in fact, dreams are a form of unconscious thinking.

Bion based his theory of dreaming and thinking on Klein's work (1975), in what Meltzer described as "Bion's modification of Klein's modification of Freud's model-of-the-mind" (2009 p. 46). Thus, these three theorists offer "… three models of the mind, the neurophysiological one of Freud, the geographic-theological one of Klein and the epistemological one of Bion, [which] can be seen to link with one another to form a continuous line of development" (ibid. p. 47).

The British psychoanalyst, Donald Meltzer (2009), describes the revolutionary impact of Klein's thinking on Bion, as reflected in Bion's development of a theory connecting dreaming and thinking. What Klein taught us, so to say, is that there is an active internal world and that dreams have an important meaning in relation to both that internal and external world. This internal world plays out in our daily reality, so that "[i]nstead of transference phenomena being seen as relics of the past [à la Freud] they could now be viewed as externalizations of the immediate present of the internal situation, to be studied as psychic reality" (ibid. p. 39). Klein created a bridge between early experiences and present realities, in that "[i]t is in the internal world of relationships that meaning is generated and deployed to relationships in the outside world" (ibid. p.40).

As opposed to Freud's concept that dream material consists of a forging of unfulfilled childhood wishes and floating dream thoughts peppered with daily minutia, Bion's view was that the unconscious elements that form dreams are related to the repressed early trauma and memories resulting from a break in the connection between the infant and its mother, as outlined by Klein. These painful bits of "raw unencoded sense data" undergo a process of "narrative transformation" into "meaningful thought" (Haartmann 2000). He termed the free-floating split-off feelings as Beta elements and those that have been processed through the mother's containment (and later the analyst's work) as Alpha elements (Bion 1962). He named the process by which this transformation takes place as Alpha Function. Dreaming is one very important way that these bits of sense data can make their way into the state of consciousness. In order to bear them, dreams, as Haartmann (2000) notes, rely on a disguise to "assuage psychic pain" that accompanies this process. At the same time, these dreams have another extremely important function, in that they pick up where the early experience left off. As Haartmann notes: "Because dreams contain messages and promote internal communication, they adopt and extend the work of maternal reverie and containment." (ibid.)

From this perspective, dreams take on a central role in mediating our understanding of the relationship between the internal world of meaning and our external world of work and relationships. What a dream does is to "represent the *meaning* of emotional experiences" (Meltzer 2009 p.44). While Klein's focus was primarily on the emotional development of the child, Bion was concerned with the link between early emotional experience and the capacity to develop the mind. As Meltzer notes (ibid.):

> *Bion's work places emotion at the very heart of meaning. What he says in effect (and this is almost diametrically opposed to Freud's attitude towards emotion) is that the emotional experience of the intimate relationships has to be thought about and understood if the mind is to grow and develop. In a sense the emotion is the meaning of the experience and everything that is evolved in the mind through alpha-function, such as dreaming, verbalizing dreams, painting pictures, writing music, performing scientific functions – all of these are representations of the meaning.*

In comparing Bion to Freud, Meltzer points out that Freud's neurophysiological model of the mind (1983 n.a.) led him to believe that "no intellectual activity or manifestation of judgment or function of judgment goes on in the dreamer" (ibid. p. 65). In effect, dreams are composed of childhood reminiscences salted with the day's "residue" (ibid.) Freud also made it clear that emotions had no meaning in dreams (Meltzer 2009 p. 67).

Although Freud linked dreaming to thinking (1900 [1976] p. 385), he considered dreaming "an unconscious process of thought, which may easily be different from what we perceive during purposive reflection accompanied by consciousness." Jung's view (1964 [1970] p. 53) was that "… a dream cannot produce a definite thought", and Klein did not concern herself with this. She essentially concurred with Freud that there is no particular intellectual activity taking place in dreaming other than what he had outlined.

Bion, on the other hand, posited that dreams contain the thoughts related to the unintegrated elements of the infant. Bion's idea was that in addition to the emotional consequence of the mother's capacity to contain split-off emotional fragments, there is also an intellectual consequence, i.e. the first roots of the baby's capacity to develop thoughts. Thus "something which in the infant was near-sensory and somatic was transformed into something more mental … which could be used for thought or stored as memory" (Crociani-Windland & Hoggett 2012 p.179). "He is describing a passage toward symbolisation and thought" (ibid. p. 170).

With the containment of the analytic setting theoretically replicating the original dyadic environment of the baby and child, the process of free association to the dreams, both by analyst and patient, was for Bion a way to make these dream thoughts more consciously available. His critical theory of thinking was based on the concept that thoughts were always in search of thinkers, not the other way around. As Lopez-Corvo (2006 p. 132) puts it: "For Bion, thinking is a consequence of thoughts and not the other way around. Thinking represents an obligatory development of the mind that is produced by the pressure of thoughts."

In relation to dreams, this meant that only through a dream could certain thoughts be made available that could then, in the properly contained analytic setting and using free association, be made available for thinking. These thoughts, therefore, were already in existence in the unconscious, but not available for thought. This naturally underpins Lawrence's concept of the matrix. Dreams contain unconscious thoughts that are, only now, under this particular set of circumstance, being made available for thinking.

Being available for thought, from Bion's perspective, meant that they could be "digested" by the patient and gradually integrated into a more robust relationship with reality (which links with Freud's reality principle, which was very helpful to Bion's thinking).

As J. and N. Symington (1996 p. 60) note:

> Bion's view was that the conscious and unconscious material was rendered more comprehensible by the dream-work, in the sense that it became processible into elements that could be used for furthering the integrating processes of thought.

The Unconscious

Freud was well aware of these historical notions of dreaming. As cited in Walde (1999 p. 121), he is quoted as saying: "I think that in general it is a good plan occasionally to bear in mind the fact that people were in the habit of dreaming before there was such a thing as psychoanalysis". Also, as a scientist, he was grounded in the notion of the scientific understanding of all things. His monumental work, *The Interpretation of Dreams* (1900), can be seen in the context of these historical and contemporary contexts.

Some cultures believed that when one had a dream, his soul had made contact with the gods and/or that the gods themselves had entered the soul of the dreamer. One example is the Maricopa Indians of Colorado, who "believed that success in life depended on the spirit, and that the spiritual is approached through dreaming" (Coxhead & Hiller 1976 p. 12). They believed that when they were in a state of dreaming, the soul would leave the body and search a spirit, who would "reveal a song or a cure." (ibid.)

This notion of the passive dreamer, whose soul meets the gods or who is visited from without, was revolutionised by Freud, in his formulation of dreaming as emanating from one's unconscious. For Freud, the dream is an expression of "the mental life of the dreamer" him- or herself (Moses 1999 p. 303). It is Freud's great achievement that "the Unconscious is not conceived as an exterior power, like the pagan gods or fate (of the Christian God), but is rather located within the human being" (Walde 2009 p. 129).

Equally revolutionary was the implication of Freud's theories of dreaming and the unconscious, i.e. that man had parts of himself that he did not know and could not easily access. This not-knowing existence challenged the prevailing positivist notions of reality and set the stage for the development of ways to access this unknown part. As Moses (1999 p. 307) puts it, Freud's thinking:

> ... completely subverted the identity of the subject and of conscious life by transporting the subject outside himself and toward a space where he no longer knows himself. Freud's division of the psychic apparatus into a conscious and unconscious system explodes the classical notion of subject and scatters its fragments in multiple psychic instances that may no longer be reassembled, as in classical psychology, into one original synthesis.

The epistemological assumption underlying this theory of dreaming is that an unconscious exists. How the unconscious is thought about is important for social dreaming. Is it something to be feared or to be embraced? Is it a source of disturbance or an important communication? Or is it all of the above?

Freud taught us that dreams are a source of tremendous information to the patient and analyst as to what repressed wish or desire has been, so to say, disabling the patient's mental health. His general view was that dreams are either composed of forbidden thoughts or unconscious desires.

As opposed to Freud's view, Jung's concept of the unconscious was of a world of infinite creativity available to be explored and, in such exploration, to expand and illuminate the quality of our conscious existence. As Coxhead & Hiller (1976 p. 15) note:

> *While Freud looked on the dream itself as a disturbed form of mental activity through which he could approach his patients' neuroses, C.G. Jung saw the dream as a normal, spontaneous and creative expression of the unconscious.*

The idea that the dream is an innovative and creative way to bring problems and anxieties into consciousness gives a different picture of its process. Lopez-Corvo (2006 p. 130) describes it as "…vindicating the unconscious from an ominous, unfriendly, and threatening nature, to a more gracious, positive, and valuable one". This notion was later taken up by Lawrence (2011 p. 333), who notes "the creative, joyful dimension of the unconscious."

Jung saw "neurosis as part of the psychic life that is trying to advance" (Coxhead & Hiller 1976 p. 16) and he valued its presence. As he wrote (as quoted in Coxhead & Hiller 1976 p. 16): "All psychological phenomena have some sense of purpose in them." From his perspective, the dream was a means of self-discovery (ibid.).

Therefore, while we all recognise Freud's enormous leap in further developing the idea of the dynamic unconscious, this view was greatly expanded by Jung to encompass its collective and creative potential.

The notion of dreams, as a form of communication and as a creative expression of the unconscious that is not easily connected to conscious experience, is central to social dreaming. This allows violent and disturbing dream material to be shared in a matrix. Sometimes dreams are shared that include other members of the matrix. This has implications for how the hosts take up their roles. They are not "charged" with attempting to understand or interpret the dream material, but only to help the matrix become aware of links between dreams and deeper meanings. This may or may not involve references to the disturbing material.

Hosts try not to run away from what is disturbing, but hold it in the larger context of all the dream material being shared. One could say, that in taking this role with this kind of discipline, whatever anxiety may arise as a result of the disturbing material is contained. However, it is not the explicit role of hosts to provide containment for anxiety. The matrix is not thought of as a group that needs a facilitator to take that role. Containment is about taking up the task.

Dream formation, production and access

Freud laid out what he terms "the psychical processes at work in the formation of dreams" (1900 [1976] p. 403), in other words the mechanics of their production, as well as their function for the dreamer. For Freud, dreams are through a variety of processes that include condensation, whereby dream elements undergo a series of transformations and are compressed or condensed into the dream as experienced.

Thus, from his perspective, "the psychical material has undergone an extensive process of condensation in the course of the formation of the dream … the dream which we remember when we wake up would only be a fragmentary remnant of the total dream work." (ibid.p. 383). Thus "… dream-condensation is a notable characteristic of the relation between dream-thoughts and dream-content" (ibid. p. 403).

Freud notes a contrast between the extensive dream thoughts in the unconscious and the relatively fewer manifest dream elements in the dream. From his perspective, the dream represents all the unconscious thoughts related to it, even though it does not and cannot explicitly contain all of them. Thus, the dream is a compromise formation. While few elements from the dream-thoughts find their way into the dream-content, those that do "represent logical relationships between the individual thoughts" (Meltzer 2009 p. 15).

Freud notes that dream material is very often quite mundane. To explain this, he articulates the concept of displacement (another process alongside condensation), whereby dream thoughts are transformed into mundane manifest dream material. As a matter of fact, the more mundane the dream content, according to Freud, the more bizarre the dream thought that prompted it. As he notes, "dreams are brief, meagre and laconic in comparison with the range and wealth of the dream-thoughts" (1900 [1976] p. 383). Either way, in the manifest dream elements or in the original dream thoughts, the unexpected and the often frightening lurk.

Freud developed free association as a way of accessing the original dream thoughts in the unconscious ("if the work of interpretation is carried further it may reveal still more thoughts concealed behind the dreams" [ibid.]). In the treatment room, the patient is encouraged to say whatever comes to mind in as uncensored a way as possible. Freud's great insight is that the way people go from one topic to another topic in a seemingly random way actually reveals an associative thought process, "a chain of ideas" (Bollas 1987 [2013] p. 9). Once the dream is made available and free association is undertaken, the dream material is "uncondensed" and the bounty and beauty of the primitive unconscious thoughts are available for exploration and understanding.

Freud's discovery of free association as a means for accessing unconscious thoughts is central to social dreaming. Hosts, in their opening statements, and sometimes during the course of a matrix, state this clearly, and often define what free association is (i.e. "free association means anything that comes to mind.").

Enhancing free association and amplification is also linked to how the chairs are placed. We cannot duplicate the standard placement of the couch and the analyst in the analytic consulting room. In social dreaming, the chairs are placed so that the familiar behavior of conversations and discussions are not encouraged and direct eye contact and socialization are minimized. Two common ways of placing chairs are in the form of a spiral and the form of a snowflake.

The goal of these arrangements gives participants their own space within the cluster of the others to access their internal and dream lives.

While Jung also took up the use of free association in his clinical work, he had his reservations about its use. From his perspective, free association runs the danger of taking the patient further and further afield from the original dream material. He developed the concept of amplification, which encourages the dreamer to connect their dream images to current cultural and social experience. His idea is "to stay as close as possible to the dream itself, and to exclude all the irrelevant ideas and associations that it might evoke" (Jung 1964 [1970] p. 12). For him, the dreams "are the facts from which we must proceed" (Jung 1961 [1995] p. 194).

This has consequences for those hosting social dreaming, where a matrix can be permeated by one clever association after another. As host, I remind participants of this potential by stating in my opening statement: "Free association means anything that comes to mind. Freud viewed free association not so much as a response or a reaction to what another has said, but as an expression of one's own inner response to the dream material." During the matrix, it is important for the host to keep hypotheses connected to original dream material as much as possible.

These notions of how dreams are produced and the ways in which their unconscious elements are accessed in the treatment room and in the matrix do not cover what actually causes a dream to happen. For purposes of working in social dreaming, how can we understand how particular dreams come when they do? What in either one's inner life or one's reality (and probably somehow both in tandem) leads the dreamer to dream such a dream?

Freud's concept of condensation suggests (metaphorically) some sort of machinery of selection. Problematically, though, this suggests that inputs from the unconscious are somehow operated upon to create consciousness. I would propose a more interactive and porous metaphor to characterise the space between the unconscious thoughts and their conscious representation, i.e. the dream. This in-between space makes possible an active interchange between these realms, similar to the fit that Freud describes between elements of the unconscious in the course of dream for-mation. We know that all of the infinite possibilities available in the unconscious cannot or need not be "tapped" for the production of a dream. In my view, it is the context of the dreaming experience that influences which unconscious elements make up the dream.

This notion of a porous membrane is central to Lawrence's concept of the matrix. He sees that matrix as the external context that influences the dream material. As he has written:

> *The existence of the matrix alters the nature of the dreams …. The matrix becomes a different "container" for receiving dreams, with the result that dream contents change.*
>
> *(2011 p. 333)*

This harkens back to the notion that dreams belong to the whole, i.e., the concept that dreaming is innately a social process and what stimulates certain dream material to be mobilised, stems from a social stimulus. The dream emerges, not as an iso-lated volcanic explosion from within, but in conjunction with the social forces and context of reality. Thus, the context for any dream exploration, whether at the individual or the associative unconscious level, influences its production. This has consequences for how a Social Dream event is thought of and communicated to participants. For example, using a particular theme for a social dreaming event may lead dreamers to bring dream material related to that theme.

The notion of a porous membrane between the dream thoughts and the manifest dream already exists in psychoanalytic theory. For example, Freud and others emphasise the influence of external factors on dream material, i.e. the state of one's body or the noises of the night. In describing the reality theory, he notes the influence of daily experiences on manifest dream material in terms of "dream-instigators" (1901 [2001] p. 656).

Contemporarily, Lansky (2003 p. 357) theorises that an "instigating disruption" is what "drives the dream into being. It is the instigator of the dream that connects the working of the inner world with events in the external world." Lansky's per-spective links up with Meltzer's idea (1983) that the dream process is designed to "solve a problem" not yet in one's consciousness.

Perhaps we can tentatively hypothesise that a dream without an external context would not emerge, particularly given the technical production processes described above. It does not just pop up due to pressure from within; it exists always in relationship to the dreamer's real experience in the external world. As Lawrence further notes (2003 p. 610): "The content of the dreaming alters to take account of its context and becomes social in orientation". This reflects an active, rather than a passive process, coming in two directions, i.e. from the outside in and from the inside out. The unconscious is an active element that participates, along with the stimulus or context of reality, in forming the seemingly chaotic material of dream thoughts into a dream.

The great mystery is how this occurs without our awareness. As Lopez-Corvo (2006 p. 209) notes:

> Where and how is the intention of the unconscious message precisely manufactured? Where and how can all of this have been decided without the awareness of our conscious self? What exactly is this concealed intelligence, capable of conceiving, so speedily, beautiful condensations and displacements in order to produce a dream? These are mys-terious questions that still lack an answer.
>
> This mystery is at the heart of dreaming and somehow, we must live with this wonder.
>
> What appears to be amazing about the process of dream formation is how such com-plex selection and transformation of memories, sensations, and metaphorical visual ideo-grams take place without any conscious intervention, behind our back, so to speak, where the whole process is generated outside of our selfness as if the unconscious was always several steps ahead.
>
> (ibid. p. 213)

In holding social dreaming events, we work to set up the best possible conditions for these processes to take place. When social dreaming is part of a larger event with its own theme, the choice of who hosts the matrix must be considered. For example, for the 2017 ISPSO regional meeting, whose theme was "Identity and

Identification in Europe in Crisis", there were three hosts, each coming from a different part of Europe. The idea behind this choice was to provide a certain amount of containment by encompassing a broad spectrum of hosts from across Europe.

This process for furthering thinking, in relation to social dreaming, takes place in reflective events following the matrix. "As I see it, the reflection group is the setting for this apparatus of thinking to undertake its task of transforming the thoughts from the infinite into actual thinking relating to reality" (Mersky 2012 p. 37). In order to reach its full potential, space needs to be taken for reflection. Without that, participants are left with many stimulating thoughts with no context for action and insight.

Conclusion

The ways of organizing and hosting Social Dreaming in whatever context are influenced by what theory of dreaming underlies the event. From the decision of what space and how to arrange the chairs; what, if any, theme to choose or relate to; who is chosen as host and what does he or she represent to the participants; how the opening statement is constructed; how dreams are associated to both by hosts and participants; how hypotheses linking dream material are formed; how to divide the available time to ensure reflection (and probably more) are all important factors to take into account.

In this chapter, I have outlined elements of the theories of dreaming developed by Freud, Jung, Klein and Bion, which form a theoretical support for my theory of dreaming underlying social dreaming praxis. In a social dreaming matrix, one is presented with rich, creative and seemingly chaotic material from the unconscious. In order to work with this material to bring insight and understanding to the system at large, hosts need to have a comprehensive internalized theory of dreaming that they can rely upon. This chapter is written in the hopes of making such a contribution.

References

Bion, W.R. (1962). "A theory of thinking". In: E.B. Spillius (1988) (ed) *Melanie Klein Today. Developments in Theory and Practice (Vol. I, Mainly theory)*. London: Routledge, pp. 178–186.

Bollas, C. (1987). *The Shadow of the Object: Psychoanalysis of the Unthought Known*. New York: Columbia University Press.

Bollas, C. (2007). *The Freudian Moment: Second Edition*. Reprint. London: Karnac, 2013.

Coxhead, D. and Hiller, S. (1976). *Dreams: Visions of the Night*. New York: Thames and Hudson.

Crociani-Windland, L. and Hoggett, P. (2012). "Politics and affect". *Subjectivity*. 5(2), pp. 161–179.

Edgar, I.R. (1999). "The Imagework Method in health and social science research". *Qualitative Health Research*. 9, pp. 198–211.

Freud, S. (1900). The interpretation of dreams. *S.E.* Volume 4–5. Reprint. Middlesex: Penguin, 1976.

Freud, S. (1901). On Dreams. *S.E.* Vol. 5, pp. 633–686. Reprint. London: Vintage, 2001.

Gosling, J. and Case, P. (2013). "Social dreaming and Ecocentric ethics: Sources of non-rational insight in the face of climate change catastrophe". *Organization.* 20(5), pp. 705–721.

Haartmann, K. (2000). *Review of Grotstein, James S. (2000). Who is the Dreamer Who Dreams the Dream?* Hillsdale: The Analytic Press. *Kleinian Studies Ejournal.* www.psychoanalysis-and-therapy.com/human_nature/ksej/hartmangrotstein.html. [accessed 08. 09. 2014].

Jung, C.G. (1930). *The Red Book: Liber Novus.* Reprint. New York: The Philemon Foundation & W.W. Norton, 2009.

Jung, C.G. (1961). *Memories, Dreams, Reflections.* Reprint. London: Fontana, 1995.

Jung, C.G. (1964). *Man and His Symbols.* Reprint. New York: Dell, 1970.

Klein, M. (1975). "Our adult world and its roots in infancy". In: M. Klein (ed) *The Writings of Melanie Klein: Vol. 3 Envy and Gratitude and Other Works, 1946–1963.* London: Hogarth, pp. 247–263.

Lansky, M. (2003). "Shame conflicts as dream instigators: Wish fulfillment and the ego ideal in dream dynamics". *The American Journal of Psychoanalysis.* 63(4), pp. 357–364.

Lawrence, W.G. (2003). "Social dreaming as sustained thinking". *Human Relations.* 56(5), pp. 609–624.

Lawrence, W.G. (2011). Intuiting knowledge from the social unconscious with special reference to social dreaming. In: E. Hopper and H. Weinberg, (2011) (eds) *The Social Unconscious in Persons, Groups, and Societies. Volume I: Mainly Theory.* London: Karnac, pp. 321–336.

Long, S. (2016). The transforming experience framework and unconscious processes. In: S. Long (2016) (ed) *Transforming Experience in Organisations: A Framework for Organisational Research and Consultancy.* London: Karnac, pp. 31–106.

Lopez-Corvo, R. (2006). *Wild Thoughts Searching for a Thinker.* London: Karnac.

Meltzer, D. (1983). *Dream Life.* Strathtay, Perthshire: Clunie Press.

Meltzer, D. (2009). *Dream Life: A Re-examination of the Psychoanalytic Theory and Technique.* London: Karnac.

Mersky, R. (2012). "Contemporary methodologies to surface and act on unconscious dynamics in organizations: An exploration of design, facilitation capacities, consultant paradigm and ultimate value". *Organisational and Social Dynamics.* 12(1), pp. 19–43.

Moses, S. (1999). "The cultural index of Freud's Interpretation of Dreams". In: D. Shulman, and G.G. Stroumsa (1999) (eds) *Dream Cultures: Explorations in the Comparative History of Dreaming.* New York: Oxford University Press, pp. 303–314.

Symington, J. and Symington, N. (1996). *The Clinical Thinking of Wilfred Bion.* London: Routledge.

Walde, C. (1999). "Dream interpretation in a prosperous age?" In: D. Shulman and G.G. Stroumsa (1999) (eds). *Dream Cultures: Explorations in the Comparative History of Dreaming.* New York: Oxford University Press, pp. 121–142.

6

AN ACTION RESEARCH STUDY OF DREAM-SHARING AS SOCIALLY-CONSTITUTED PRACTICE

Ruth Balogh

Introduction

My purpose here is to open discussion on the implications of framing processes for sharing dreams as "social", through inquiry based in action research. In newly emerging fields of discourse, many questions may naturally arise regarding the developing epistemological basis. For research in social dreaming, all these areas of discourse are tentative since we base our thinking on a very small body of litera-ture. Yet critical analysis (e.g., Manley 2014) has already begun to inform our work; explication and analysis of the philosophical roots of our thinking is one approach (e.g., Long & Harney 2013), but we can complement this by examining taken-for-granted positions and implied epistemologies that underpin existing accounts. The discourses appropriate for such inquiries are social scientific, cultural and ethnographic. In this chapter I aim in a small way to open up the development of this kind of perspective on social dreaming, using a "first-person" action research approach that is grounded in practice.

As an action researcher, my curiosity naturally turns to questions of processes and practice. If we take the purpose of social dreaming as: "to provide a forum for the sharing of hidden or unspoken thoughts and feelings about the social circumstances of the social dreaming participants" (Manley 2014 p. 323), then how we construct the "social" through social dreaming practice becomes a matter of interest. Action research explicitly sets out with the intent of improving aspects of situations felt to be unsatisfactory. It is a form of practice based inquiry using dialogue as a vehicle for taking action. As Kemmis, argues, following Habermas's theory of communicative action (Kemmis 2006 p. 104), it takes place in the "(overlapping) organizational and lifeworld settings in which people live and work together."

Unlike conventional positivist research, which averts its gaze from the research-er's social engagement, trying to minimise it through de-contextualisation and procedural standardisation, action researchers explicitly acknowledge that they operate within social systems. Instead of distancing ourselves from others, we attempt to work collaboratively, working *with* rather than on people. Thus, the processes of collaborative action research not only produce findings and insights for change but through the active participation of those involved, these processes are the means by which inquiry engenders change. And they are themselves matters for study.

Therefore, every action research project is an exploration of some aspect of its socially situated nature, and our findings are shared more through portrayal of the particularities and contextual details of research accounts than from attempting to generalise. Action research processes reflect the multi-faceted nature of reality as they draw on multiple perspectives, including the voices of researchers themselves; and the nature of the knowledge so generated is recognised as provisional, so that research accounts are more inclined to open up debate and invite critical connection than to present statements of general truth.

Social dreaming and action research

The social dreaming literature has identified action research as appropriate for researching social dreaming (Lawrence 1998, Baglioni & Fubini 2013, Balogh 2015). Published action research studies on social dreaming, however, are few. The action research practice alluded to by Lawrence (1998) draws its inspiration from the Tavistock Institute with whom Kurt Lewin, one of the founders of action research, also collaborated (Marrow 1969, Neumann 2005).

While action research – precisely because it is recognised as socially and culturally situated – must necessarily draw on a range of different philosophical perspectives, the work of the pragmatist and educational philosopher Dewey with its focus on learning is considered fundamental by many action researchers. Dewey's work embraced an ethic of education for social change. It is in this light that he has been credited with using a more sophisticated form of action research even before Kurt Lewin coined the term (Harkavy & Puckett 2014). As a pragmatist his insistence is on creating knowledge that is useful in terms of the context in which it is generated. From this perspective, the pragmatists' approach is rich in insight both for action research, and also for social dreaming research. When social dreaming is considered as a form of socioanalysis (Long 2013), the pragmatist Peirce's notions of abductive logic and the newly coined associative unconscious have been found useful for developing the philosophical basis of social dreaming (Long & Harney 2013).

The Tavistock approach typically works through consultancy, where, in its initial formulation an action researcher worked within an organisation or social system to "study what was being enacted in the social situation, to hypothesize how that enactment might be related to unresolved psychological issues … and to craft social experiments … intended to resolve psychological issues" (Neumann 2014 p. 758). Later it encompassed a wider, more socio-ecological approach, but it has always focused on unresolved psychological issues using psychoanalytic concepts and group relations. Lawrence's development of the ideas and practice of social dreaming took place within the context of his own work at the Tavistock (Manley 2014 p. 326) and this is the form of action research he envisaged as his eighth "working hypothesis" for social dreaming (Lawrence 1998 p. 139).

For this chapter, a more important distinguishing characteristic of the Tavistock, and Lawrence's approach to action research is of the outsider role of the action researcher, albeit collaborative, containing and facilitative in nature – but not originating from "inside" a system. This results in a tendency for its action research reports to be written in the public voice, where third-person and passive voice constructions dominate. This is at odds with current critical action research practice where the "reflexive turn" – or "the ability to reflect on our own reflections … to examine our own attitudes, assumptions and prejudices" (Ledwith & Springett 2010 p. 18) has become an essential element of action research accounts and any claims to "validity" (Winter 2002, Dadds 2008, Heikkinen et al. 2012) – with the main authorial voice in the first persons singular and plural (Green 2006).

The act of positioning oneself inside the research process brings a shift in voice from the "deity mode" of speech, where knowledge is framed as propositional and the dominant voice is passive; towards the first person, active voice, and the examination of one's own theorising through reflexivity. Such positioning is, however, far from straightforward. Torbert distinguishes between first- second- and third-person research/practice (Torbert 2006).

As much as we may like the idea of action inquiry [a form of action research], we rarely actively wish to engage subjectively in first-person research/practice in the present. At least that's what I've found … … Not only are we as individuals unpractised and unpolished in the domain of inquiry in the midst of our daily lives, but so also are our intimate relationships, our organizations, and social science itself.

(op. cit. p. 208)

In addressing such difficulties, action researchers have drawn on different ways of knowing that derive from the world of the imagination, using creative expression to disrupt – or at least unsettle – our habitual, persistent and indeed *dominant* discourses of rational argument and logical analysis. Winter et al. describe how this approach has enabled practitioners to "draw on the full range of their cultural resources and the full range of their capacities (including emotional empathy)" (Winter, Buck & Sobiechowska 2001 p. 2) to "express and evoke feelings and to explore value conflicts and ethical issues" (op. cit. p. 185).

The prominence of these issues in action research, and the challenge they present to creating appropriate communicative spaces to draw on these "cultural resources" prompted me to wonder whether dreaming could provide action research with one such cultural resource. I offer the following developmental account of my interest in social dreaming and its practice as a "first-person inquiry". This approach stands in contrast to Lawrence's work, positioned as an outsider consultant in the Tavistock tradition; his voice separate from that of the social dreaming matrix participants in his accounts of social dreaming. However, this position was also a source of discomfort to him as revealed in his dismay over the readiness of group relations' consultants to move to interpretation on behalf of the group: "Interpretation is about 'I've got the power'" (Lawrence, quoted in Manley 2014 p. 336). This points precisely towards the reasoning behind action researchers' impulses to undertake inquiry inclusively. In putting forward a first-person account, I hope to extend the range of possibilities for social dreaming practitioners to use action research to inquire into their practice in a more participatory way.

The roots of my inquiries into dreaming and action research

My inquiries began to take shape when a dream "irruption" occurred, obliging me to understand it in terms of my research and working life. I had long been interested in dreams as a source of personal insight, but confined my view of what constituted "personal" to a construct that focused on my immediate emotional attachments to family and friends through a loosely articulated psychoanalytic perspective. The idea that they might illuminate my working life only occurred to me when I returned to work in social research in health after a break of several years and had the dream that directly invoked my current research. Even then it did not occur to me to study it until several years later when I mentioned it to my co-researcher and supervisor who expressed interest (Balogh 2010 p. 518).

A later dream provided further impetus:

> *I was lost in a building at my workplace, looking for the inaugural lecture of my colleague Professor David Manning. As I searched, the building ceased being a modern one and became an Oxford college. I came upon an old man, the Principal, asleep on a window-seat in a long white night-gown, and I woke him up. In doing so I woke myself, and found myself sitting bolt upright in bed. I was full of outrage about an event I considered unjust that had just taken place in my working life.*

Such was the strength of my feeling, I knew I had to take action over this matter, an employment issue affecting my work. I called my trade union representative who advised me to address the issue, and with great care. The action I took as a result led me to discover an institutional procedure for dealing with the situation, and by following this, my colleagues and I eventually resolved things successfully.

I was struck by the way the dream communicated something to me without my needing to analyse it. However, successive conversations with friends revealed multiple levels of meaning. First, the building's history was significant: it had recently been built on the site previously occupied by the human resources department – the very department I needed to contact. I then recalled that longer ago it was where the college principal lodged. The building itself, and its layers of history, mapped directly on to the context and nuances of my feelings. In further tellings, a friend noticed the additional meaning of "principal" as "principle" and I realised the name "Manning" signified employment.

As I write, two further connections indicate the dream's significance for my future work: I recall this academic's work was in Imaging Science, a reference both to the imagination, and to systematic, scientific analysis. I also recall an occasion when visiting Keble College Oxford and being shown the pre-Raphaelite William Holman Hunt's painting "The Light of the World", (a white-clad Christ-figure holding a lantern), and my puzzlement about the picture being displayed in a side chapel rather than in public view, as though (like our dreams) it had to be hidden.

I began to grasp how dreaming could be directly helpful in my work situation, especially over issues about which I felt uncomfortable (Balogh 2010 p. 518). I also began to grasp the Freudian notion of condensation, whereby "two (or more) images combine (or can be connected) to form a composite image which is invested with meaning and energy derived from both" (Rycroft 1968 p. 22). Making this connection, between my work and my dreaming, enabled me to encounter resistance in myself to extending the way I thought about dreaming, and the "lifeworld" of my dreams grew larger, beyond my own internalised dynamics.

My understanding of the power of dreams also drew on the 1960s and 1970s movement (pre-dating Lawrences's work), of sharing dreams in groups (eg., Williams 1980, Shohet 1985, Goodison 1995). I had occasionally taken part in such groups and this too helped me grasp the potential for sharing dreams in public spaces. However, my anxiety that "any terrors that arose in my dreams might call for disclosure that I might not be ready for" (Balogh 2010 p. 522) made me uncertain about venturing in to such spaces. But experiencing a well-facilitated group helped me learn how imaginative techniques could lead to a better understanding of the commonality of human emotions without such disclosure. Realising that personal contextual details could be set aside in sharing dream insights enabled me "to connect to other people's dreams, and in so doing invite them into my own" (op. cit. p. 522).

But the meanings generated from such group activity always seemed to relate to personal issues despite being publicly articulated. In some group dream sharing this is explicitly reflected in the group's operation, e.g., for Ullman "it was the function of the group to be helpful without being intrusive, respecting the dreamer's privacy yet engaging actively with the dreamer" (Ullman & Zimmerman 1979 p. xix), and "there is a gradual recognition that the true leader of the group is the dreamer" (Ullman 1996 p. 230).

My inquiries were taking me more deeply into my work as an action researcher, and I sought to study and engage in dialogue over ways for dreaming and meaning-making to become more collectively constructed, even addressing the field of the group-as-constituted, as we occasionally see in social dreaming accounts (e.g., Baglioni 2010 p. 165) and as occur in irruptions from more conventional group-work, leading participants into "collective retroflection" about issues in their shared social milieu which refuse to be ignored (Grey 2005 p. 210). In communicating this intention within my "lifeworld", I encountered the literature on social dreaming.

Exploring dream-sharing as social dreaming practice

A number of questions concerned me in my inquiries into social dreaming. One revolved around the differences between reports of social dreaming matrices (Lawrence, 2005, 2010) and my experiences of group dream-sharing using the Gestalt "I Am" approach where "everything in the dream represents a part of yourself, projected outwards" (Friedman 2007 p. 98). How, I wondered, do different arrangements / activity systems for group dream-sharing play in to the kind of knowledge they generate? Contemporary anthropological literature on dreaming regards "dream interpretation systems as complex communicative processes" rather than "treating dreams like museum objects" (Tedlock 1987 p. x), breaking down both the distinction between "the dream" and its telling and inviting consideration of the social space and communicative interchanges in and through which dreams are told. In representing dreaming as taking place within a bio-psycho-social system this also gestures to the phenomenological continuity between dreaming and waking life (Boss 1977 p. 25; Bastide 1966 p. 203). This lens – of continuities rather than binary oppositions – offered a route into analysing both reports and direct experience of such processes.

A second question was more of a general uncertainty about expertise and the extent to which a grasp of the psychoanalytic approach of Bion, central to the theorising and practice of social dreaming, might be necessary for the successful conduct of a social dreaming matrix. Lawrence reported a related tension over expertise when he introduced social dreaming in the 1980s in a milieu where "the received truth was that dreams and dreaming could only be conducted by a psychoanalyst and an analysand" (Lawrence 2005 p. 3). In contrast, the group dreamwork movement familiar to me uses non-hierarchical self-help principles (see Williams 1975; Shohet 1985; Goodison 1995); while Ullman rejects the necessity for psychotherapeutic expertise: "serious dreamwork could be pursued without a background in psychiatry or psychology if the interest and motivation were there" (Ullman & Zimmerman 1979 p. xix). To what extent, I wondered, could social dreaming be undertaken by someone like myself without psychoanalytic training, still less a sophisticated understanding of Bion's ideas?

My studies revealed a further tension. I was working at the edges of two discourses: social dreaming, where action research was privileged but barely explored, and action research where dreaming seemed to deserve inclusion in the "creative turn" but was absent except at the margins (e.g., Convery 1996) or by allusion, e.g., in Burchell's use of "reverie" as energising practitioner research through poetic expression (Burchell 2010). Aware that disciplinary boundary-crossing – well-established in action research – brings both difficulty and reward, I resolved to tread carefully and study widely.

Learning how to practise

I found the social dreaming literature was rich in first-hand accounts of social dreaming matrices enabling groups in a wide variety of settings to discuss strong emotions openly, "allowing access to the depths without disturbing the surface" (Fubini 2010 p. 146). Questions of practice were alluded to but without systematic or situated analysis. One discussed learning to conduct a social dreaming matrix (Eden 2010), reporting on an apparently incomplete development of a certification process for hosts. I recognised it was based on Kolb's experiential learning cycle (Kolb 1984) of "concrete experience, observation, reflection, and further experimentation" (Eden 2010 p. 178), a coherent theoretical position about learning but not articulated as such.

This version of a learning cycle which begins with direct experience (as opposed to traditional pedagogy which starts with theory) is particularly useful when imaginative techniques are employed to explore emotional and ethical issues (Winter, Buck & Sobiechowska 2001). The key difference between Eden's conceptualisation and that of action research lies in the inclusion of theorising in the action research cycle. Her implied position, being congruent with mine, was therefore encouraging

Experiments in dream-sharing

Unable, at this time, to identify any learning opportunities within the social dreaming movement, but enthused by the potential of social dreaming, I started experimenting with fellow action researchers. Such existing social spaces can offer fertile ground for opening up new "communicative spaces" in the Habermasian sense (Kemmis 2006). Feeling unready to enter into more than one new territory, I set aside trying to facilitate a social dreaming matrix and instead articulated these experiments as "social dreaming sessions". I grounded them in experiential learning, briefly introducing my inquiry, setting ground-rules, negotiating consent for using the material, and embarking directly on the experience of dream-sharing. The ethical framework was greatly assisted by the professional and action research values underpinning the events where I offered these sessions, as was the voluntary nature of participation, given that other opportunities were available.

I conducted the first among a small group of Collaborative Action Research Network (CARN) members gathered for a weekend on Hadrian's Wall in the English-Scottish Border Country to discuss "Boundaries and Debateable Territories". After introducing the idea of "breaking down the barriers between night and day by studying our dreams collectively" on the Saturday, I invited my seven colleagues on Sunday to share some dreams and free-associate to them. The ground-rules followed those of the event, based on CARN values (http://carn.org. uk/about 2017). I invited my colleagues to contribute dreams around a focal question: "what our dreams might tell us about our practice as action researchers" and to associate to them as in a social dreaming matrix but without the usual Matrix seating arrangement. Dreams with powerful personal meanings emerged. One participant reported that (like me) she had never considered bringing her "private and personal into my work life like that before" (Balogh 2010 p. 527). The strength of the experience was such that six were willing some two years later to contribute further by associating to an image that arose during that session – that of a house in a forest, which had emerged again in slightly different form at a subsequent social dreaming session that I held at a later conference. These dreams and their associations represented my first attempt to develop a collective meaning from dream images, which I called "In the forests of the night" (Balogh 2015).

My schemes for making meaning from shared dreams varied with circumstances. For example, in a conference with half-hour slots I occupied separate ones for dream-sharing discussion. Conference timetabling allowed only partial overlap of participants between the two sessions but in the discussion, I recapitulated some of the dreams, with the original dreamers contributing, thus inviting newcomers into the imaginative world we had created. Their responses to the material were treated as equally legitimate as the dreamers'. I framed each dream-sharing session by a question or issue I considered engaging, and this proved an essential focus for me in guiding our attempts to make meaning. When longer sessions were available I split them into two, sharing dreams for the first part and opening discussion in the second. I operated alone and made no records beyond brief written notes. By collecting (as far as possible) participants' contact details, I was able to perform, in a limited way, some checking of the meanings I made from specific images and associations. Collective meaning-making for the group-as-constituted was not feasible under the conditions of these early inquiries, but was something I aspired to undertake.

Observations

Although I had invited participants to shift attention "from the dreamer to the dream" (Lawrence 2005 p. 14) and was impressed by their willingness to share dreams, I also made some observations regarding my main questions. I found I needed a fair amount of active facilitation to maintain the focus on dreams, as my colleagues' interest in the material led them into discussing and theorising *about* dreaming. In addition, I found I had made an erroneous assumption that the notion of "free-association" would be familiar to my colleagues.

Such observations began to shape the nature of the gap I was trying tentatively to bridge, between socially constituted dream-sharing and action research, and I modified my practice. I realised the notion of free association is not prominent across the breadth of action research discourse and therefore needed explication. I attempted in one session to introduce it experientially by providing a set of photographs, inviting members to choose one, and the group to free-associate to it. But creating a narrative explaining their choices tended to dominate interaction: as with dreams, the image-makers sometimes marginalised the images. Disparities between the two discourses became apparent: apart from the Tavistock approach, attention to psycho- and group analytic concepts within action research is limited. I have found a few instances, e.g., the Francophone "psychosociology" literature (Chevalier & Buckles 2013 pp. 16–21); and isolated examples, e.g., Shepherd's use of Bion in action learning (Shepherd 2016), and Carson's use of psychoanalytic theory to "extend the meaning of critical self-reflection in action research" (Carson 2009 p. 348).

I observed the tensions between my request to restrict participants' contributions to dreams and associations, and tendencies to focus more on the dreamer, bringing rational discourse into the group. Thus, my observations seemed to support Lawrence's argument in favour of dream-sharing not to be conducted in a conventional group which "tends to fill with finite knowledge as the participants exercise their authority and leadership" (Lawrence 2005 p. 57) but instead as a "collection of minds opening and being available for dwelling in possibility" (op. cit. p. 40). My groups had operated in the egalitarian manner of action research where overt power-play is unacceptable and there is mutual expectation for participants to behave with respect and curiosity (Balogh & Springett 2014). However, I was aware that the collective intent to observe such rules does not deny the complex, shifting, and contingent nature of the group dynamics at play. But in line with my intention to frame such matters through a social scientific lens I was less inclined to turn to Lawrence's group-relations approach for articulating the nature of this complexity, instead turning to Lave's ethnographic and relational perspective of "situated activity" to analyse praxis in dream-sharing / action research (Balogh 2010), where:

> the notion of situated activity assumes that subjects, objects, lives, and worlds are made in their relations. That is, the contexts of people's lives aren't merely backdrops, nor are they simply whatever seems salient to immediate experience. Persons are always embodied, located uniquely in space, and in their relations with other persons, things, practices, institutional arrangements.
>
> (Lave 2011 p. 152)

Reflections

In my facilitation, I noticed I was occasionally enveloped by moments of panic as dream contributions grew ever more diverse and I feared an expectation I might have to interpret them. But my learned confidence as a practitioner and belief in the value of experiential learning enabled me to return, within the act of facilitation, to a kind of emptiness of purpose, knowing that such expectations derived from my own fears and the experience itself was sufficient for us all to learn from. Keeping this as a kind of anchor, I allowed silences, and occasionally I broke them.

Reflecting on the way participants behaved, I was impressed by their eagerness to share dreams. Our familiarity with Freud's idea that dreams are the royal road to the unconscious and to repressed feelings and pathologies seemed not to obstruct our desire to risk revealing such material. I was also struck by the appearance, in most groups, of someone who claimed not to dream. This suggested a curious magnetism surrounding our dream-worlds that extended even to those with nothing to contribute. There were instances when participants clearly felt they had learned something new about themselves and their personal relationships through sharing a dream. Once a participant became tearful during discussion, but she confirmed my reading of these tears – which emerged on reporting a "big dream" – as relating to a deeply felt resolution rather than distress. Some participants responded to my invitation to consider dreams as relating to their working lives. And there were further instances when I felt my aim of creating collective meaning could be realised as I discovered continuities between the groups' images so that, for example, I could speak of action research as like a house in a forest.

Social dreaming within a Social Dreaming Matrix

I felt able to experiment with the "snowflake" arrangement for a social dreaming matrix once I had experienced taking part in one. Between my third social dreaming session and participation in my first SDM, I dreamed the following:

> *Suddenly I receive a series of texts on my phone … it's an avalanche. I open the final text and it's a dense list of words, lots and lots of them, all separated by punctuation marks. "Echo" is one of them. I scroll through the texts from back to front, skimming through them. Words first, then images and finally a little movie …. It started with some bees buzzing round my head. We are standing at the edge of a pool and I am batting them aside. Looking at it I immediately feel this as a real experience ….in the movie I plunge into the pool and the bees are gone.*
>
> (Balogh p. 23)

This dream deepened my understanding of the relationship between dream and wakeful life as a "continuous yet fragmentary process" (Balogh 2015 p. 317). It also provided me with a clear image of taking part in a social dreaming matrix as moving away from being an observer of images reflected on a screen towards plunging into a different reflective surface, one of "immersion" – a term sometimes used in experiential learning.

When I took part in a day-long social dreaming event I paid attention not just to the dreams and associations but also to our behaviour and my feelings about being in this different kind of space. In a conventional "circle" arrangement, the collective gaze is towards the centre and members are in a position directly to "read" the posture, gesture and talk of a segment of circle members in view. The centre, towards which everybody faces, is thus implied, with people's attentions darting across it. In the "snowflake" the gaze of co-participants was directed to the centre but their appearance to co-participants was fragmented. Opportunities for eye-contact were disordered and it felt more natural to direct my visual attention to the emptiness of the central space – as in meditation practice, I thought – and to pay greater attention to what I was hearing from the populated space around it. I felt isolated within the group yet in connection with everyone else's isolation through listening and uttering. The notion of "pooling" our dreams and associations was compelling. It became clear to me how the snowflake disrupted performances of group turn-taking and conversation. I also noticed participants occasionally made utterances on the matrix margins. For example, one contribution was introduced as doubtfully legitimate since it was not a dream, nor maybe a free association: it was a song – which would have re-drawn the boundaries between visual and auditory imagination had it been sung.

My "apprenticeship" as a social dreaming matrix facilitator moved into a new phase now that I had undertaken "legitimate peripheral participation" (Lave & Wenger 1991) in social dreaming matrix practice. I had grasped at the outset that I was trying to understand how to persuade group participants to restrict their contributions to dream images and associations, and had discovered more about social dreaming practice. Once again, at an action research conference, I had a practice development opportunity. I invited colleagues again to share dreams around a focal question, but within a snowflake seating arrangement and discussion programmed in a later slot. As people arrived, some began to move the chairs. The unfamiliar arrangement and my requests to maintain it seemed in itself to invoke entry into a different type of social space. People contributed dreams and images with less digression than previously. But further to this, the researchers presenting after me (it was a double session) took a huge risk and, abandoning their initial plan, decided to work with our dream material (they had taken part in the matrix) in their theatre-based workshop "Reclaiming the imagination" (Patterson 2011). They provided a scheme for us to enact in mime our dream images, initially in four separate groups and then, using movement performance as communication, step-wise into an integrated dance that flowed between the groups. Not only had I successfully "held" a social dreaming matrix, but I received the chance to think about collective meaning-making and the complex communicative processes in the dream-sharing system, in a very different way.

Theorising

I needed to inform my research through the literature, but was daunted on several fronts. The major psychoanalytic thinkers are prolific, and to me sometimes obscure. Although I had some familiarity with the object-relations school having used Menzies-Lyth's organisational perspective in nursing research (Balogh & Bond 1984), I was aware of how scant was my theoretical understanding and, given its importance to me, how completely lacking was my experiential understanding of the professional knowledge-base of clinical practice.

Whitehouse-Hart refers to the tension between clinical practice and the use of psychoanalysis as a culturally situated interpretive approach (Whitehouse-Hart 2012). Feeling the need to ground my studies, I turned to *The Interpretation of Dreams* (Freud 1900) and found Freud's literature review enormously helpful, resonating with my own attempts to resist separating dreams from waking life, well expressed as he quotes Hildebrant about:

> the completeness with which dreams are secluded and separated from real and actual life and on the other hand their constant encroachment upon each other and their constant mutual dependence.
>
> *(Freud 1900 p. 8)*

This need to ground my thinking also derived from the risks associated with research in a subject area where the marginalisation of dreaming in dominant rational discourses is mirrored in academic discourses (Balogh & Getz forthcoming). The very open-ended – and perpetually puzzling – nature of dreams seems sometimes to be reflected in the literature, so that even Lawrence strays into disciplines where the connection to social dreaming is either tenuous, as in his abstract connections between quantum physics and dreaming (Lawrence 2003), or when based on inaccurate testimony as in his espousal of Kilton Stewart's attribution of social dreaming-type activity to the Semai Senoi of Malaysia (Manley 2014 p. 328, Balogh 2015 p. 321). The inter-disciplinary position seemed nonetheless to offer the potential to bring together thinking from the edges of different disciplines, including literature and sur-realism, into social dreaming research, and I studied widely.

My position that experiential learning, informed and tested by theory, offers a further source of grounding, invoked my connection with Gestalt approaches and propelled me towards Jung – not a prominent figure in social dreaming research, but whose stature on dreams gives him natural prominence. In the anthropological as well as the Gestalt literature I encountered some practically useful Jungian concepts including "active imagination" (Price-Williams 1992, Grey 2005). This refers to a way of paying attention not just to images but also to emotions "to be identified with, to be treated as though they were objectively present" (Price-Williams 1992 p. 247). This concept seemed to register into practice relating directly to the "emptiness of purpose" or "meditative state" described above.

By situating my studies in the foundations of psychoanalysis I felt better equip-ped to encounter those who had inspired Lawrence: Bion and Bollas. Both have helped to frame social dreaming as a source of new knowledge. I found Bion's focus on the knowledge that can arise in groups where unconscious material is allowed play, and Bollas's notion of the unthought known enabled me to see how a social dreaming matrix could have the potential to constitute research in its most fundamental sense, of creating new knowledge directly from the resources of par-ticipants. It seemed to me that since anybody can dream, and the telling of dreams is universal, social dreaming could offer a unique practice for one of action research's most pressing problematics – that of creating conditions for knowledge democracy in an unequal world where rational modes of expression dominate (Openjuru, Jaitli, Tandon & Hall 2015).

Bringing dream material into public discourse

The question of how to understand the social in social dreaming comes into sharp focus when we consider processes for understanding, using and sharing in public the material from a social dreaming matrix. As I continued to take part in and facilitate these I encountered diverging approaches. In one matrix I experienced I observed that the hosts were continuously recording data in writing, without negotiation over ownership. On my inquiry into this it emerged that notwith-standing the generally accepted principle that the dreams belong in and to the matrix, data-recording was framed as one of the hosts' tasks and not amenable to sharing. Seen in terms of an analytic/therapeutic relationship between hosts and participants, such practice is perhaps understandable. As action research it misses a chance for dialogue grounded in data held in common. In a different matrix the discussion phase was led by the host (Julian Manley) who invited group members, now outside the snowflake, to contribute ideas and write them on a flipchart in public view. This stimulated thinking and discussion about relationships between the concepts portrayed. I have since used this technique and found it useful not only to think about our dreams but also to surface, for discussion, some troubling material which arose. Opening discussion and inviting in-depth reports on these issues will, I believe, enable hosts to clarify the way they choose to construct their practice.

Important in my own experiments was the strong mutual trust, voluntarism, and commitment to shared values that underpinned them. This is not necessarily the case for would-be social dreaming matrix hosts. As in action research, the development of trust between participants is essential as a basis for productive dialogue. The best examples of dream material playing into contexts of mistrust come from literature. In Sylvia Plath's *Johnny Panic and the Bible of Dreams* the protagonist maintains guard on the therapist's filing cabinet of patients' dreams, fearful for their safety. In Ismail Kadare's *The Palace of Dreams* a Kafka-like bureaucracy systematically and forcibly collects its citizens' dreams. On the other hand, Ursula Le Guin's *Social Dreaming of the Frin* and *The Word for World is Forest* portrays dream gathering as socially embedded and trustworthy practice (Plath 1977; Plath 2008; Le Guin 1980, 2003). Such material is valuable because it takes us into imagined worlds of unethical practice that is impossible for practice accounts to consider. For my account, the examination of such issues has not arisen, but this in no way diminishes their critical importance.

Concluding remarks

In this chapter I have been trying to resist the binary distinctions of dominant discourses that separate dream and wakefulness; theory and practice, mind and body and so on, and to look for ways of expressing continuities of persons, relations, and activities as situated.

The questions that pre-occupied my first inquiries have become more nuanced as I have explored this emerging field in my life-world. Questions of expertise thread through my account, which I hope shows how wide-ranging and self-critical study on and in practice provides a way to learn, otherwise unsupported, to conduct a social dreaming matrix. I also hope it raises issues for the conduct of research and training in social dreaming. In re-visiting my initial questions, I also hope I show how there is no compelling argument to restrict the social dreaming matrix to working within the Tavistock external action research approach, and nor is the focus on unresolved psychological issues a *sine qua non*. In taking dream-sharing into different realms of action research, into more openly collaborative communicative spaces, inquiry becomes possible into how collective meaning-making could become more fully available to participants themselves.

References

Baglioni, L. (2010). "Dreaming to Emergence in a General Hospital" in W. G. Lawrence (ed) *The Creativity of Social Dreaming* pp. 147–167. London: Karnac Books.

Baglioni, L. & Fubini, F. (2013). "Social Dreaming" in S. Long (ed) *Socioanalytic Methods* pp. 107–127. London: Karnac Books.

Balogh, R. & Bond, S. (1984). "An analytical study of a joint clinical teaching / service appointment on a hospital ward" *International Journal of Nursing Studies* 21(2) 81–91.

Balogh, R. (2010). "'In dreams begins responsibility': a self-study about how insights from dreams may be brought into the sphere of action research" *Educational Action Research* 18(4) 517–529.

Balogh, R. (2013). "CARN Conference: dreams and the gift of data" in CARN and C. Moules *Action Research in Diverse Contexts: Contemporary Challenges. CARN Bulletin No. 16.* pp. 21–24. Manchester: Manchester Metropolitan University.

Balogh, R. (2015). "In the Forests of the Night: an inquiry into the relevance of social dreaming for action research" *Educational Action Research* 21(3) 312–330.

Balogh, R. & Getz, C. (forthcoming). "Dreaming across continents: a collaborative inquiry into dream-sharing as a resource for action researchers" *Action Research.*

Balogh, R. & Springett, J. (2014). "Collaborative Action Research Network" in D. Coghlan & M. Brydon-Miller (eds) *The Sage Encyclopaedia of Action Research (vol 1)* pp. 119–121. London: Sage Publications.

Bastide, R. (1966). "The Sociology of the Dream" in R. Caillois & G. von Grunenbaum *The Dream & Human Societies* pp. 199–211. Berkeley & Los Angeles: University of California Press.

Boss, M. (1977). *I Dreamt Last Night.* New York: Gardner Press.

Burchell, H. (2010). "Poetic expression and poetic form in practitioner research" *Educational Action Research* 18(3) 389–400.

Carson, T. (2009). "Teaching and Cultural Difference: exploring the potential for a psychoanalytically informed action research" in S. Noffke & B. Somekh *Handbook of Action Research* pp. 347–357. London: Sage Publications.

Convery, A. (1996). *Identity Issues in the Conduct and Reporting of Teacher Research* unpublished PhD thesis University of East Anglia Norwich.

Dadds, M. (2008). "Empathetic validity in practitioner research" *Educational Action Research* 16(2) 279–290.

Eden, A. (2010). "Learning to Host a Social Dreaming Matrix" in W. G. Lawrence (ed) *The Creativity of Social Dreaming* pp. 176–186. London: Karnac Books.

Fubini, F. (2010). "Totalitarian toddlers: Consulting in the mental health service" in W. G. Lawrence (ed) *The Creativity of Social Dreaming* pp. 131–146. London: Karnac Books.

Freud, S. (1900). *The Interpretation of Dreams SE Vol 4.* London: The Hogarth Press and the Institute of Psychoanalysis.

Friedman, J. (2007). *The Dream Workbook.* London: Carroll & Brown.

Goodison, L. (1995). *The Dreams of Women.* London: The Women's Press.

Green, K. (2006). "Defining the field of literature in action research: a personal approach" *Educational Action Research* 7(1) 105–124.

Grey, L. (2005). "Community building viewed from a group dream perspective" *Gestalt Review* 92, 207–215.

Harkavy, I., Puckett, J. (2014). in D. Coghlan and M. Brydon-Miller (eds) *The Sage Encyclopaedia of Action Research* (vol 1) pp. 252–256. Los Angeles, London, New Delhi, Singapore, Washington DC: Sage Publications.

Heikkinen, H. L. T., Huttunen, R., Syraljala, L. & Pesonen, J. (2012). "Action research and narrative inquiry: five principles for validation revisited" *Educational Action Research* 201) 5–21.

Kadare, I. (2008). *The Palace of Dreams*. London: Vintage.

Kemmis, S. (2006). "Exploring the Relevance of Critical Theory for Action Research: Emancipatory action research in the footsteps of Jurgen Habermas" in P. Reason & H. Bradbury (eds) *The Handbook of Action Research* pp. 207–217. Los Angeles, London, New Delhi, Singapore, Washington DC: Sage publications.

Kolb, D. A. (1984). *Experiential Learning: experience as the source of learning and development*. Englewood-Cliffs: Prentice-Hall.

Lave, J. (2011). *Apprenticeship in Critical Ethnographic Practice*. Chicago & London: University of Chicago Press.

Lave, J. & Wenger, E. (1991). *Situated Learning: Legitimate peripheral participation*. New York: Cambridge University Press.

Lawrence, W. G. (1998). "Social Dreaming as a Tool of Action-research" in W. G. Lawrence (ed) *Social dreaming @work* pp. 123–168. London: Karnac.

Lawrence, W. G. (2003). *Experiences in Social Dreaming*. London: Karnac.

Lawrence, W. G. (2005). *Introduction to Social Dreaming: Transforming thinking*. London: Karnac.

Lawrence, W. G. (2010). (ed) *The Creativity of Social Dreaming*. London: Karnac.

Le Guin, U. K. (1980). *The Word for World is Forest*. London: Granada Publishing.

Le Guin, U. K. (2003). "The Social Dreaming of the Frin" in U. K. Le Guin (ed) *Changing Planes* pp. 64–67. London: Harcourt.

Ledwith, M. & Springett, J. (2010). *Participatory Practice*. Bristol: Policy Press.

Long, S. (2013). "Introduction: Socioanalytic Methodology" in S. Long (ed) *Socioanalytic Methods: Discovering the hidden in organisations and social systems* pp. xix–xxx. London: Karnac.

Long, S. & Harney, M. (2013). "The Associative Unconscious" in S. Long (ed) *Socioanalytic Methods: Discovering the hidden in organisations and social systems* pp. 3–22. London: Karnac.

Manley, J. (2014). "Gordon Lawrence's social dreaming matrix: background, origins, history, and developments" *Organisational & Social Dynamics* 14(2) 322–341.

Marrow, A. J. (1969). *The Practical Theorist: the life and work of Kurt Lewin*. New York & London: Basic Books.

Neumann, J. (2005). "Kurt Lewin at the Tavistock Institute" *Educational Action Research* 13(1) 119–136.

Neumann, J. (2014). "Tavistock Institute" in *The Sage Encyclopaedia of Action Research* (eds) D. Coghlan and M. Brydon-Miller (eds) (vol 2) pp. 758–762. Sage Publications.

Openjuru, G. L., Jaitli, N., Tandon, R. & Hall, B. (2015). "Despite knowledge democracy and community-based participatory action research: voices from the global south and excluded north still missing" *Action Research* 13(3) 219–229.

Patterson, R. (2011). "Reclaiming the Imagination (abstract)" in Bringing a different world into existence. CARN Conference, 4–6 November, Vienna.

Plath, S. (1977). "Johnny Panic and the Bible of Dreams" in S. Plath (ed) *Johnny Panic and the Bible of Dreams and Other Prose Writing* pp. 17–33. London: Faber & Faber.

Price-Williams, D. (1992). "The Waking Dream in Ethnographic Perspective" in B. Tedlock (ed) *Dreaming: anthropological and Psychological interpretations* pp. 246–262. School of American Research Advanced Seminar Series: Santa Fe New Mexico.

Rycroft, C. (1968). *A Critical Dictionary of Psychoanalysis*. Harmondsworth: Penguin.

Shepherd, G. (2017) "'From where I'm looking it just seems like two people have missed the boat…': understanding set behaviour from a socioanalytic perspective" *Educational Action Research* DOI: doi:10.1080/09650792.2017.1399921.

Shohet, R. (1985). *Dream-sharing: a guide to the understanding of dreams through the experience of sharing*. Wellingborough: Turnstone Press.

Tedlock, B. (1987). "Preface" in B. Tedlock (ed) *Dreaming: anthropological and psychological interpretations* pp. ix–xiv. School of American Research Advanced Seminar Series: Santa Fe New Mexico.

Torbert, W. (2006). "The Practice of Action Inquiry" in P. Reason & H. Bradbury (eds) *The Handbook of Action Research* pp. 207–217. Sage publications.

Ullman, M. (1996). *Appreciating Dreams*. Thousand Oaks: Sage Publications.

Ullman, M. & Zimmerman, N. (1979). *Working with Dreams*. London: Hutchinson.

Whitehouse-Hart, J. (2012). "Surrendering to the dream: an account of the unconscious dynamics of a research relationship" *Journal of Research Practice* 8 Article M5.

Williams, S. K. (1980). *The Jungian-Senoi Dreamwork Manual*. Berkeley: Journey Press.

Winter, R. (2002). "Truth or fiction: problems of validity and authenticity in narratives of action research" *Educational Action Research* 10(1) 143–154.

Winter, R., Buck, A. & Sobiechowska, P. (2001). *Professional Experience & the Investigative Imagination: The ART of reflective writing*. London: Routledge.

7

FESTINO DI SAN SILVESTRO

Rites and social dreaming

Domenico Agresta

Introduction

This chapter examines temporality as the essential connecting element that binds the relationship between ego-identity, the sacred and the social dreaming matrix (SDM) with regard to the creation of a founding myth. By "Founding Myth", I mean the basic elements of the constitution of a community starting from the imaginary. That is to say, the relationship of the community with a cultural context and its connections with an experience of historical events. I will call these elements as they appear in social dreaming, "dream icons". With this term I define the theme of the SDM (or a specific object that is present in a sequence of dreams during the work of free association and the constitution of a pure mental object) that is the connection between the unconscious and the inner matrix of the community (Amaro 1995; Menarini & Montefiori 2013; Agresta 2015). The same objects – the dream icons of the SDM – are present too in the rite. The theme of the SDM is the synthesis of the aggregate icons. I suggest that we have three kinds of icons: family matrix icons that represent the basic affective meanings of internal objects; dynamic matrix icons that express the relational values of those objects; the icons of the self that express the deep meaning of the story of the subject in the past and in the present.

The SDM reveals such dream icons and through the social dreaming process; the researcher is able to build a mythical and imaginary map of the community. Because a rite has to find its link in the body of the community, the icons – using a SDM – help us to view a topography of the mental field we are studying.

In the traditional context of the Italian community described in this chapter, "icons", such as the wood, the voyage, the cross, the parents – and specifically San Silvestro as the anthropological and psychological *father* figure or the symbol of the representation of time – are perceived by the community as sacred structures that represent the creative dimension of the collective and express a sacred mystery of origins. I am assuming that if the community dreams the rite, the community can have a direct contact with the imaginary in all its parts. I will be suggesting in this chapter that it is through the work of the SDM that we can find those "dream icons" that lead us to an understanding of the quality and nature of community-based beliefs in sacredness and mystery. In the SDM, a peculiarity of the dream icon is that it visually constructs the sacred object which it represents and of which it is also the origin, since it possesses a similar nature and quality. As a construction, it acquires a symbolic and creative value and hence a transformative dimension which is present in the here and now of the SDM, thanks to the constellation of associative content that is an essential part of the social dreaming process (Giovannini & Menarini 2004).

Being a production of the unconscious, the dream icon is a purely mental form. It exists but it is not directly present. I think that a rite of passage has the same common function in the sense that a community tries to stay in contact with its memories and emotions through a rite. A rite of passage is also a metaphorical way to be part of history, and then to exist in the present. I consider an SDM as a rite. The SDM and its process is like the process that the body of the community will do to find something new. Maybe, then, an SDM could itself be a rite of passage through the experience of sharing dreams.

The rite of "Festino di San Silvestro"

Starting from these elements, this study describes the use of the SDM in a rite of passage in Sicily. The rite is called "the Festino di San Silvestro". San Silvestro was a Basilian Monk and Patron of the Town of Troina in the Province of Enna.

Every year, all the men of Troina start from the Church of San Silvestro and embark on a difficult journey to the Sacred Wood of Nebrodi. The pilgrimage, which starts on a Thursday night and finishes on Sunday afternoon is the process that creates a relationship between the community and the territory of the journey and in doing so combines present experience with memory and history. In this sense, the rite is an experience that engages with the sense of time; a way of creating contact between them as part of the land and within a cultural context. As De Martino (2002) described in his studies we can consider this experience as "being in history". De Martino states:

> The fundamental constitution of being is not being in the world but having to be in the world ... The worldliness of being refers to having to be in worldliness, having to be according to a community project of being .... The catastrophe of the worldly does not therefore appear in analysis as a way of being in the world, but as a permanent threat, sometimes dominated and resolute, sometimes triumphant.
>
> (2002, pp. 669–670)

The most important phase of this rite is in the middle, when the best men in the group must touch the laurel in the deepest place of the valley and come back to the camp to show the rest of the group that they are alive. It is in this place that the body of San Silvestro was found, according to legend, completely intact. In touching the laurel the men of the village become heroes and contribute to a myth that brings together the past and the future. Becoming a hero means having a direct contact with the sacred. The body contact with the laurel determines the belonging with the territory and history. The testimony of touching the laurel is proof of the testimony for the future generations.

Introducing social dreaming into San Silvestro

During the three phases of the rite of San Silvestro, I hosted an SDM with some of the participants: one at the beginning of the journey; the second in the middle; the last one after the end of the rite. Within the rite of passage of San Silvestro, the SDM created a place in which a community could uncover something inside their shared sense of life and existence. In this case, I did not use the technique of the dream reflection group, because the important thing was to focus on the observation of the representation of the foundation myth from the matrix.

My aim is to consider the SDM as a psychological device that helps the researcher to capture something of the present in the primordial matrix of the community and the sacred and identify how the community organises roles, rules and relationships from the creation of a specific imaginary in the shared dreams that uncover something of the origins and nature of a Founding Myth.

Starting from the matrix and its characteristics I will try to suggest some new reflections on SDM and research. In the connections between the SDM and the rite of passage I will also be suggesting new concepts influenced by anthropological and psychological studies, which I have called the "anthropopoiesis of the mind" and the "semiophoric function" of dreams, or "semiophores".

SDM as a rite of passage: anthropopoiesis and semiophoric function of dreams

Every social group builds and creates rites and myths of origin with the aim of establishing, representing and controlling its own identity (Agresta 2015). A rite could be the expression of an unconscious representation, a social psychopathology, or a conflict. Following Francesco Remotti (2013), I call such concepts of rite the "anthropopoiesis of the mind". Remotti introduced the concept of anthropopoiesis as a way of understanding the human being in social contexts. According to this idea, every community is born twice: the first is biological and the second is social, determined by cultural actions. For the purposes of my research, the "anthropopoiesis-of–the-mind" entrusts itself to culture by means of the study of dreams through SDM, and leads to a manifestation of the multiplicity of man, characterized by different ways of living. Theoretically, a rite of passage could be one of the most important examples of the anthropopoietic process, since the "body" of the community, in the case of San Silvestro, changes during the rite. It becomes a new "body" (as a metaphor) that the new community has created through the bodily exertions of the community representatives in the form of the "Heroes" who touch the laurel and give birth to a new "community body".

My idea, starting from the SDM, is to consider an "anthropopoiesis of dreams" as a metaphor about how a culture/group creates thought while they are acting a social drama like a rite of passage. I think that this is the same concept as Bollas' "unthought known". As Lawrence (2007, p. 15) says:

> Bollas has written about the "unthought known" (Bollas 1987). Each of us carries in the recess of our inner world traces of memories of experience, which are never thought about and are, therefore, out of consciousness. However, in later life we can have an experience which will trigger the unconscious, vestigial memory bank. Once this happens, we think about it. Once thought, it becomes known to us.

Metaphor and dreams

According to Nisbet (1969, p. 4),

> Metaphor is, at its simplest, a way of proceeding from the known to the unknown. It is a way to cognition in which the identifying qualities of one thing are transferred in an instantaneous, almost unconscious, flash of insight to some other thing that is, by remoteness or complexity, unknown to us. The test of essential metaphor is not any rule of grammatical form, but rather the quality of semantic transformation that brought about.

By focusing on this quality of semantic transformation, I want to consider dreams in the SDM, as "semiophores". The semiophore is an object that becomes a "bearer of meaning" when it loses its usefulness and acquires a pure semantic function. This notion, introduced by Krzysztof Pomian (2007) is attributed to all material objects with a meaning. Finding the original application of a semiophore in literature, Pomian extends it to all visible objects. So, the function of the semiophore is to be an intermediary between the visible and the invisible, a bridge between the spectator and the hidden, the distant or the absent. The semiophore reveals its significance only when it is exposed to the gaze (in our setting the dreams of an SDM linked with a specific place or referring to a specific period of time), and this significance is given it to the extent that it corresponds to expectations, questions, and new needs which originate from present society and its reporting through time and via the society it is witnessing.

As such, the invisible is so in different meanings: because it is placed in a time or place other than the past or present because of limited duration or because it is elusive to our knowledge. The SDM is the place of the "Myth of Origin" of the community we are looking for. The dreams are the objects – the connection between the invisible and the visible – and the work with the SDM is the social process –- through the use of unconscious thought – that now we can call specifically the "liminality experience". This liminality emerges in the SDM which is "purposely convened in the here-and-now, [and] is a reflection of the primordial matrix of humanity" (Lawrence 2003, p. 3).

Manley (2014) suggests that Lawrence chose the idea of "matrix" to define a containing space of potential birth; the birth of new thought and ideas; or to explore a space that enabled him to explore other areas of potential taboo, such as the possibility of allowing a spiritual, even mystical dimension to his work (pp. 329–330). And indeed, I think that the idea of the "infinite", which Lawrence located in the matrix, is very close to the liminal phase that the community engages with during the rite of passage. Similarly, I think that during the SDM the participants inhabit a "threshold" area. If we did not use the SDM, the semiophores (meaning the relics in our case) would risk being only empty structures. Thanks to the shared dreams, these structures are filled with the most diverse entities: ancestors, gods, people, events and circumstances. The dreams allow the exchange between the visible and the invisible; they take shape in the SDM and create a connection between the receivers and the senders.

The shared unconscious of social dreaming and the rite of passage

According to Van Gennep (1981) the rite of passage represents the change of an individual from one socio-cultural status to another. Therefore, the study of a rite of passage within a social dreaming matrix is more than a "simple" study of relationship. If a dream is a semiophore, the process we use with an SDM in the context of a rite is its structural representation in terms of the imaginary.

In my opinion the SDM reveals this function on the basis of the hypothesis that the dream is formed in its potential for social action expressed in the drama of the rite of passage (Agresta 2015). The matrix is a container but it is above all a psycho-sensorial experience with an affective base. This leads to the formation of a "structure process" that can be defined as the building of meanings by means of dreams (Agresta 2010). It enables us to represent "ideal anthropological structures". So, in terms of groups, it gives maximum facilitation to the group capacity to dream and then to access knowledge. This considers the SDM to be the device that facilitates the creation of an anthropopoietic process thanks to the shared unconscious activated by the dreams as semiophores.

With an SDM we are able to describe and stay in a liminal space – like in a rite of passage – and observe the process of building and making memory. In terms of myth and with reference to his theory of thinking, Bion asks:

> to what extent is myth-making an essential function of α? It may be that the sense impression has to be transformed to make it suitable material for dream-thought, but that it is the function of dream-thought to use the material put at its disposal by α, the units of dream-thoughts so to speak, in order to produce myths. Myths must be defined; they must be communicated and have some of the qualities of common-sense-one might call them 'common non-sense'.
>
> *(1992, p. 192)*

The shared unconscious of social dreaming (perhaps Long and Harney's "associative unconscious" (Long & Harney 2013)) is a way of analyzing the constitution of a myth. Bion starts with the concept of the Alpha function that makes it possible to transform sensory impression into suitable material in the dream thought. He advances the hypothesis that the thought of the dream so transformed is used as material to produce, at the social level, the myths (Nebbiosi & Petrini 1997). The myth therefore has to do with shared community sensory experiences that draw on unconscious elements that have not undergone a transformation, and, therefore, following Bion, have not found a "sense" yet.

The group which creates, lives, produces and performs the rite is a group which decides to remain at the *threshold*, the liminality of experience. How is this liminality observed? Every rite has its "dead" times which are actually moments of great empirical significance for the structuring of the primary structured process we can observe during the SDM.

The "dead time" of social dreaming within the rite

The following sequence of dreams is from the SDM before the men started the journey.

> I dreamt San Silvestro said: 'Don't worry'.
>
> I find it hard to be present at this festival. It is as if the festival had gone and I am not able to catch up with it and be with them. If possible, with great sacrifice I manage to catch up with them but not in a correct way. I lose the things I have, my comforts, I lose my rucksack … I find it difficult to do what I do every year.
>
> Jesus Christ and San Silvestro say to me: 'Set out on the journey and be strong'. I was pushing my father in his wheelchair and my Dad was giving me strength. At a certain point Dad got up and came towards me. He came to me and hugged me.
>
> San Silvestro saw me and said to me: 'You must carry me on your back'. I said to him: 'How can I do it?'– and he said: 'Don't worry, you will be able to carry me on your back!'

This sequence of dreams reveals to us the nature and trepidation of the rite: will they be able to do that? Do they have the strength? This sequence might be an exact replica of the feelings of this stage of the rite, because the matrix has its anthropological configuration and it is linked with the context we observe. The icon of San Silvestro is present in many dreams and the feelings that men have in the dreams are the same as the affection they felt for San Silvestro too.

I think that like a myth the dreams have a specific structure we can refer to in the SDM, which corresponds to the imaginary with the rite. As the physical body of the community moves to the process of the rite and feels many emotions, the SDM shows us the process of the unconscious of the community in the rite, in their transformation and in their phases just through the dream-work.

I dreamt that San Silvestro said to me: 'Tomorrow you will find something in your new house'. After this, I ran to my old family house and I said to my Mum: 'I found the way to be happy! I must respect you all and start to be more active!'.

San Silvestro helps me to be a better man. In the dream I was like a thief because I stole to many sheep and now I must find the right direction. I must be a better man if I want to die with my family and my wife.

After I met my wife, San Silvestro invited me to work hard for the future. I was really feeling bad: I saw my son Lucio in big trouble and only after the voyage I found the solution to help him and myself.

It seems that the time experience of the SDM is the equivalent of the time of a rite of passage because the process of the dreams replicates the emotions for the community and their responsibility to make a good journey respecting the connection with the traditions of the territory to create new heroes.

Social dreaming matrix as a fractal

SDM is a system but it is also a structure and anti-structure (Turner 1969; 1974). The work with free association is like the infinite renovation of the rite and the infinite regeneration of the experience of the rite that is always the same in its structure. In this sense I think that the SDM is like a fractal and in this sense the process moves towards something like a Mandelbrot set (Mandelbrot 2000). In my opinion the SDM is a non-linear fractal of an isotopic nature at a linguistic or semantic level even though we are working with dreams. The overlapping of the common semantic signs (semantic overlapping of dreams icons or the theme created in the SDM) of two or more lexemes will form an amalgam of which the isotopy is the result (Volli 2004). This is the way I use SDM in this kind of study. I consider a sequence and I investigate using the icons which are more present in the sequence of dreams as the equivalent of the lexemes that form the amalgam.

In my opinion SDM interpreted as a fractal is similar to this semantic field, a geometrical organization (but as a mental field) of the dreams reported in the section in a specific space time. For example, the semantic field of the SDM focuses on this type of isotopic characteristic and is built on the rule of free associations, for example, around the icon of San Silvestro that is present in several dreams.

Social dreaming and the anthropology of rite

I feel that Gordon Lawrence (2010) did not completely understand – in the sense that he had not structured – that the function of the SDM is nothing more than the way and the place in which the mind, in its most archaic form, is developing. I have the simple idea that sharing dreams in the matrix is a way of creating something waiting to be realized but not captured yet. In this sense I think that we need to create a Myth in a ritual process. Alternatively, we can find out what dreams or metaphors want to show us when they are like a Myth in Bion's conception of

Myth as a "non-common sense" as I said above. This is clear with the dreams of San Silvestro, who is always a guide for the men who have to become heroes.

> *I saw San Silvestro and he told me to go out and call everyone to go to the wood.*
> *San Silvestro gave me a pat on the back and said: 'You're making a mistake.*
> *San Silvestro told me to go to my land in the country to help plant laurel saplings. There was me, him and another person.*
> *I dreamt that San Silvestro told me to call a boy (who had recovered from a bad illness).*
> *I dreamt about the square in the village; some people are arriving with laurel. My daughter comes up to me.*

Lawrence and Long (2010, p. 231) propose the hypothesis that: "The dream provides the link between the conscious observer (embedded in his or her system of language and culture) and the unknown, spontaneously organizing system of thinking that is the human ecological niche". This ecological niche is the background of the feelings present in the dreams. The dreams are in turn a part of the experience of the rite as a metaphor of life and death.

> *I saw San Silvestro comes back from the wood. He told me to be ready to travel and say hello to all the strangers I will see during the journey.*
> *I have a dream. When I was child I started to cry after I found my father with another wife. San Silvestro helps me and He gave me the solution to save my father and invite him to come back.*
> *I saw my friends ready to go to the wood. They told me that if I do not come with them I was in trouble. I have no power to do that but San Silvestro told me that my father was in the wood waiting for me.*

I think that the ecological niche is present in a rite of passage by the fact that this symbolic action in a human society is like dreams or dreaming. Acting a rite or dreaming a rite is very similar. The experience is linked directly with the inner feelings and emotions, like in a dream or in a sacrifice. The connection between SDM and the anthropology of the rite is that the SDM could be the ecological niche of the dreamers in the SDM, which in turn is the ecological niche of the icons present in the trans-generational space/time of the community. The SDM could be the place in which we can find the ecological niche of the dreams of the community we study. This is why it is very difficult to use an SDM out of its context or cultural set. I think this is the connection between the rite of passage and the SDM as the experience to be in contact with the sacred and De Martino's general concept of "being in history" (2002). This ecological niche creates an anthropological place in which dreams could be allocated like objects in a rite of passage thanks to the symbolic action of a community.

In the following sequence of dreams, the last of those from the SDM used in the rite of San Silvestro, there is another common element linked with the idea of the ecological niche as the manifestation of the anthropology of rite studied with a

SDM: the icons of Family, the Boy and again the icon of the Church. These icons represent not only the trans-generational process of a group or community. They are also a reflection on how to observe the unknown, the sense of creation (Agresta 2015; Menarini & Montefiori 2013; Menarini & Marra 2015). These icons, in my opinion can be compared with the idea that the dreamers are connecting with each other and with their inner life and institution.

> *I dreamt that a woman, regarding the boy mentioned above, told me to go to Padre Cosimo. We all went to the sanctuary at Tindari to pray together.*
>
> *I dreamt I saw a boy who had to go to a hot place to do something and he was wearing a blue swimming costume with red stripes.*
>
> *At my house there was this enormous party and there was San Silvestro who told me to go to a boy and tell him he would do a miracle if he came to my house to thank him.*
>
> *I dreamt about my mother. Me, her and my brother got into bed. She told us the story of San Silvestro.*
>
> *I see myself as a giant and another rebels against me and starts to hit me. Even though he often falls to the ground, he always gets up and attacks me. Immediately afterwards I see myself in a river with water which is falling onto me. I feel a sense of peace and tranquillity.*

The icon of the boy suggests that the field of the SDM, and its ecological niche, are close to the experience of what the community *live* in their perception of existence in history during the process of the rite of passage. To become a Hero you must die but you must tell the story and show yourself to the community. The passage between the visible and the invisible – the semiophoric function of the dream and its anthropopoietic feature – occur with the creation of the theme of the matrix in its form and identification of oniric icons, that is of mental objects which express the psychic intentionality of dreamers. As icons are mental events, they are potential symbols.

Conclusion

The social dreaming matrix creates a mental space at a conscious level which provides a container for the social unconscious to be addressed through dreaming and free association (Lawrence 2007) The focus in this study was not on the individual but on people in their culture. In this sense, social dreaming engages the cultural aspects of dreaming with culture as present or as represented in a rite. I have also shown that if social dreaming is in a field of dramas; ie., social metaphor in a symbolic action in human society – like a rite of passage – it is a device that has not only the same function of a rite but the same constitution and the same structure.

As Manley (2014, p. 337) suggests about Gordon Lawrence and SDM, "Lawrence went to identify four areas belonging to this unconscious 'sphinx-like' space: 'being', 'becoming', 'unthought known', and 'dreaming'. His idea was that these four areas could be visually represented as four faces of a single three-dimensional pyramid".

Like a rite of passage, we have a similar structure about the creation of Myth of Origin and a space in which a community can find solutions. Working with dreams means working with culture and its relation with the context and its relation with history. Dreams are the manifestation of the sacred intended as a perception of time experience and the possibility of transforming the sense of existence of a community in common imaginary in a rite of passage as their psychosomatic drama. As we have seen, the sense of the sacred and the observation of a rite as a sequence of "being in the History" suggest that social dreaming is a rite of passage from the invisible to the visible. In this sense, I consider not only the use of SDM as a specific device for this kind of research but also a manifestation of the rite its self.

The SDM is the device that creates a visible connection and a link between what is in the unconscious, what is in the history and what is in the rite in term of symbolic social action. That phase structure of social dramas is not the product of instinct but of models and metaphors carried in the actors' heads (Turner 1974, p. 34).

In conclusion, therefore, the historical question of the imaginary overlaps with the relations and historical facts shared by the community that enacts the rite, but that shares the dreams in an SDM. We can talk about controlling time because we observe unconscious shared matrices represented semiophorically by the dream which is the anthropopoietic foundation of the community mind in the constitution phase of a founding myth in the question of recognition of the ego-identity. Our reflections stress not so much the "obvious" awareness of historical knowledge as unconscious knowledge, but rather the possibility of having identified an observational method that focuses attention on this correspondence: viz. unconscious time and ritual time are the same thing in terms of constitution of the ego-identity as a metaphor of a rite of passage of imaginary. The icons present in the dreams create this connection and representation. I consider this experience very close to the sacred because the matrix creates the space to see the sacred and to be in contact.

Given the anthropopoietic nature of the dream and its semiophoric function, a double imaginary coincides in an historical and shared mental field (matrix), in which the mental and the cultural fields, as the expression of a founding myth of the social group, start from the unconscious dimension. In this sense, history too enters the imaginary and takes its form in the dream. It can be transformed affectively in its institutional dimensions (laws, museums, events, anniversaries and rites) and is no longer experienced in a single historical fact (memory). The SDM can observe its own creation of the ego-identity.

References

Agresta, D. (2010). "Il Social Dreaming come strumento di ricerca-intervento" *Rivista Doppio-Sogno*, [online] Volume 10. Available at: www.doppio-sogno.it/numero10/ita/15.pdf. [Accessed June 2010].

Agresta, D. (2015). "The anthropopoietic question of the mind: considerations on dreams, rites, and history within the unconscious. The Mlawa Battle in the Social Dreaming Matrix." In: D. Agresta, Z. Leszek, and M. Grzywacz (ed.) *The Battle of Mlawa 1939 in the Collective Memory*. Poland: Mlawa Edition, pp. 32–37.

Amaro, C. (1995). "La terapia gruppoanalitica: campo mentale del transpersonale e della pólis". in F. Di Maria and G. Lo Verso (ed.) *La psicodinamica dei gruppi*. Milano: Raffaello Cortina Editore, p. 210.

Bion, W. (1992). *Cogitans*. London: Karnac.

Buttita, E. I. (2002). *La memoria lunga*. Roma: Meltemi Editore.

De Martino, E. (2002). *La fine del mondo. Contributo all'analisi delle apocalissi culturali, a cura di Gallini C.*. Torino: Einaudi.

Giovannini, V. and Menarini, R. (2004). "Icone oniriche: costruzione di significato, valore e senso in gruppo," *Funzionegamma*, [online] Numero 2, Sogno e Gruppo 2. Available at: www.funzionegamma.it/icone-oniriche-costruzione-di-significato-valore-e-senso-in-gruppo.

Lawrence, W. G. (2003). *Experiences in Social Dreaming*. London: Karnac.

Lawrence, W. G. (2007). (ed) *Infinite Possibilities of Social Dreaming*. London: Karnac.

Lawrence, W. G. (2010). (ed) *The Creativity of Social Dreaming*. London: Karnac.

Lawrence, G. and Long, S. (2010). "The creative frame of mind." In: W. G. Lawrence, (ed.), *The Creativity of Social Dreaming*, 1st ed. London: Karnac, pp. 213–232.

Long, S. and Harney, M. (2013). "The associative unconscious." In: S. Long (ed.) *Socio-oanalytic Methods*. London: Karnac, pp. 3–22.

Mandelbrot, B. (2000). *Gli oggetti frattali: forme, caso, dimensione*. Torino: Einaudi.

Manley, J. (2014). "Gordon Lawrence's social dreaming matrix: background, origins, history, and developments," *Organisational & Social Dynamics* 14(2) pp. 322–341.

Menarini, R. and Marra, F. (2015). *Il bambino nella casa dello specchio*. Roma: Borla.

Menarini, R. and Montefiori, V. (2013). *Nuovi orizzonti della psicologia del sogno e dell'immaginario collettivo*. Roma: Edizioni Studium.

Montefiori, V. (2015). *Dentro il tempo*. Roma: Edizioni Magi.

Nebbiosi, G. and Petrini, R. (1997). *"Il significato teorico e clinico del concetto di "senso comune" nell'opera di Bion"*. Available at: www.sicap.it/merciai/bion/papers/nebbio.htm.

Nisbet, R. A. (1969). *Social Change and History: Aspects of the Western Theory of Development*. London: Oxford University Press.

Remotti, F. (2013). *Fare umanità. I drammi dell'antropopoiesi*. Roma: Laterza Editore.

Ricoeur, P. (1986). *Tempo e racconto. Volume uno*. Milano: Jaka Book.

Van Gennep, A. (1981[1909]). *I riti di passaggio*. Torino: Bollati Boringhieri.

Turner, V. (1969). *The Ritual Process, Structure and Anti-Structure*. London: Aldine Transaction.

Turner, V. (1974). *Dramas, Fields and Metaphor, Symbolic Action in Human Society*. London: Cornell University Press.

Volli, U. (2004). *Manuale di semiotica*. Bari: Laterza Editori.

8

LOOKING FOR TREASURE IN DREAM WATER

Francesca La Nave

> I am walking or swimming at the bottom of the sea. I look up and see light shining through liquid stained glass or precious stones. The edges move slowly like oil, or a jellyfish.
>
> *(This was a dream the author had sometime during training in Group Analysis)*

Introduction

This chapter introduces a working development of the accepted practice of the social dreaming method (Lawrence 2007), involving the use of art-making to complement and amplify the task of the social dreaming matrix. It is not a departure from the social dreaming model as developed by Lawrence and his collaborators, but rather an optional extension of the model, setting into an experimental course and in concrete terms, the connection between social dreaming and creativity, which has been documented in the literature (Lawrence 2007; 2010).

This development is built on the backbone of previous work, undertaken before 2010, when I introduced a number of social dreaming principles, such as free association and dream amplification in a collective setting, to the practice of art psychotherapy and, more specifically, to the structure of art psychotherapy groups. The published result of this work (La Nave 2010, 2014) aimed at strengthening the way images are routinely viewed in art psychotherapy groups, by integrating aspects of the non-clinical methodology of social dreaming with the clinical methodology of group art psychotherapy, whose primary objective is therapeutic improvement, including increasing patients' resilience and decreasing their bonds to symptoms.

Art making is already at the centre of the art psychotherapy methodology, which, broadly speaking, aims at supporting patients' epistemic capacity, interactive abilities and emotional literacy, through supporting the development of imagination. The social dreaming ethos of sharing dreams in a transpersonal way, focussing on the dream, not the dreamer, struck me as significant in its lack of personalisation and gave rise to a hypothesis that if something similar could be done with the art made in art psychotherapy groups, it could increase patients' ability to view and draw from each other's art, something relevant to themselves. This idea gave rise to modifications in the structure of my art psychotherapy groups, where interactive aspects of making, viewing and discussing images were given priority through the introduction of more robust conditions for the presence of images to be acknowledged and used more interactively during the course of therapy. This has the objective of drawing patients' attention away from preoccupation with symptoms and dominant pathologies and towards creativity.

While, at first, the flow of information was from social dreaming towards art therapy, it later formed the groundwork for thinking about further cross fertilization between the practices of art therapy in groups and social dreaming. At the origin of this chapter is the hypothesis that the phenomenon of art making as a communication about intra and interpersonal constructs and notions, held in the unconscious-conscious continuum, could be fruitfully applied to the thinking of social dreaming. This could be a way of contributing to the elaboration of the themes and ideas presented by the matrix. I stress that I have not altered the original structures of the social dreaming method and have not substituted art making for any known part of the process, such as the matrix, the dream reflection dialogues or the system synthesis; art making has been added as a complementary addition to the dream reflection dialogue, effectively extending the dialogues' verbal work into a non-verbal register.

Congruous with social dreaming ethos, this is a work-in-progress hypothesis, whose outcomes, or even principles, are still under scrutiny; any further development of this model will need systematic research. The hunch that art making can concretely add something of value to a social dreaming programme may find agreement as well as objections. Over roughly a ten-year period, during which I have taken tentative steps towards a more coherent conceptualisation of this intervention, the greatest challenge has come from the logistics involved with this method: art making, even when produced at fairly basic levels, requires additional degrees of organization. In the case of social dreaming and art making, it translates into additional time, appropriate space and art materials being made available.

Independent organisations and university departments specializing in art related studies, such as those training in the arts therapies, have art making spaces and materials as part of their ordinary activities; this and their professional interest in the unconscious and in social dreaming, made them able to host this version of social dreaming with relatively little change to their normal resources. It has therefore been with this type of organization that I have had the opportunity of hosting social dreaming programmes with art making. This has been either as part of art psychotherapy training courses at a master of arts level, or as experiential interventions for national and International art therapy conferences, or as team building activities in staff training programmes.

This chapter therefore is a brief account of an experiment which, historically and across different organisations and contexts, has so far, not been carried out according to a standardised procedure: as such, it has the function of benchmarking the stage of its development, with the understanding, as mentioned earlier, that it will need systematic research and standard implementation of a coherent methodology, to collect and interpret outcomes and translate them into a body of evidence for its usefulness. Limited as it is, this chapter includes examples drawn from practice such as descriptions of proceedings and of visual imagery. It also includes one image taken during the middle stages of an art making process following a social dreaming matrix (SDM).

I have permission from the authors to use this image, anonymously in confidence for this publication. Throughout the chapter I shall make reference to social dreaming (SD) and art therapy (AT) literature and I shall use the terms "image making" and "image" to describe the process of making art and any of its products, regardless of whether they are two or three dimensional, permanent, or transitory.

Dreams and art

Before discussing how art making could be integrated in social dreaming programmes, I want to consider what I see as a natural alliance between social dreaming and art-making. The context for the art making I describe here is that of art therapy; it is here and particularly in art therapy groups, that images may be used in ways comparable to the way dreams are used in SD.

The SDM is understood as an assembly for the social sharing of dreams, their associations and amplifications, to access collectively held, unconscious knowledge. As Lawrence describes it:

> the matrix is used to capture the space of thinking and free associations. It is a space that mirrors, while awake, the space of dreaming while asleep, giving rise to images, metaphors, analogues and symbols.
>
> (Lawrence 2005, p. 37)

At the same time, at the core of disparate AT methodologies lies a consensus that the making of art can be part of a process of shoring up expression, communication and joint reflection to bring into being forms of knowledge which would not be available through solely verbal means (Edwards 2004; Dalley 1987; Schaverien 1992). Rose (1980) quoting Barnes (1937, p. 111) says that any art image is "a stop the mind makes between uncertainties", which I understand as describing the capacity images have of holding, expressing and communicating information, not definitely known, or yet fully understood.

While SD and AT rely on quite distinct theoretical and functional paradigms, they nevertheless appear to share common areas, particularly in what concerns their relationship with the unconscious and creativity. One of social dreaming's explicit objectives is to gain access to realms variously addressed through concepts such as Bollas's *Unthought Known* (Bollas 1987), or Lawrence's continuum of *Unconscious* and *Infinite* (Lawrence 2007). These expressions, drawn from psychoanalysis, describe metaphysical constructs and phenomena within which individual and collective ideas, assumed to be unconsciously held, symbolically meet and interact, to generate knowable versions of themselves.

In the clinical practice of AT groups, images emerging from individual and collective activities, hold explicit and implicit information about their makers' emotional condition, their personalities and relationships. These pieces of information are held and communicated through various parts of a process including making and viewing images, according to procedures inherent to the session's structure and described in the literature (Skaife & Huet 1998). These structures have at once facilitative and restrictive functions: by creating and holding boundaries and limitations, such as, for example confidentiality and time limits, they allow the flow of communication to happen at levels which can be tolerated both emotionally and cognitively, as fitting specific, clinical contexts. For example, in AT groups with emotionally unstable adults, structuring the session in finite and definable parts will support both, therapists and clients, to manage emotional regulation during the more difficult, intersubjective exchanges. In even more specific ways, art making allows experience to be externalised and, to an extent, objectified, by being held in a physical object, "so that it becomes possible to reflect upon it" (Edwards 2004, p. 10). This is crucial in making the process emotionally and practically safe while achieving specific therapeutic objectives.

As in all psychodynamic group work, the size of AT groups influences the dynamics and quality of group processes; larger groups, such as those attended by more than thirty people, tend to focus towards less personal and private concerns in favour of larger and more collective narratives (Skaife, Jones & Pentaris 2016). In practice, when dealing with images, this means that images are looked at for their transpersonal value and significance, rather than analysed with a view to interpreting intrapersonal issues. This would be closer to the ethos of SD where the focus is always on the dream, not the dreamer (Lawrence 2005; 2007; 2010). To apply this way of looking at images, that is, to focus on the image, not the image maker, is one of the ways art can be naturally viewed, as for instance, in a gallery. We can appreciate and resonate with a piece of art while knowing nothing of its author.

Art psychotherapy is a broad church with different clinical applications and orientations; approaches vary according to the client groups they aim to serve and one of the many ways in which they differ is how deeply and explicitly they engage with the unconscious dynamics of transference and counter-transference. Current practices include some that are strongly informed by psychoanalytical methodology (Mann 2006) as well as others doing so to a lesser extent (Springham 2012), as, for instance, when informed by mentalization based practice (Bateman & Fonagy 2006) a treatment paradigm focussing on emotional regulation and particularly effective with emotionally unstable personality disorders. Varied as they are, AP practices share common denominators and among them, the central importance of the presence and emergence of unconscious material from images and from image-making processes. The empirically observed connections between making art, the mobilisation and development of more creative states of minds and the increased capacity for emotional regulation and recovery, which have been the basis for the clinical practice, has more recently been corroborated by neuroscience (Hass-Cohen & Carr 2008; Oppenheimer 2005).

I opened this chapter with the *Treasure* dream, with minimal explanation, to let the reader meet the dream from a free associative position, similar to the one we assume in the SDM and, by the same token, making it their own. At the time of the *Treasure* dream, I was concluding my group analytic training, which had followed my art psychotherapy training by about ten years and, coincidentally, I was becoming aware of social dreaming. The dream appeared to authorize a synthetic view of these paradigms: the flexible and latticed structure, connecting individual cells into an organic-looking unit, was reminiscent of the group analytic matrix (Ahlin 1985), as well as of the aesthetic correlations and differences of artworks made within art psychotherapy groups.

My dream experience was one of fascination with the beauty of the vision while at once feeling, more than thinking, a notion that art works, in art therapy groups, could be illuminated (*sunlight through the glass*) by being viewed as clusters of connected ideas (*jellyfish structure*), where the focus is on the image, not the image-maker, mirroring the SDM ethos of the focus being on the dream, not the dreamer. The dream created meaning at theoretical and professional levels in the notional possibility of cross-fertilisation between the paradigms of SD and AP, which was first put to practical use in my work with art therapy groups (La Nave 2010; 2014). While other, more personal readings would no doubt be possible for this dream, to my mind its poignancy rests in the way it was instrumental in creating new thinking, even though I was considering it in isolation and not in association with other dreams.

The (2009) social dreaming programme in Rome's botanical gardens, explicitly set out to explore the question of what conditions are conducive to a creative mind-set. In *Infinite Possibilities of Social Dreaming* (Lawrence 2007) most chapters refer directly, or indirectly to creativity, but Zarbafi, Clare and Lawrence specifically address the emergence of creativity as implicit to the experience of the matrix itself (Zarbafi, Clare & Lawrence 2007). One entire publication, *The Creativity of Social Dreaming* (Lawrence 2010) is dedicated to this relationship and authors show diversely how in theory and practice, social dreaming is never far from creativity, whether we view it as a constituent principle, a contributory to, or a product of the practice.

Four chapters in the volume directly link SD to specific art forms; respectively Slade's to Drama (pp. 25–49); Selvaggi's to children's drawings (pp. 53–64); Manley's to the iconography of slavery (pp. 65–82) and Werdigier's to the art of Rap (pp. 169–176). Only Selvaggi, however, describes a mixed-methods approach with primary school children, who, ostensibly due to a natural, age related limitations in verbal skills, use drawings in the actual matrix and discussion, to describe and associate to dreams. The resulting product strikes me as a mixture of social dreaming, social didactics, art and group relation experience, confirming the possibility of modifications in the core model of SD to adapt to different situations.

There are confluences as well as differences in AP's and SD's theoretical use of abstract concepts such as creativity, the unconscious and the unknown. Broadly rooted in psychoanalytically informed ideas, these concepts are transformed by their use within different frameworks. At its closest to individual psychotherapy, AP links the unconscious with deeply individualistic and intrapersonal narratives. Like dreaming, the process of art-making is also, to a great extent, a deeply personal and private one, drawing us in a meditative closeness with our art-object. However, just like SD finds a way to assign trans-personal meaning to dreams, so we can argue that the implied sense of ownership of an object by an owing subject through the words *our* and *art-object,* confines our understanding of the creative process phenomenon; where the boundary between our subjectivity and the objectivity of our art dissolves at certain points and we enter in such a deep state of resonance with it that we may indeed experience losing our sense of where we finish and our art begins.

When art is made in therapeutic groups, intersubjective phenomena add a further layer of experience to the one involved in making art. Recognised therapeutic factors in AP group practice include the opportunity to interact through artefacts, equally through their making and their sharing, leading group members to meta-physical forms of reciprocity, where resonance to the "unthought known" (Bollas 1987) extant in the art, whether or not consciously acknowledged, allows new ideas and thoughts to emerge. This way of relating to art, to ourselves and each other through art, involves what David Maclagan calls, with an adept pun, *wondering about,* in an image, a kind of imaginative inhabiting of it, which, with its *continuous psychological lining,* gives our response to images its depth and resonance of meaning (Maclagan 2001, p. 36). He goes on to describe this experience – which, in my view involves resonance, free association and amplification of images – as both learned and shared and as a phenomenon which is half-way between the solitary and the collective, between subjective and trans-subjective (Maclagan 2001, p. 37).

It is this capacity that art has, of placing us between states, not definitely intra-personal, or interpersonal, but rather at once individual and collective, that has been recognised as an important therapeutic factor, to be exploited in AP groups through explicit or implicit technical strategies. While therapeutic change is AT groups' unequivocal aim, the achievement of personal transformation essentially depends on formulating more adaptive ideas and creating new narratives through exposure to the emotional and aesthetic phenomena of making and jointly viewing (Isserow 2008) art in a collective setting.

As products of secondary processes, art images involve degrees of planning and determination and, even at their most spontaneous and immediate, emerge intrinsically more separate from their makers than dreams do from the dreamers; having said that, and despite losing some of their personal connotation when exposed in the public arena, images spontaneously made and viewed in smaller, group like settings, continue to be connected with their authors and, like dreams, may also be perceived as intensely personal and private. It has been my expectation that applying SD's approach to the spontaneous making and viewing of images in a collective setting, can transcend the limitation of individual, visual narratives in favour of collective ones, while making it possible to focus on the patterns connecting the various images to each other, just as it does with dreams.

My understanding of Lawrence's description of this process (Lawrence 2005, pp. 14–15) is that by keeping with the themes that link the dreams in the matrix, we move from the subjective preoccupations of the individual dreams to the nodes holding meaning between the dreams. This is an area beyond the limits of the personal and individual unknown, where information may be sought in terms of the shared cultural and trans-personal.

Creativity and art are not in a symmetrical relationship because the latter always derives from the former, while the reverse is not true. Similarly, the relationship between art and dreams is not causal, or symmetrical. There are, however, factors placing dreams and art images closer to each other. One is the pictorial nature of dreams. Although as phenomena, they convey feelings, sounds, body sensation and even smells, their telling and their listening to in the matrix is mostly conveyed through pictorial descriptions. Another factor is the open nature of art. What David Armstrong said about dreams, that they are the carrier *for* meaning, not *of* meaning (Armstrong 2005) is true of art as well. No dream can be truly seen in its integrity, like a work of art can. We tell and listen to them in their subjectivity, and we lend to other peoples' dreams our own sense in colours and feelings and in so doing we make them briefly our own. I think it is precisely at the point when participants experience this transient, shared ownership, that a temporary elision takes place around personal boundaries, as if a small portion of the energy holding individual psychic skin was diverted to form another connective medium, the matrix, where spontaneous associations are made.

The continuing relevance of these ideas to my thinking is illustrated in the *Treasure* dream given at the beginning of this chapter, which guided my thoughts around image making; it seemed to be moving its influence slowly (*like oil on water*) until it had reached a tipping point and there was a departure in my thinking, in a different direction: I was looking at the *sunlight through an aggregation of cells*, separate and yet welded in an inseparable network. This description fits both the *jellyfish* and the *stained-glass panel*, which were in the primary experience of the dream: the former are colonies of specialised cells, rather than one individual in the true sense of the word, and the latter are collections of glass pieces held together by a net of welded lead. I perceived the precious stones as something valuable and attractive: group analysis and social dreaming. I was immersed in the unconscious (*water/ ocean*), but in a shallow, pre-conscious state and available to thinking; the light of reason/illumination, was through a semi-transparent membrane which was identified with distinct and yet interchangeable objects. In a sense, the dream synthesised the idea of the matrix, organising the shared ownership of the oneiric material wherein and the possibility that art could be a conduit for that material's further amplification, illumination and understanding.

Art making response

As mentioned above, art making requires essential equipment, which even at a basic level includes paper, different mark making materials, and space which can accommodate, and tolerate, a degree of temporary disorder, or mess. Although we already have examples of SD programmes running in diverse contexts, such as Museums and Art galleries (Manley 2010), the need to cater for these requirements has restricted the range of contexts where SD and art making response have been used so far. I routinely host SD and art making response (AMR) programmes respectively for students and training teams of art psychotherapy training courses and for conferences hosted by organizations and universities connected with AP training programmes. These contexts share an ideological and constitutional investment in art as a reliable conduit for the expression of pre-conscious and unconscious material, such as ideas, emotions and ultimately information.

Placing the AMR within an SD programme is a technical issue, but often, as I also mentioned earlier, it is governed by practicality. I have always thought of it as a semi-independent component, following both matrix and the dream reflection dialogues (DRD). However, the question of how closely it does so it may depend of the amount of time available and on the structure of the event hosting the SD; due to this the way AMR has articulated within SD sequences has been inconsistent. For example, at two international conferences of art therapy, held in London in 2013 and 2016, we hosted ninety minutes long SDMs and DRDs with up to seventy-five participants per matrix, on each morning of the three-day conference, in parallel and separately from a number of other experiential workshops. At the closure of each day, we had a large, art therapy, studio group (Skaife, Jones & Pentaris 2016) where both, art-making and verbal inter-actions took place, with more than three-hundred delegates. All conference interventions and presentations, including the SDM, were processed here through free ranging interactions including image making, dialogue and free association.

These were important experiences in the development of my thinking about AMR, being instances where the art making was not dedicated to the SD, but rather linked to it through belonging to a larger event of which SD was part. It demonstrated that art-making would not need to substitute any part of the SD process, but could would work as an independent, yet connected part of the SD process, through a different symbolic order. In 2013 the SDMs had generated dreams with themes about *fragmentation* and *opposition*, gesturing towards an increase in difference and reduction in homogeneity in the art therapy practice; this was also corroborated by the widely different and innovative example of practices present at the conference. In the large art therapy group two art works stood out: one was a very large, cardboard and paper canoe, worn by its maker around her hips, while walking around the room, paddling imaginary water. The other was a trailing fabric, worn like a shroud by someone striking dramatic poses. The two images, as well as others, derived from dreams, integrated the SDM experience for those delegates who had not been part of it. They also embody, rather than describe, different experiences in a space (*world*) filled with art pieces. Being approached by the shrouded figure felt disquieting to many and associated to both the anxiety of needing to remain professionally functioning while working at the edge of the unknown, as well as the persecutory experience of vested authority. The circling canoe connected with ideas about distance travelled by what was once a young profession, which had now perhaps reached a stage both, maturity and complexity. The large art group, overlapping in function with the AMR, felt like a cross between a different kind of matrix and a system synthesis, redistributing the conference disparate experiences, including art-making, things heard and things misheard, hypotheses and hunches, so they could be exchanged and known by all; this large group functioned as a meta-visual, end of the day digestive system, for all oneiric, visual, verbal and non-verbal material.

As described in SD literature (Lawrence 2005) dream reflection dialogues (DRD), sometimes also referred to as dream reflection groups (DRG) (Lawrence 2007) are brief meetings in small groups, whose function is to move us from the free ranging ethos of the matrix to a more reflective position in order to identify and process the dreams, stories and themes emerged therein. They are point of transformation, taking our energy from a trans-personal position to one suitable to the emotional and conceptual examination of the emergent thematic narratives. This is an important nodal point, allowing us to take a rest from the roller-coaster of the matrix and enter a domain where we can think about our feelings and experiences of the dreams. The brevity of the DRDs contributes to their spontaneous focus function; quite different from that of image-making which is a protracted process involving time for making as well as viewing what had been made. When, opposed to the example described above, a period of art making can be integrated with the SDM process, it could do so by following the DRD.

Bringing art making response into the social dreaming process

In my experience SD is an explorative tool, which can operate as a self-standing activity, as well as part of organizational consultations, or against defined topics, or questions. Following from the dialogues, AMR continues the matrix discourse bringing into being a new relationship between image making and the stories told by the dreams and their associations. The integration of a non-verbal component to SD is still being studied (Berman and Manley, forthcoming 2018) and there is, as yet, no definitive procedure to analyse its content. The initial hypothesis is that the making and joint viewing of art, in the context of a SD programme, will serve the function of supporting, amplifying and in some cases, make more explicit, the connection with unconscious and pre-conscious content, already found in the matrix (Wright & La Nave 2016, unpublished report).

In the interest of coherence and boundaries, I ask participants to focus on the themes and feelings identified by the DRD and limit the time available for visual elaboration to forty-five minutes. Art-making revisits all available experiences of the matrix, including residual pre-conscious connections between the matrix and the wider context to which the dreams and associations may be speaking. The symbolic order to which this process belongs is non-verbal and meta-visual, fruitful in addressing the more difficult-to-define thinking of the matrix.

Case example 1: the mountain

For a number of years, I have been hosting a SD programme for the second year of training of a three-year MA in art psychotherapy. The overarching question for each training group, usually around twenty-three people, is "What is it like to be half way through this training?" One year a group generated an abundance of dreams themed *around monsters and vampire elders, transformations that could not be controlled and laboured journeys over mountains and glaciers.* During the DRD the students were increasingly recognising feelings of ambivalence towards the demanding and often persecutory rigours of the training, with an emphasis towards mutual support and sadness for a small number of trainees who had not been able to continue.

The images included monsters in various media, and the majority of the work was large, expressive and detailed, with large amounts of wet and pliable materials, which the students associated to the transitory, yet difficult to control, sense of dismay the course inspired at that point. A two-foot high, cardboard and paper piece, shaped like a mound, had a number of small dolls made with paper and pipe-cleaners, attached to the sides, with one doll perched on the top. As one student was recalling one of the matrix's dreams, about being on top of a mountain and then falling, the doll at the top actually detached and fell to the ground. The impact of this synchronous event was at first surprise and hilarity, but subsequent observations turned the conversation to the presence of other, less benign feelings, about envy and the reality that what had been up to that point, a supportive group of peers, would soon become a group of professionals competing for jobs; someone mentioned feeling a sudden sense of satisfaction at the sudden fall of the doll and becoming aware of their desire to identify with the demanding and persecutory staff group and examiners. By making aggressive fantasies explicit, instead of creating division and mistrust among the students, this realisation appeared to lower their anxiety and reclaim some of the emotional energy, until then held in the attacks towards the course and its demands.

Case example 2: joint work

The following vignette is from a SDM for the same institution, during a different year. The first dream was "not being able to find my car. I am in a dilapidated car-park and cannot remember where the car is parked. I look around to get help" from this point the matrix moved through themes of building dilapidation and dead fathers and grandfathers, to floods and buildings under water, underwater worlds, Chocolate and faeces, giants, reinforced and giant penises, then a series of very violent dreams and dreams where parents and siblings turn into monsters, dead and buried bodies, spiders, being a spider, pushing through intestine like tunnels leaving a spider-web behind.

In the DRDs the students expressed difficulties in making sense of the themes and seeing how the dreams could help them find new ideas about their mid-training reality. As they set out to the art making, they appeared to move almost in unison in creating a square room within a room (Figure 8.1), by joining several pieces of paper together. The images were made quickly, mainly using the paper structure as

FIGURE 8.1 Dream reflection: Art Making Response

ground, medium and boundary and followed the dreams in illustrative ways. It looked as if the students were making up for their difficulties in considering the dreams, by trying to build a protective, powerful and fortified unit (reinforced penises and protecting selves and siblings from violence). The ambiguous shape, straddling notions of defence and containment, became a conduit for reflection on the year group internal dynamics, revealing a degree of fragmentation and lack of solidarity among the students. One of the concluding observations was that they had experienced the SD task, including image making, as a cohesion building process.

Case example 3: NY conference

This example is drawn from a recent SD programme that Tim Wright and I hosted, as part of a large conference in New York, themed around the relationship between mentalization and the arts. We hosted two SDMs, each attracting approximately forty to fifty people, equivalent to about half of the candidates, with DRD and AMR and final discussions, tasked with attempting a system synthesis. Mentalization (Bateman & Fonagy 2004; 2006) is an important psychological paradigm, connected with robust evidence for manualised, clinical protocols, based on empirical research.

The question for the SD was "What is the relationship between the arts therapies and mentalization?", reiterating the conference central matter. The stated mission for the SD programme was to function as a search engine for ideas about what position art therapy should assume in relation to mentalization, which would be fed back to the larger conference body through its various workshops and plenaries. The dreams brought into view emotional experiences about the rise of importance of mentalization related techniques, held by various sections of the professions, but only partially acknowledged by the more conscious part of the system. The images supported the emergent ideas of the matrices, but also identified shadow aspects of the relationship: several dreams as well as images appeared to suggest considerations of shifting landscapes. The use of collage in this context seems meaningful as possibly representing the grafting of different paradigms over each other. One dream of an elephant walking in the temple and crashing the temple's pillars, while intensely associated with, during the matrix, was not reproduced, in any of the images. This absence was noticed and ironically linked to the phrase the elephant in the room, in this context the reluctance experienced by many in the profession to change, or adapt their practice, as well as to declare it explicitly. Several images allude to states of aggregation while others represent vortices, some giving birth to birds. These last would appear to emerge from associations with bird dreams in the SDM and with the linked themes of peer support and of the experience of danger and dissolution as well as opportunities associated with change. Some images show well integrated areas, others retain articulated, but clearly differentiated parts: visual representations, we hypothesise, of the different states of integration of the mentalization paradigm within the arts therapies (Wright & La Nave 2016).

Discussion

The three examples given are quite different from each other, despite being organized within similar frameworks and structures in terms of duration and procedural aspects. From the point of view of reflecting on the art made during the AMR, numbers greatly affect the way it can be done, and certainly the possibility of recording it. Additionally, the way images are arranged for viewing contributes further levels of complexity to the global thinking of an SD programme, in addition to the images' individual content. The example drawn from the second AP training programme shows all pieces of work on paper are joined in a solid looking, oblong frame, containing both 2D and 3D images in an entirely enclosed space, effectively creating a single, collective piece, encompassing all other, individual pieces. While the photographic recording was simplified by its compact shape, the significance of the arrangement spoke to the year-group's system's internal dynamics and in particular to a hitherto felt, but not fully declared until then, desire for a solid holding (*frame*) capable of containing and protecting the individual students from the difficulties of the training.

When SDMs are small, say up to fifteen people, images can be arranged in such way as to be easily viewed from a relatively stationary position. When SDMs are larger than thirty participants people need to move around the images in order to see them. Far from being a value-neutral activity, it may expose important aspects of the system linked to the politics of space, reluctance or tendency to be, or to make something visible, internal relationships with authority and hierarchy: expressed by the way space is used, apart from having practical consequences for the amount of time necessary for the process. In cases such as the large art therapy group described earlier, part of a larger event where the art-making was the main task and distinct from the SDM, further thinking needs to take place on how to examine the way it may have been directly and indirectly informed by the matrices' dreams. The greatest difficulty in this case is represented by the fact that the body of the conference delegates, of the SDM's and of the large art therapy group's participants, only partly overlap.

Different from dreams which are narrated, images need to be seen to have any meaning, and how they can be seen, changes their impact and, consequently, what they can offer. Images from the AMR cannot be discussed in reciprocal, free associative terms because they have been made simultaneously and not in a free associative sequence, in the way the dreams are in the matrix, but they function as amplifications and associations to the dreams that preceded them. While art images are no more linear than dreams, they create visibility for some of the matrix's unconscious material through their collective lens. The function of their visibility is dependent on the way in which we view them and what kind of position we need to assume towards them, especially at a point when we need to reach working hypotheses or intuitions on the state of the system. Again, no systematic research has been done, so far, on the best way to do this. In a relatively small assembly individual images may be introduced by their makers. While this is perfectly legitimate, to prescribe it would contradict the free ranging/free associative, SD ethos of focussing on the story/dream, not the narrator/dreamer, amplifying, instead of reducing, the importance of the image maker's intentions and personal relationship with the image. In a large assembly, such as the fifty-plus SDM described above, such direct representation would be impossible to achieve.

One alternative and possibly fruitful way, which I have only just begun to explore, could be to place images in small groups, according to main thematic categories. As categories overlap and also have internal contradictions, images need moving and replacing several times, in a process of continuous visual re-location and re-classification, which could prove distracting as well as useful in equal measure. To let images be gathered together, in clusters shaped more by impulse than determination, seems to make altogether more sense. All participants may look at all the images together, explore and/or ignore possible connections and associations. Since it is at this point that hypotheses and new ideas can be identified and conclusions be drawn, it is crucial that participants can enter in a state of shared, reflective attention to their comprehensive involvement with the SD process, including discoveries, surprises and learning.

Conclusion

In this chapter I have proposed a development of the traditional social dreaming model involving the adjunct of an additional phase during which participants make art based on their experience of the matrix. This development finds origin in pre-existing observations about the links between social dreaming and art psychotherapy groups, but departs from clinical applications of creativity and strives to remain coherent with the ethos of social dreaming. I have discussed similarities and differences between art therapy and social dreaming, between art and dreams and how image-making may be integrated, or partially integrated in SD programmes. Such integration may be challenged by logistical factors such as time and the type of space available. I have described experiences made in the course of providing social dreaming programmes and art making response for different organizational contexts, with substantially differing briefs. In some cases, the requirement has been to provide experiential workshops where the organisation's main task has been the education and training in the arts and the arts therapies; in these cases, the SDMs have been relatively small, with less than thirty participants and sufficient time allocated, for the AMR to be "bolted-on" to the SDM and DRD. In other cases, such as large international conferences, where SD programmes attract between forty and fifty participants per matrix, AMR may follow the SDM immediately, or in some cases, be brought into line with a pre-existing, end of the day, large art making group, where both, SD participants as well as non-participants, are present. These different structures do not only offer purchase to the AMR, but in their diversity, are affected by and affect the way it can operate.

The initial hypothesis, indebted to art psychotherapy, was that the joint making and viewing of art, following an SDM, may embody aspects of the matrix, through a re-elaboration which is not just illustrative, but actually contributing new information to our understanding of the dreams, by making their visions visible in physicality of matter, structure and colour.

My experience of creating and implementing AMR has been, overall, rewarding. Due in great part to it being at an experimental stage, its returns are a mixed bag of hurdles, learning solutions and discoveries. To state, incontrovertibly, how strongly AMR extends the range of knowledge SD provides in its purely verbal version, is not possible at this juncture because it needs a systematic research to be designed, implementing the process with controllable parameters and indicators, including SDM size, space conditions, range of art materials and time allocated to the distinct phases. I suspect that a comprehensive study of the function and outcomes of AMR in SD may prove very challenging, particularly because of the disparity of indicators it will need considering.

Particular attention needs paying to the time ratio art-making and system-reflection. Lately, for medium size SDM (between twelve and twenty-five), I have restricted the art-making period to forty-five minutes, and extended the final reflective part to up to one hour. This has proved beneficial in a number of ways: it allows due attention to be given to the images, which in turn will have been made more instinctively than deliberately, retaining, through being less refined and corrected, a greater degree of primary connection with the matrix dreams. In addition, more time for discussion settles participants into a reflective mood and familiarises them with the progression of their thinking from dream association to dream and image association, which many may not be acquainted with.

Feed-back from past programmes has corroborated the original hypothesis that AMR enhances the process of SD. There are, as I have described and discussed, applications and restrictions to this method, including the challenges involved in the making, reporting, studying, classifying and analysing of visual art, which contributes complexity as well as richness, to the verbal narrative of SD.

Links to reports

La Nave F., Frizel C. http://ojs.gold.ac.uk/index.php/atol/issue/view/33. Vol 8, No 1 (2017).

La Nave F., Wright T. (2016). *Social Dreaming Report* for ICAPT@Pratt Institute: The Arts and Mentalization: Communicating at the Edge of the Unknown. Pratt Institute, Brooklyn, New York, October 2016 (unpublished) https://1drv.ms/w/s! Atdbzdci-RdtlQTwlayRyy_FsRth.

References

Ahlin, G. (1985). "On thinking about the Group Matrix." *Group Analysis*. Vol. 18(2) pp. 112–124.

Armstrong, D. (2005). *Organization in the Mind: Psychoanalysis, Group Relations, and Organizational Consultancy*. London: Karnac.

Barnes, D. (1937). *Nightwood*. New York: New Directions.

Bateman, A.W., & Fonagy, P. (2004). *Psychotherapy for Borderline Personality Disorder. Mentalization Based Treatment*. Oxford: Oxford University press.

Bateman, A.W., & Fonagy, P. (2006). *Mentalization-based Treatment for Borderline Personality Disorders*. Oxford: Oxford University Press.

Berman, H., & Manley, J. (forthcoming 2018). "Social Dreaming and Creativity in South Africa: Imagi(ni)ng the Unthought known" In J. Adlam, J. Gilligan, T. Kluttig, and B.X. Lee (eds). *Creative States: Overcoming Violence*, Vol 1, Part 4, Ch 2. London: Jessica Kingsley.

Bollas, C. (1987). *The Shadow of the Object: Psychoanalysis of the Unthought Known*. London: Free Association Books.

Dalley, T. (1984). *Art as Therapy*. London: Tavistock Publications.

Edwards, D. (2004). *Art Therapy*. London: Sage Publications.

Hass-Cohen, N., & Carr, R. (2008). *Art Therapy and Neuroscience*. London: Jessica Kinsley.

Isserow, J. (2008). "Joint Attention in Art Therapy." *International Journal of Art Therapy*. Vol. 13(1) pp. 34–42.

La Nave, F. (2010). "Image: Reflections on the Treatment of Images and Dreams in Art Psychotherapy Groups." *International Journal of Art Therapy*. Vol. 15(1) pp. 13–24.

La Nave, F. (2014). "Theatre of the Image and Group Interaction" in D. Waller (ed) *Group Interactive Art Therapy, Its use in Training and Treatment*, pp. 153–164. London: Routledge.

La Nave, F., & Wright, T. (2016). Social Dreaming Report for ICAPT@Pratt Institute: The Arts and Mentalization: Communicating at the Edge of the Unknown. Pratt Institute, Brooklyn, New York, October 2016 (unpublished) https://1drv.ms/w/s!Atdbzd ci-RdtlQTwlayRyy_FsRth.

Lawrence, W.G. (2005). (ed) *Introduction to Social Dreaming; Transforming Thinking*. London: Karnac.

Lawrence, W.G. (ed) (2007). *Infinite Possibilities of Social Dreaming*. London: Karnac.

Lawrence, W.G. (ed) (2010). *The Creativity of Social Dreaming*. London: Karnac.

Maclagan, D. (2001) *Psychological Aesthetics, Painting, Feeling and Making sense*. London: Jessica Kingsley.

Mann, D. (2006). "Art Therapy: Re-imagining a Psychoanalytic Perspective –A Reply to David Maclagan." *International Journal of Art Therapy*. Vol. 11(1), pp. 33–40.

Oppenheimer, L. (2005). *A Curious Intimacy; Art and Neuro-psychoanalysis*. New York: Routledge.

Rose, G.J. (1980). *The Power of Form, A Psychoanalytic Approach to Aesthetic Form*. New York: International University Press.

Schaverien, J. (1992). *The Revealing Image*. London: Routledge.

Selvaggi, L. (2010). "Low-shot on Reality: Dreaming in a Primary school" in W.G. Lawrence (ed) *The Creativity of Social Dreaming*, pp. 53–63. London: Karnac.

Skaife, S., & Huet, V. (ed.) (1998). *Art Psychotherapy Groups*. London: Routledge.

Skaife, S., Jones, K., & Pentaris, P. (2016). "The Impact of the Art Therapy Large Group, An Educational Tool in the Training of Art Therapists, on Post-qualification Professional Practice." *International Journal of Art Therapy*. Vol. 21(1) UK: Taylor & Francis.

Springham, N. (2012). "How can Art Therapy contribute to Mentalization in Borderline Personality Disorder?" *International Journal of Art Therapy*. Vol. 17(3).

Werdinger, W. (2010). "Social Dreaming with Black Rappers in New York" in W.G. Lawrence (ed) *The Creativity of Social Dreaming*, pp. 169–176. London: Karnac.

Zabafi, A., Clare, J., & Lawrence, W.G. (2007). "'Don't Explain, Just Go': The Creative Process and Social Dreaming" in W.G. Lawrence (ed) *Infinite Possibilities of Social Dreaming*, pp. 79–98. London: Karnac.

SECTION III
Social dreaming practice

9

"ARE YOU SHARING A DREAM?"

Social dreaming in a community

Hanni Biran, Judith Ezra, Or Netanely, and Hanan Sabah-Teicher

> I dreamed that people ate other living beings and treated them with terrible cruelty
> while leading them to slaughter, and then I woke up and realized it wasn't a dream.
> *(Told in Tel Aviv, January 2016)*

Introduction

This chapter describes our initiative to use the social dreaming matrix as a method to open an alternative space for dialogue in our community in Tel Aviv, Israel. In this chapter we will: 1) explain the violent discourse in the Israeli society, which was the context in which we felt the need to promote public dialogue; 2) explain how we view the social dreaming matrix as a method that could promote such dialogue; 3) analyse the form and content of four social dreaming matrix sessions in which we applied this method in our community (our main purpose); and last, 4) we will discuss the effects these sessions had on the participants, our new understanding from these sessions and their analysis, and lessons we have learned about the use of the social dreaming matrix as a method to promote public dialogue in a split society characterized by violent discourse.

A violent discourse

In our initiative, we ventured to deal with the Israeli public discourse, which is heated and emotional, full of magical expressions which incite action, or summon a very strong emotional reaction. Such heavily loaded words may be Jew/Arab, left/right, war/terror/peace, Ashkenazi/Mizrahi (referring to Jews descended from either European or Arab countries) – and when used in a discussion, a strong "us or them" connotation arises. It is also a discourse full of harsh words and aggression, prompting violent physical action, such as "death to traitors". Political debates are conducted *ad hominem*, delegitimizing the counterpart as a traitor, corrupt, fanatic, or not human enough. This discourse does not promote mutual understanding, insight, or even a serious clarification of issues and problems (Gitay 2010).

The Israeli society is deeply traumatized, by catastrophic disasters such as the Holocaust and total wars that threatened its annihilation and defined its identity (Volkan 2009), and by ongoing violence and terror attacks that keep it in a constant state of vigilance against the other. This ongoing existential dread narrows views on reality, and its complex inter-subjective dimension. It creates a symbolic equation in which words and symbols become concrete and omnipotent – as if the other's perspective is not just another partial view of reality, but rather an act, that has to be defended against, as if it has been realized. Any dialogue threatens such a society with negation of its identity, and annihilation of its existence, or at least invalidates its very right to exist. Such dialogue is unbearable, and so there is no space for examination and observation as a basis of integration of various aspects of the complex reality.

Dreaming a social change

In this atmosphere, we asked if and how it would be possible, to *dream* this social reality (Ogden 2010). That is, to transfer the political–militant subject matter and aggressive-anxious emotional import of the Israeli discourse, into the unconscious realm where the rules of primary thinking processes may undermine the concreteness of the content, and hint towards the deeper origins of the emotions involved. With the technique of a social dreaming matrix, we hoped to dream what has not yet been dreamt. We asked to find out how social dreaming may allow us to unravel new thoughts seeded in the dream imagery.

We hold that social dreaming is a method which allows the creation of a new space that contains a dialogue between two states of consciousness, expressed in two modalities of discourse that we term "Waking Discourse" and "Dreaming Discourse". The waking discourse is concerned with what exists – a sort of pragmatic realism (Arieti 1961). The dreaming discourse takes place in a potential realm, a world of possibilities, visions. The dreaming discourse expresses an implicit inner reality and inter-subjective dimension that raises questions regarding what is perceived as objective reality, and reveals its layered and constructed nature. The oscillation between these two consciousness states creates a *fuzzy* attention space in which perceived objects do not exclude or replace one another, but rather co-exist, and a suspension of understanding allows each idea to have the possibility of existence. Such a space allows the participants to let go of conventions, and the need to organize ideas in terms of development from beginning to an end, and allows any end to become the beginning for something else. And so, since thoughts and ideas become more abstract and less bound to physical objects and actions, they can also be shared more easily between people. This ability for *abstraction together* has the potential to change reality since reality is more than physical things and their properties, but also what people perceive and what people agree upon.

We hold that sharing a dream within the matrix is an act of faith; an essay to create a state of suspension – personally and socially – of the immediate judgment of reality. This suspension undermines the conventional ways of thinking (or actually of not-thinking), which would hinder any attempt to participate in a fertile political dialogue. It makes no sense arguing with a dream. The suspension space allows us to differentiate the idea from its realization, as any idea is valid for thinking even if it is not possible to realize it.

The social meaning of the matrix

What we have described so far may characterize a dialogue between two or more people, or an intra-psychic dialogue. Therefore, we must explain the meaning of the social dreaming matrix; viz., as a sample of individuals from a society who work together to interpret the larger whole to which they belong. The underlying rationale of the social dreaming matrix is that the mental content that an individual person represses has a social meaning and that through the associative thinking in the matrix (Manley this book) this social meaning can be brought to consciousness.

Under this view, the unconscious within each of us, named as the "associative unconscious" (Long & Harney 2013) means that every individual holds a partial piece of a broader social puzzle, and only the collaborative effort of numerous individual perspectives can begin to delineate society as an object. If in the past, being part of a social whole was a spiritual or an ideological experience, it is now a very real experience when people's identity and lives are rooted within a global network. Information-sharing technologies allow for ever more complex connections between people. Technological initiatives such as open source coding strive to create a world of shared ideas, a greater whole via collaborative effort of independent agents. However, this collaborative effort of many individuals may give birth to a higher level of consciousness which cannot be conceived by the individuals that created it. To become part of the social matrix, is to put aside individuality.

The method

The social dreaming matrix is constructed in a way that allows for individuals to relinquish ownership of their dreams and share them with the members of the matrix, as a form of open source authorship of dreams. The participants sit scattered across the room in a snowflake formation and the hosts are also dispersed among them. The formation allows voices to come up anonymously, as one cannot always see the face of the person who is talking, and the one talking does not always see how his or her delivered dream or association is received, so subtle conformity cues that are used for editing oneself are missing. Common themes may be an uncanny experience (Freud 1919), getting lost, and emergence from a structure. The matrix itself aspires to infinity, coming up with riddles only.

All the four matrices described in this chapter took place in a community centre in Tel Aviv. Tel Aviv is considered the liberal, urban, and cultural centre of Israel. Tel Aviv attracts young people and culture, and is the centre of protest against the national politics on the one hand, and a target for criticism and scorn for being a detached *leftist bubble* on the other hand. Throughout the time period the matrices took place, Tel-Aviv was subject to terror attacks and high political tension. The matrices attracted participants from other cities in Israel. Each session had about thirty to forty participants, from a range of ages from teenagers to seniors, of various professional fields – therapists and non-therapists.

Delayed afterthoughts

We transcribed the dreaming sessions verbatim, and returned to the transcriptions in our discussions between sessions. We also came up with new associations, inspired by the matrices. Overall, the sessions are made up of highly condensed mental imagery. We were driven to give it meaning in two axes: by researching new ways of thought and new forms of logic that the matrix aroused in us, and by associating to meta themes that were present in the matrix. And so, our analysis of the raw material collected in the matrices followed two main axes: an analysis of the matrix's discourse modalities, and a thematic analysis. In both axes we searched for new thoughts that were born in us.

Analysis of the four matrices

The first matrix – January 2016

> *Last night, I dreamed that there was something wrong with the ceiling in my parents' house. Something was leaking, some kind of wetness. And this was interrupted by an entirely different scene – this foreign woman came to stay as a guest at my place in order to attend some event, and another woman was there, a colleague from my workplace, who was caring for an elderly woman. Then, my colleague had the nerve to tell my guest that she can leave, just go back to Sweden without saying Shalom [the Hebrew word used for Hello or Goodbye, as well as Peace].*

This is the dream that began the matrix. It leads to two emerging themes: leakage and peace. The theme of leakage evoked water, as a many-faced symbol. Water, symbolizing life and growth, may also be disturbing and elusive as a leaky faucet at the edge of one's hearing at night; water can be a source of infection and poisoning; a large amount of water can flood and drown. It seems that the water motif evoked a disturbing emotional sense of leaking water, of death and disgust, as expressed in the following dream:

> *There was this artificial, man-made lake. It was small and pretty shallow. There were animals swimming in it. My girlfriend talked me into swimming in those shallows, dragging myself around in the water; that swamp water. At some point I saw orange water-tigers. They grossed me out and I went out and washed myself at the nearby park.*

This dream lead to associations about disasters that involved Tel Aviv's Yarkon river, which is very polluted. During an international sporting event, a group of Australian athletes crossed a bridge over the contaminated river as part of the opening ceremony; but the bridge was poorly built and it collapsed, and three of the sixty athletes who fell in the water died of infections caused by polluted water. The other tragedy mentioned was that of a little girl, who went missing, and it was eventually discovered that she had been murdered by her father, shoved into a suitcase and thrown into the dark waters of the Yarkon. The theme of water evoked a disturbing emotion that seemed hard to digest.

The second thematic axis that was evoked by the first dream, concerned the dove of peace. The dove is the ultimate symbol of peace, but one must keep in mind the kind of peace involved – in the bible, the dove symbolizes the extinction of sinful humanity by a flood, and the possibility of a fresh start. It is a symbol of an apocalyptic peace. It began with an association of eating a live dove as a test of manhood, which then led to a memory about a dove that entered a consultation room and couldn't get out, frantically flying about until the two patients caught it, calmed it – and the therapist – and let it fly out safely. Later in the matrix, doves resurfaced as a filthy animal that filled an entire attic with its droppings. Then, they were nostalgically linked to pre-statehood Israeli society, in which doves were used by the Palmach militia as a secret means of communication. Nostalgia then evaporated as another participant mentioned that in those days of Zionist Socialism, social oppression and the limitations on free speech were much harsher.

As hosts, we formed certain working assumptions regarding the thematic development of the matrix. For instance, we suggest that stopping on the way to peace [Shalom/Goodbye], creates a dangerous situation. Processes that often began very hopefully came to a halt and are now polluted and poisoned. Standing still leads to stagnation and entails dangers that are difficult to notice. This is a mere assumption that allows the next step to take place.

Another assumption was that the matrix tells about a state that is more acute than simple stopping or slowing down; we have already reached the place we are afraid of and the previous divisions that provided a sense of order and progress no longer exist.

More dangerous rooms or houses were depicted in the dreams. From the first dream, which featured a leaking ceiling, to the dove who flew into the room. Dreams of fitting rooms which are small, closed off spaces which cut a person off from social space, indicating some kind of split or detachment between the individual and society at large.

However, the attitude towards these rooms was altered throughout the matrix. The desire for a room is expressed in a dream where many people were standing in line to book a hotel room; everyone got their room except for the dreamer. The next association offers a way to transcend the static structure of rooms: "it's like this paradox, when someone goes to a hotel and there are no vacancies, so he says, if everybody just moved one room over, there would suddenly be a vacancy" – movement itself seems to create space.

The final dream of this session suggests that we should move and travel as light as possible. This dream presents the younger generation's variation of this movement.

> *This reminds me of a dream I had about … this thing about traveling on, of wanting to move to Berlin, of course, but I'm from a kibbutz, I want to leave but I know that I won't have anybody there, but I'm a street cat, but then I realize that I need to bring a cow from our cowshed to Berlin, but how will I get a cow around Berlin's subway system, and my father is working in the cowshed and I tell him, you know what, I'll take one of the calves to Berlin.*

Here we may suggest that the generation of the Holocaust has clung to Israel as a safe haven, turning it into a place of redemption, where one holds fast to the soil; the younger generations, however, feel at liberty to move about and live abroad, even in places such as Germany, refusing to shoulder that heavy a burden (a calf instead of a cow), while keeping a more compact, but meaningful element with them. The matrix, that began with going back to one's parents and ended with a young woman leaving for Berlin without the burden of the Holocaust that is weighing heavily on the older generation. This indicates a transformation that was made possible within this generational discourse, through the matrix's preoccupation with the question of inter-generational relations.

The second matrix – May 2016

The second matrix, as the first one, opened with dream concerning intergenerational connection:

> *In my dream, I have to buy stamps. My son decided to cancel his internet subscription and wants us to communicate through letters, like in the old days. I am driving a car through darkness, rain and fog. I can't see anything, it's like driving blind. I have to get to the store. On my way, my windshield-wipers made a kind of square, just like a stamp, through which I could see where I was going.*

The course of the matrix can be seen as a development of the theme of a very mortal woman's struggle with titanic elements, often symbolized as feminine. Intergenerational and inter-gender tensions are also explored further in the matrix. In the very next dream, the rising sea threatens to flood Tel Aviv, and the female dreamer escapes the flood with a young female politician who happens to drive by, leaving the man who was with her to drown. When they reach refuge, a fatherly politician offers them his hand, and they complain together about the neglecting male Prime Minister who didn't prepare to help the survivors. The idea of female power is elaborated, and raises the questions of whether to spare men or whether men will be needed. Other associations recall the apocalypse and the end of the world, and the idea of limited survival such as in Noah's ark. The sea (a symbol of the unconscious as well) is threatening to engulf the land (the conscious). In one of the dreams, the danger is so great that people cling to little cube-like houses, which may represent social fragmentation.

The woman driving in the dark out of dedication to her son in the opening dream also recurs, in certain variations, throughout the other dreams. In a song that comes up in one association, a woman is standing on the seashore and her heart shines as a lighthouse to guide her lover home from sea. But as he keeps going out to sea, her heart burns and she dies. In another association, a woman saves her husband from being suffocated at night. And in another association, a mother saves her army-refusing daughter from drowning. The mother thus saves her daughter from the "system" or the masculine army. Either way, we can see these women in leading positions, ostensibly fighting social blindness and conventions. It would seem women represent both a very personal, emotional attachment to the other that holds people together, as well as a cosmic wholeness that threatens to tear us apart, and that women struggle to balance the pull of these two extremes.

Then this horrifying tension embodied in womanhood finds a manic solution, as the matrix encounters a sudden change. One participant says that she is a "lucid dreamer" and that in her dream she is angry that someone wants to charge her money for seeing a show. As a very long fence pops up and blocks her way and with the feeling of helplessness this evokes, she suddenly gains awareness inside the dream. She then begins a kind of grandiose onslaught of super powers that enable people to levitate and fly like super-heroes. The motion is very hectic and one can never know what the restlessness that is overwhelming the matrix will result in. But when she reaches the clouds, some man that was with her turns out to be her male double and they kiss.

Perhaps this is an omnipotent escape from the raw power of the sea to more lofty domains, where one can have magical control, as well as a refusal "to pay the price" for participation, that turns into a withdrawal into oneself, when the couple turns into a single, androgynous person. The resolution of this conflict is the unifying pairing of male and female, it is a romantic notion that salvation comes through coupling. Still, this solution hints that gaining the knowledge that is obscured by two mutually negating perspectives, requires a superpower to allow integration.

Then comes a torrent of associations about the holocaust and its effect on second and third-generation survivors, and a twisted romantic solution is offered. One dream offers a clear example:

> *In my dream, me and my family are going to visit my grandfather, who is a holocaust survivor, and had already passed away. He lives on the top floor and I realize that that is heaven, the afterlife. My grandfather married my grandmother after losing a wife and a daughter in the holocaust. In my dream, he has a new wife. Living with my grandmother was hard for him, it was a marriage of survival. In my dream, me and my father come and sit on the couch in grandpa's living room and we go into his new wife's robe. I put my arm in the left sleeve and my father puts his in the right sleeve and we slip into it together.*

In this dream we see the romantic solution to the apocalypse is to start anew – a man and a woman who survive and become a couple, and bring offspring to out-live the disaster, thus symbolizing unity and continuity in the face of chaos and trauma – as in Noah's ark. However, in this dream we also begin to witness a merger of different generations, the cancellation of the generation gap and even of sex differences, as everything is sucked into the holocaust and the following gen-erations are trapped within their parents' past. It seems that both father and daughter are trapped in the grandfather's memories of the holocaust. The new wife has vanished altogether and the burden of the holocaust is portrayed through the act of entering the robe on the grandfather's couch, which twists time into a trapping loop. The encounter between a man and a woman – who bring forth the next generation – means resisting death; but when we recall the traumatic destruction that the survivors still bear and pass forward to the next generation, is there any fruitful potential here for something lively and new?

The third matrix – June 2016

The third matrix was conducted a day after a terrorist attack took place not far from our meeting place, and in which several people were killed.

The opening dream:

> I wanted to start but I blacked out, I remember only one dream that keeps recurring, it's a nightmare, that I am traveling, it's always abroad, I live here, but the dream is always when I'm away; I leave a place, a flat or a hotel I am staying in, and as I leave, everything seems very clear, the streets and the people are very familiar to me, and then suddenly it gets messed up and I completely lose my orientation, every street that's supposed to be X changes to something else, and I can't find it, and at the end after a lot of trouble and fear within the dream, there's always some sort of solution, but I feel depleted of energy.

The opening dream's theme of being lost brings to mind the opening lines of Freud's essay "The Uncanny" (Freud 1919), where he recounts an experience where he wanders randomly in an Italian town and mindlessly but surely, he keeps returning to the same place – where prostitutes are to be found. Getting lost can be seen as a departure from rationality to an uncanny encounter with the strange-yet-familiar elements of reality. In the very next dream that comes up in association, the dreamer says that when she was in Berlin, she dreamt that she was lost in the corridors of The Hebrew University in Jerusalem; she is trapped there and cannot find the way out. And so, a tension is building between clinging to familiar cities, and the anxiety of getting lost in them. This last dream can also be seen as repre-senting the social split between the academy, a symbol of the old, preexisting establishment – such as the academy in Jerusalem – and Tel Aviv and Berlin which mark the direction and the motion led by the younger generation. Or perhaps, this dream suggests two failed solutions – she is unable to escape the Israel that haunts her in her dreams, and she is unable to find an academic, intellectual resolution.

The next shift in the matrix direction would suggest that in the state of loss and being lost, the matrix seeks growth and continuity and struggles against trapping loops. When dreams exhibit considerable splitting between perfect order and chaos, known/familiar and foreign/menacing, left-wing and right-wing, it appears then that inter-generational splits leads to difficulty in perceiving creative and fertile continuity. This lack of social fertility is manifest in the next dream through the figure of a young woman who repeatedly serves as a surrogate mother for her own mother and, on the other hand, through another dream of an older woman who is no longer fertile but gives birth to a huge child who speaks Hebrew but appears to suffer from some kind of mental impairment and abnormality.

One of the associations mentioned was the "Ballad of the Lady and the Bird". In this ballad, a young boy and girl are trapped in adult bodies and their voices cannot be heard. In the end, they manage to come out as birds on a bridge – they scream but are unheard. They then decide to jump in the water and commit suicide. This association heightens the alienation between children and adults and brings to mind the voices that are not heard and end up being lost. It seems that the matrix is touching on the anxiety surrounding the inability to hear novel voices – these are born, but fail to develop. Another association was to a poem by poet Boaz Yaniv, which reads: "When I was born, I told the midwife everything, but she forgot and I am stuck in the same conversation ever since". This poem also related to the inability to be heard. The feeling is that the generations are not moving forwards and that generations pass and nothing is learned.

This difficulty in inter-generational transmission also appears in the matrix as a failure to communicate, phrased in one of the dreams in the words of the book of Psalms – "let my tongue cleave to the roof of my mouth" – which means that one is mute. This calls to mind things that cannot be spoken of in the Israeli society, for example the participants' choice to ignore the previous day's attack.

Another dream came up, in reference to current events. In the dream the Prime Minister sends the dreamer on some mission, despite the dreamer's objection, and commands the dreamer to board a boat. Whilst on the boat, the dreamer fears that the Prime Minister sent him away to get rid of him, and so he calls his father and gets off the boat, while he sees a couple of his friends boarding a similar boat. If the beginning of the dream may remind us of Hamlet's being sent to England to meet his own death because of his loyalty to his father that threatens his uncle the king; the second part of the dream – seeing a couple boarding a similar boat, may remind one of the tale of Noah's Ark, in which God wishes to do away with society, and those sent on the boat in couples are meant to be spared. This duality of connotations may bring about the question of trust in authority – are the survivors banished or saved? After this dream the atmosphere in the room changed, and a tense and bitter debate of political positions began – a sort of a reverse Tsunami, in which land (the realism of wakeful discourse) attacked the sea (the unconscious depth of dream discourse).

The matrix concluded with the dream of a granddaughter walking down the beach with her deceased grandfather and asking herself when would be a polite enough time to tell him that he is dead. Thus, the wisdom of the elder generation becomes a nostalgic burden. It appears that alongside the difficulty in letting future aspects be born and grow, it is likewise difficult to let past aspects leave and die. Nevertheless, the concluding dream shows an emerging connection – the shoreline connecting sea and land – and the creation of an inter-generational discourse that allows these split off parts to come together through the ability to acknowledge death and allow the transformation from past to future.

The fourth matrix – July 2016

This final matrix can be described as a kind of implicit dialogue between the two axes – that of themes and that of discourse modalities. On the thematic axis, we find dreams of children getting lost alongside the struggle between the secular, religious and military cultures; in terms of dialogue modalities, we find an abundance of dreams and associations. The first dream, shared by a woman, was of having her small son disappear, apparently kidnapped by some religious community. She described the culture of this community as one which keeps men and women completely separate: the women work menial jobs and have much lower status than the men. The dreamer comes to this community and is given a child who is supposed to be her son, but she feels that he is not her son.

This first dream is about a conservative community with strict rules which admits a boy who cannot grow as a subject in his own right and must become a small part of their collective identity. This dream can also represent the army, where the uniforms erase the subject. This notion is supported by an association offered later on by a man who said that, when he was a child and his father first came home on leave from the army, he did not recognize him and said, "mommy, there's a soldier at our house!".

Throughout the matrix, children are getting lost and their mothers go looking for them, with much anxiety and distress. Whereas in the previous matrix the speakers were those who were lost, this time, they care for others who are lost. Still, getting lost is a relative experience, a lost child may say to his mother, who just found him – "*I* wasn't lost, *you* were lost".

In Israel, mothers must bear their anxiety about the wellbeing of their children who join the army. Men, however, display certainty and knowledge, with less signs of distress. This is prominently manifest in David Grossman's aforementioned novel, "To the End of the Land". It seems that mothers whose children become soldiers take on a social role of "anxiety-containers", thus allowing men to stay practical and focused on the actual goals.

The associations offered in the matrix featured the orthodox Jewish community living in the city of Bnei Brak several times. They raised questions about foreignness and belonging. The encounter with the other may fail because the stranger who is trying to initiate it may feel detached from their natural habitat. One association offers an example: "hair on your head is natural and sensual, hair in your soup is disgusting". The question is how can one create an encounter with the other that is both natural and humanizing. The matrix began with a dream about a strange community that threatens to swallow up the young subject and ends with another social dream that tells quite the opposite story about the encounter with the other:

> I am going to Egypt and I am worried. I am afraid that the Egyptians will see that my face looks like my father's – and he fought in Egypt, in the Sinai. I can see that there are women and children there and that their faces all look like my father's. They can see that I look like him and, to my surprise, respect me for the fact that my father fought for something he believed in.

This dream possibly expresses the notion that conflict, of all things, can lead to connection.

The conclusion of the matrix, through an encounter with the other, also indicates the human resemblance that is found between enemies. There is a connection that transcends ethnic belonging and this connection can lead to an encounter between the two peoples. The dream is also suggesting that the other holds a key component of one's identity, through memories that hold both the reminiscence of similarity and intimacy, and that of fighting. The willingness to look directly at the other and to assume responsibility for the consequences of violence creates the ground on which a new and surprising encounter can take place. The price and the challenge that one must face is overcoming fear, which is related to guilt and the fear of revenge. The result is the potential for sharing an encounter and expanding one's memory to include the implicit possibility that the shared past entailed not only war, but also love. The young dreamer fears being associated with his father's violence, but this association eventually leads to friendliness and respect. Violence may well be a denial of our inter-being with the other, and always a double edge sword, but it may also be a precondition for such recognition, as the destruction dynamic with the other and his survival lead us to realize the limits of our projections on the other. Once more, this new opportunity is made possible by the journey of the younger generation into old/new territories.

Conclusion

In the analysis of the four sessions presented in this paper we ask how the social dreaming matrix may offer its participants a space for transformative discourse in the context of the split society in Israel. Through our analysis of the four matrices, we discover that the material and the themes that may be found in the sessions share two main aspects. First, we find a tension between difference and identity. Throughout the four matrices we see the traces of categorical differences that are difficult to bridge, such as political right and left, Jews and Arabs. Interestingly, most references to such differences seem designed to validate the assumption that they exist. In contrast, some differences hold a potential for connection, such as that between men and women or between generations (parents and children). These differences hold the potential for a fruitful connection seeing as, while participants outlined such differences, they were also looking for connections through them.

The matrices elaborate these differences as keys to very profound apocalyptic solutions. When violence and destruction are overwhelming, as in the chaos that ruled before the creation of man and woman, a recreation is sought, to give new purpose. The romantic coupling of man and woman to bring a new life is a poetic solution to the complexity of life and its devastating pains. But as we see, this symbol of hope is based on denial – we hope that the next generation will change the world, but the task is greater than any generation can achieve on its own. The older and the younger generations do not cooperate, but rather rest their hope or blame on each other. Perhaps because the intractable Israeli-Palestinian conflict, lasting six generations now, undermines hope for the change time will bring.

Second, we found that the emotional effect of the matrix was a significant factor for the participants – the abundance of material and emotional connotations emerging in each matrix gave it an emotional charge, allowing for a deeper connection to more compressed and intricate emotional meaning. Just as dreams may be but means for our repressed emotional reactions to be experienced safely, under the guard of the mechanism of censorship that confuses and codes meanings in rich imagery, so we can view the social dreaming matrix as a safe place to experience anxiety and not knowing, and perhaps own these.

It seems these two aspects – the differences and the emotional impact – mark the challenge and the potential offered by the social dreaming matrix. In a traumatized society such as in Israel, pain takes a central place – so much so, that it subsumes the whole identity, and denies and suffocates the ability for complex dialogue. In the violent political discourse found in Israel, social identities are based on exclusion and negation of the other. This discourse adopts a pseudo rational pretense, which is in fact a means of denying other ways of thinking.

On the one hand, right-wing politics serve a paranoid rationale, which gets ever more irritated, and cuts off complexity itself, poking holes in the fine lines of new thoughts before they may emerge. And on the other hand, we see the righteousness of the liberal left, which assumes universal, humanistic values, and goes against the separatist, hierarchic values of "us or them" of the Israeli right-wing politics. Still this sort of righteousness is self-affirming, lacks compassion and does not allow dialogue, as it removes itself from the main argument and means of validation of the right-wing discourse – the raw pain. The left's agenda is thus reduced to mere patience in the face of violence. Thus, these two camps are intransigent and entrenched, agreeing only on a technical, neutral militant viewpoint in which the Palestinians are a threat to be neutralized or a problem to be solved, rather than a counterpart to be recognized, who may even define us.

The method of social dreaming allows for movement to occur between states of consciousness, thus creating a unique container that allows the participants to come in contact with deep levels of the raw human pain and fear, and recognise the mutual suffering, as well as the deep existential wish for peace and security. In the sake of this very wish, the right-wing politics in Israel is willing to cut away all otherness, and the left-wing politics is willing to retreat from reality. Sharing these ideas, and allowing them to move about in the room, between the discourses of waking and dreaming, enables transformation to occur. Such is the transformative use of the dove which symbolizes peace in Israeli current culture. In these moments concepts emerge, only to be reversed in meaning. The matrix struggles to hold the linear continuum of logical constructions, but the dreaming discourse creates a reverse perspective that undermines the existing order, and the signifiers lose their validity and become exposed as partial and unstable.

We hold that social dreaming is an act of hope, a method that aspires to create a moment in which opposites are held together; a moment in which each person may see his side and the other person's side as connected, the unimaginable integration as possible, and the divides of fear and hostility as less than crucial. In these moments of incoherence lay the power and inspiration of the social dreaming matrix.

References

Arieti, S. (1961). "The Loss of Reality." *Psychoanalytic Review*, 48C (3): 3–24.

Freud, S. (1919). "The Uncanny." *S.E.*, XVII (1917–1919): *An Infantile Neurosis and Other Works*, 217–256.

Gitay, Y. (2010). *The Israeli Discourse: Rational Versus Emotional Argumentation*. Haifa, Israel: Pardes Publication.

Long, S. and Harney, M. (2013). "The Associative Unconscious" in S. Long (ed) *Socio-analytic Methods*. Chapter 2. London: Karnac.

Manley, J. (2019). "Associative Thinking: A Deleuzian Perspective on Social Dreaming" chapter 2 this volume.

Ogden, T.H. (2010). "On Three Forms of Thinking: Magical Thinking, Dream Thinking, and Transformative Thinking." *Psychoanalytic Quarterly*, 79: 317–334.

Volkan, V.D. (2009). "Large-group Identity: 'Us and Them' Polarizations in the International Arena." *Psychoanalysis, Culture & Society*, 14(1): 4–15.

10

LONDON DREAMING

Nuala Flynn and Ruth E. Jones

Introduction

In 2012, spurred by a new social dreaming host looking for a community of practitioners, a group of six including Gordon Lawrence met to explore the possibility of setting up a monthly social dreaming matrix (SDM) in London. There was a mutual desire to connect, to create a community for social dreaming in London and to hold a space to see what dreams were saying about social concerns in the city and beyond. The London "Social Dreaming Hub" (London Hub) was born and hosted at the Working Men's College in Camden until Gordon's death in 2013. A new phase opened in 2014 and a new home was established at a community centre near St Pancras, where a monthly SDM has been held ever since.

This chapter will be a review of the evolution of the London Hub and the dreams, themes and new perspectives that have emerged. It will reflect the hopes and the context of the London Hub, the impact of Gordon Lawrence's death and the purpose, meaning and future of the incumbent "London Dreaming".

Initially, a mixture of ideas and intentions, including the potential for research and events to promote and grow social dreaming theory and practice, echoed the aims of the emerging Gordon Lawrence Foundation (GLF). From 2005, a series of social dreaming training workshops created a pool of "trained" hosts looking for opportunities to practice the hosting role. And specifically, there was a desire to establish a supportive community for social dreaming practitioners. With hindsight, it could be said that the matrix formed itself in this conducive environment.

This chapter follows the organic process of sustaining an open access social dreaming matrix by a core of determined social dreamers. Dreams will be reported as spoken, in italics with a minimum of interpretation so that the dreams can continue to resonate and evoke fresh multi-dimensional associations, and retain the potential for new meaning to emerge with each reading.

Working Men's College – the first location for the London Hub

The London Hub was well supported by a range of participants who had learned social dreaming methods either by association with Gordon, or through the training work- shops or who had learned through the experience of participating. There were different personalities bringing a range of background and emphasis, so inevitably there were differences of style in the way the matrix and the ensuing dream reflection dialogue were held. In the London Hub a supportive practice emerged of pairing new or less experienced hosts with more experienced ones. Their shared reflections before and after each matrix provided a creative space for further learning, synthesis and reflection.

The challenges ahead were portended by a dreamed response to the first London Hub Matrix:

> *I had a dream last night after the meeting that I was playing on a square guitar which was on my lap and horizontal. It felt very difficult to play.*

Occupy – seeking new social forms and structures

As the monthly social dreaming matrix was coming into being, work was also underway to establish the GLF. In the summer of 2012, in the overlap of these two initiatives, a small group working with Gordon organised a social dreaming study and practice day to explore social dreaming related to the "Occupy Movement" (for an account of the social dreaming which took place there, see www.tavin stitute.org/projects/social-dreaming-at-tent-city/). This event was well attended and provided a vehicle for newcomers to join the London social dreaming impetus. The following dream was shared:

> *A car is driving up a winding mountain road, the older occupants enjoying the ride and the view. Another car comes up behind but can't get past as the road is too narrow with too many bends and there is a steep drop to one side. The middle-aged occupants of this car are fru- strated, stressed and tailgate the first car, driving dangerously close, tempers fraying. More cars come up behind, and their young occupants see there is no way to speed up the pace or get past, so they either turn around and take a different route or else purposely fly off the edge.*

The dream proved to be prophetic. Matrices took place regularly with a commit- ment to consolidating and continuing Gordon's social dreaming legacy until summer 2013 when the GLF was established and Gordon's health was failing. Participation began to be less sustained and several meetings were cancelled at short notice. By late 2013, the Hub as an emergent community of practitioners had begun to dwindle. Some new professional social dreaming projects started and the formation of the GLF did not actively include the co-evolution of the Hub. A distinction began to make itself felt between two different emphases: the matrix as an autonomous process which had been midwifed into the current social dreaming form by Gordon Lawr- ence, and the social dreaming matrix as ward of the Gordon Lawrence Foundation.

In the first matrix after Gordon Lawrence's death, the themes of loss and legacy and the colours of mourning from different cultures were present in the dreams and associations. The question of inheritance and succession, and the interplay of colour and gender appeared repeatedly.

> *A dream tells of going to Gordon's study to find everything has been removed except some African masks. Dreamers find they are black and enjoy it. A father turns out to be a black man and a book is discovered entitled "Nature's Informer" which brings about feelings of elation.*

Other dreams remind us of the fragility and vulnerability of the body, held within the skin which can easily be cut or damaged, whatever its gender and colour. Things can appear dead when they are not, the "thread" can easily be lost or missed, and the African ritual masks, together with the knowledge left from Gordon's research in the book called "Nature's Informer", can raise the spirits. Gordon referred to dreams returning us to our primordial origins, drawing from Jung, who said "Dreams are pure nature: they show us the unvarnished natural truth, and therefore fitted, as nothing else is, to give us back an attitude that accords with our basic human nature" (Jung, 1964). (The meaning of nature arises from *natura* – birth, and *inform* means to give shape to, or to communicate news.) The matrix is letting us know of its primary spirit, which brings forth new life through dreams.

Matrices continued to be cancelled during this period of grieving and realignment whenever attendance looked likely to be low, which meant that some new dreamers found their efforts to get involved were repeatedly thwarted. Frustration grew in a smaller core of hosts who were keen to continue with the monthly London SDM. Without the reliable involvement of established participants, questions arose about the value of the open London Hub in and of itself: Can the matrix sustain itself without a father figure "sponsor" and without an institutional container? What is its purpose when the matrix is not informing a conference or other predetermined organisational context? Where and what is the "substance" of the matrix? Is it viable or worthwhile with smaller numbers of regular participants?

A cultural vision and a working model for the Hub was inspired by a meeting of those wanting to continue. The following hypotheses were formulated: that social dreaming is one way in which we can facilitate renewal in society (this is an expression of a sense of purpose, not a definition); that the London Hub complements the GLF research activities with ongoing social dreaming practice; and that participants in the Hub must take responsibility for its continuity and not look to others to carry it forward.

There were sufficient new participants and sufficient interest in an open process of social dreaming to see a small number of hosts take up the reins and set about finding a venue to reliably accommodate a monthly London Hub matrix. At this stage, it could be said that the matrix itself exerted a primary urge to exist which possessed some of the hosts with the enthusiasm to continue. A sense of dreams looking for an open place to be dreamt as collective social dreams, free of institutional strictures, was emerging as a distinctive vision.

Nomadic – looking for accommodation

Initially a matrix was held in a garden room at a psychotherapy organisation, where bees and their hives were recurrent images. Initially the preoccupation was with bees as endangered creatures, exploited and abused – queen bees being parcelled up and sent round the world through the mail. But these concerns gave way to a marvelling at the complexity of the social structure of a hive, the role of worker bees as creative functionaries in the bee-community, and then the sense of the matrix as a hive, in which participants, like worker bees gather the nectar of dreams and transform it into the honey of new thoughts. The matrix ended with lines from a Rilke poem "We are the bees of the invisible. We wildly collect the honey of the visible, to store it in the great golden hive of the invisible ..." (Rilke, 1963).

Over the summer a more suitable space was found, offering skyscapes over the city. Shockingly, just days before the September matrix, the whole building was suddenly closed down and an emergency alternative offered instead. This turned out to involve a descent into a windowless bunker along labyrinthine corridors several floors below ground, which reverberated with every passing tube train. (On seeing the concrete walls, we wondered whether the dreams would get through!)

> *I feel sunshine and a warm breeze on my skin, and feel happy and blissful. Slowly I realise that I am standing on tip toe on top of the Shard. I have a basket on my arm. Balancing becomes more precarious and air feels cooler as the sun starts to set and the wind picks up. A winged figure approaches, wanting to put something in the basket – I realise this is impossible as I am increasingly precariously balanced and anything more would make me fall. The only way is down – I don't have wings.*

Themes in the dreams and associations at this time involved rhizomes and mycelium; the emphasis is on the worker bees who do not reproduce but live to serve the hive; women as benign and malevolent figures; fossilised footprints of a family on a beach which get covered by the tide; runaway trains and people wearing vibrant colours full of life. Young artists who attended spoke of dancing a wake all night for the victims of current appalling events, as though dreams were not sufficient to cope with the seemingly daily reports of planes falling out of the sky, mass exodus across borders, and bombings and explosions in the Middle East.

Subsequently, a dance school provided an accessible venue for the London Hub that autumn. But, with between six and ten people coming, this was too expensive to be more than a temporary home.

During this period of looking for a place to settle, which coincided with the gathering refugee crisis, there was a determination to sustain the supportive practice of co-hosting, and also to ensure that the London Hub remain as democratic and accessible a process as possible in the face of pressure for someone to assume a leadership role. There was a commitment to keeping more complete notes of the dream material for sharing, and a forward schedule of named hosts offered some stability. An open mailing list quickly released flurries of emails, welcomed by some who felt this kept them in touch with the Hub and angering others who did not want their in-boxes clogged up with unsolicited traffic. The hosts began to experience a tangible strain from holding an open process where the *raison d'être* was for the matrix to create the opportunity for dreams and their associations to communicate. The pressure to lapse into a support or social group was never far away and newcomers had to be aided to appreciate that the primary tasks of social dreaming are not personal.

Home

From the beginning of 2015, the London Hub moved to the pleasant basement meeting room in a not-for-profit community project near St Pancras station. By asking participants to make a small voluntary contribution, a flexible donation is given to the organisation each time for the use of the room. Thus, the Hub requires no accounting or administration other than holding an e-mail list for sending reminder notices. This has made the London Hub sustainable, accessible and community based, so that participation can be truly open and democratic.

This modest and sustainable setting made it possible to see that the richness and depth in a matrix does not equate to the number of participants. The matrix was reliably bringing forth dream images which informed on many levels. There was also a parallel process between the search for a steady location for the dislocated London Hub and the burgeoning migrant crisis. Dreams and associations referred to the Large Hadron Collider – a cavernous building where particle physics is exploring invisible dimensions; to parallel universes right next to each other and their further dimensions; to the experience of "not knowing" and to the dreaming mind. There is something scary and exciting about the dimension of dreaming which confronts us with the limits of our understanding: there are doors of the mind we can't (yet) open, and multiple, seemingly contradictory meanings co-exist.

> *With a teacher and friends, I was walking outdoors by a waterfall and along a stream. We were making our way down into a building; an echoing cavernous building, with enough rooms for us, but not enough bedrooms. I recognise this place from previous dreams. There's a dusty secret annex that was forbidden before, now it's an abandoned annex that we can make our own.*

Increasingly present was the question of how to read what the matrix reveals about that which has not yet happened. Like Charlotte Beradt collecting dreams under the Third Reich (Beradt, 1985), what are we to do if the matrix is foretelling as well as reflecting what is already known? Can the matrix dreams only really make sense in retrospect? What difference does it make to history and culture to witness these social dream images and make links to them? What if witnessing and discovering new ideas and bearing the feelings in social dreaming is a form of activism? Can we gain new insight and perspective? What would become available to inform us if the dominant noise and voices of our culture quieted and we paid greater attention to dreaming?

One morning in London there is a sea of daisies everywhere, like an infection? I am walking through endless daisies. There is such a sense of silence, no cars, serene, transformative but I also felt lost.

Someone dreamed of the answer to everything, which was 'forgiveness' and woke up to find she had had a stroke and couldn't speak.

Reflections pondered whether forgiveness would silence us at a stroke? What if silence spoke? What would we lose? Does the matrix ask or only inform, and from where?

Democracy – leadership – ownership

In 2015, having achieved a self-sustaining model with rotating pairs of hosts and a viable venue, some of the hosts again questioned the usefulness of the matrix if it was not to inform a specific setting, still concerned that there were not more regular participants. For others it sometimes felt like a struggle to protect the matrix from being closed down before it had fully made its identity felt. What was it *for?* remained an open question. Was *being* an open question what it was for?

At a party, there were two venues: inside with a lovely couple, kind and friendly and comfortable, or outside with the vibrant, less comfortable, rebellious ones, more risky and dangerous, rolling joints maybe? I couldn't decide where to be.

I am driving a large vehicle, heavy to manoeuvre; takes driving skill, it's challenging to keep going – hard work but I am in control and will make it.

I woke up feeling pregnant, although there is no morning sickness or movement and yet I know I am pregnant.

Both new life and death seemed possible for the matrix, with hosts feeling burdened by the anxiety that there were not enough participants. This led to a period of experimentation with setting themes as though this could save the Hub. Two participants established a separate venture, *The Queer Social Dreaming Matrix*. In case the London matrix was going to languish, could it be seeding new offshoots to assure its continuing existence?

Themed matrices

As the humanitarian crisis of people caught in or fleeing from conflicts intensified, a group of politically engaged therapists were wanting a space and a deeper way of thinking about the problem. A new idea to use the matrix to help contain participants' feeling of powerlessness in response to this crisis was taken up. This raised concerns for some that having themes would distort or exploit the ongoing matrix process. Others felt that themes could facilitate a form of Asclepian dream incubation with the matrix as sphinx or oracle. The invitation to two linked matrices on the theme "Dreams of Home – Refugee Crisis" was an experiment which increased attendance to over twenty. These were followed by a third themed matrix "Terror on the Doorstep" just a few weeks after the Bataclan attacks in Paris.

The immediacy of the primal need for home in the first matrix was striking:

> *I'm in a house I want to buy but can't afford it. I have to leave and have shat my pants. There is a hole in the fence where the cats come in, the gap has got bigger. A golden retriever comes in, I like it but its taking too much, I don't want it there. Do I stop the gap?*

Homer's Odyssey came up, giving a mythic European perspective on leaving and returning home and all the ordeals involved on the journey. The matrix is a mosaic of dream fragments which together form a bigger picture of collective trauma which requires painstaking effort and determination if it is to be witnessed as a whole and not split off parts. Ancient treasures are buried and forgotten, children steal and deface passports. The empty sacred womb-space of the feminine (Hagia Sophia) stands in contrast to a dream which puns on the name of the town Motherwell, a place that is not well but devastated and desecrated.

> *It is night, there's a path, and a woman in a cloak, who came from the left? She takes me to the Dome and points to the floor, there are mosaics of the most horrific gruesome scenes of torture. Holding my hand she says 'This is what you might have to face, and you might not survive it.'*
>
> *I am showing children the empty space inside the Hagia Sophia – it is a safe space.*

In the second "Dreams of Home" Matrix, the dreams have a different tenor from the first: the level of fear and horror is less, there are surprising turns, concealments and revelations.

> *Two black men are sleeping in a car outside a childhood home, one asks for my suitcase, the other is subtly protective.*

Associations are made to Kindertransport and someone new to social dreaming asks if the matrix is a safe place to unpack a suitcase of dreams.

> *There's a very old house full of mystery and presence and rich heritage. The dreamer is shown things in the house, a painting. A lonely boy has a red boil on his arm, the old house is lost and burnt down. On a journey to find home, two lights are hanging where the house once was. There's the same sense of mystery and presence, the boy sat down having found home. I woke sobbing.*
>
> *I am in my own space. A complete stranger appears. Who are you and what are you doing here? We are taking each other in – where do we go from here?*

This second themed matrix seemed to register resistance to opening up to the fears and losses. Then a sense of mourning and the need to face change began to come in, with a wider range of feelings, and repeating the allusions to Odysseus' mythic journey of transformation and homecoming. There was palpable anger about the loss and destruction of the ancient places and an emerging perplexity and complexity, where strangers can be threatening and helpful and resource laden.

The matrix informs us of its nature

There's a ship on the ocean, trawler sized. The sea is rough and one side is open. There is no captain – the vessel is going somewhere by itself.

After the themed matrices in the autumn of 2015, the new year saw the format spontaneously revert to the open matrix, now with one host rather than two, and with between four to nine of the active participants coming each time. Several participants from the themed matrices joined the mailing list but few returned. A trickle of new dreamers were being directed to the Hub by the GLF, while some longer standing participants decided to leave. In the face of this fluid and migratory attendance, the hosts met to discuss perspectives and concerns. Feelings of disengagement and ongoing disappointment at the perceived lack of participants were shared, as well as a counter-balancing feeling of hope and of a slow process evolving. Each of the rotating hosts reported feeling a particular sense of burden and responsibility before each Matrix, like labouring uphill. They all had also experienced surprising feelings of renewal and meaningfulness after the SDM, having been moved by the rich, unexpected communications between the participants and between the dreams. Discovering that this was a shared experience generated sufficient curiosity for another three months block to be scheduled, with a review meeting at the end.

I am walking up hill, it's snowy and icy, and then I come across Aude, who is delighted to see me. I looked after her when she was a child – she is now a young woman with her old school friends. I feel overwhelmed with love. Aude is holding an olive coloured letter, apparently it is from friends in the Gulf States, people I don't know.

When the remaining hosts met in the summer to again decide whether to continue, they all arrived feeling burdened and resigned to letting the London Hub close. However, the atmosphere and energy of the meeting shifted radically at the suggestion that the matrix was actually in a context after all and that it was responding to the question "What is London Dreaming?" Although voiced previously, only now could this pivotal open question be thought and heard, as if a state of individuation had been achieved, with the matrix asserting its own trajectory.

It could be said that the phrase "London Dreaming" returned the focus to the primary spirit or implicit intelligence of the matrix, bringing a sense of relief and satisfying the wish for clarity of purpose. One explanation was that it was like being re-tuned to the radical listening in the liminal aesthetic register that social dreaming offers. In this way serving the matrix becomes a radical act of hospitality! The matrix is an uncolonised place for making contact with wild animating dreams, where renewal happens. Something had been getting in the way of simply listening to London's dreams as "Nature's Informer", without having to do anything other than be moved by them. The hosts became aware that their anxiety and feelings of responsibility or disappointment could push them into prematurely foreclosing their willingness to simply attend to the matrix and its emergent processes.

The realisation that the London Hub had evolved into a different entity brought a collective shift and released enthusiasm for another term of rotating hosting. From this point, the small matrices, small in terms of number of participants, have felt much bigger, somehow autonomously alive, and rich, steady, and good.

The new chapter

At this juncture, dreams started to speak of safe places which were no longer safe, and of underworlds opening up where tasks are night time tasks, not rational day time ones. Persephone is snatched away into the earth and there are monsters inside our homes, even when we try to carry on as usual. In the latter part of 2016, after the Brexit referendum, the theme of facing new kinds of reality was asserting itself. The matrix informed us of the impoverishing effect of established or institutional powers. The dreams challenged our assumptions, and stretched our comprehension towards new dimensions, where the world splits apart, where sink holes open underneath us, and where we are faced with thinking and feeling more deeply and creatively.

> I saw another world in a gap below this world. It was a night journey with four tall athletic young men, like gods. We walked through a small city. It was war torn and getting more and more impoverished. We came to a huge concrete building/ monument, and we knew there was the source of evil and we had to diffuse it.

The dreams began to articulate a strange new quality of our human relationship with animals – the creatures seem frightening, ferocious, wild but then it becomes clear that they are actually curious and observing, watching what we humans are doing. There are terrifying snakes which are distressed to be in receipt of human projections – the animals are continually being misunderstood, and not being seen in their true nature.

> A friend's cat Fred is unhappy – people are not relating to it by its inner cat name – the dreamer commiserates with the cat – people usually are not interested.
>
> It's an Alpine scene, lush grass, lots of families, with picnics. My own extended family is there. From the woods comes a loping figure, a beast on four legs so I stand – I am so scared, I want to run but he will destroy my family so I stand my ground. The hyena comes and I see his face and nose. He is 6 feet tall on hind legs. I feel a mix of deep fear and love towards the animal, there is a sense of pride and strength. The hyena turns and returns to the forest.

Auden calls dreams the "fauna of the night" (Auden, 1992) and these seemed to address our cultural ambivalence towards dreams – the "animals of the night" – and to animals as "other", with both dreams and animals as threats to the safety of attachment figures. In today's zeitgeist, there is much to be disturbed about and so the matrix communications can be hard to bear, hard to be born. An association to "The Second Coming" (Yeats, 1990) asked "And what rough beast, its hour come round at last, Slouches towards Bethlehem to be born."

Conclusion

While the initial impetus for the London Hub was to network, nurture and share practice as social dreaming *practitioners*, it has become clear that social dreaming *itself* is the preferred medium for support, insight and communication. People who mainly do not know each other find themselves nourished by engaging at emotional depth with the finite and the infinite, the personal and the cosmic in the SDM. Perhaps initially serving as a container for emergent thinking in relation to the GLF and later for facing Gordon's debility and eventual death, the London Hub Matrix has increasingly asserted a different legacy. A spirit of its own has made itself known as a practice form rather than an instrument, which is too difficult to play when used for pre-determined or psychological purposes, as presaged by the first recorded dream. This shift from *activity* to *adherence* parallels the contemporary paradigm shift, as twentieth century institutional and national structures give way to the twenty-first century fluidity of globalized networks and migrations. Today people face the challenge of redefining their purpose and identity, facing into the fear of loss evoked by leaving home and established assumptions, and making new beginnings.

It is pleasing to note that the monthly social dreaming matrix that began in 2012 is ongoing in 2018. The process has seen cycles of languishing and renewal, with ever present uncertainty and always close to the edge! The Hub has evolved a space of radical hospitality offering hosting for London's dreams in response to the open question "What is London Dreaming?" It has required hosts to continue while bearing uncertainty about what this is and what it is for, and to be prepared to play with that. The original spark, incorporating Gordon's ailing body and inspiring spirit, enthused a community of social dreamers new and old. With his loss we separated, like bees swarming and searching for a new hive.

In the beehive, each bee can only exist as part of the whole hive, and the majority are short lived worker bees. Similarly, with dreams and their associations in the matrix "hive", each dream is a fractal of the whole. Dreamers come together to serve the ongoing impetus of the dreaming colony, and to gain sustenance from the dream nectar. A shift of paradigm in the matrix has been effected, and the dreamers have become attendants, waiting on the matrix, committed to a practice of listening and seeking to understand what is conveyed.

A new phenomenon has been making itself felt since the summer of 2016. There have been dreamers with dreams to share which somehow cannot find their way into the matrix, remaining unspoken. This phenomenon has come to awareness in the dream reflection dialogues. Over the same period, the matrix is vibrating with a palpable sense of urgency, with more esoteric content, and non-material dimensions of experience. This is an interesting development, recalling the "shard dream" and its warning against, or the necessity of being thrown off balance by accepting Hermes' offerings.

This chapter could not have been written without the records of the themes and dreams in the monthly matrices. With them, it has been possible to make sense of the new thinking that has become clear over the lifespan of this matrix. A truly social purpose is achieved by steadily serving the matrix, over time, in a space where the dreams can be welcomed for what they are. As the core group of hosts has again suffered a loss, the future is as edgy as ever, with the ongoing open question of survival, and whether it is necessary to reach a wider audience, by using social media platforms or contemporary themes. It is unclear whether this concern is fuelled by the seductive trope that "bigger is better" which colludes with late capitalism's imperative of perpetual growth. However, the generosity of the matrix, birthing London's dreams, will always be available when people are willing to be of service as hosts and dreamers, and offer radical hospitality to the matrix material.

For now, "What is London Dreaming?" abides in a spirit of alert openness, listening for the matrix to inform the next steps.

Postscript

In an era of shifting paradigm, the world is emerging as a more profoundly and mysteriously interconnected place than scientific knowledge has hitherto allowed for. As an afterword, we wonder whether David Bohm's understanding that there is a hidden reality to quantum theory, "the Implicate Order", is returning from exile (Ananthaswamy, 2017) bringing to light his view that non-locality means every entangled particle influences every other particle in the universe. This refugee science emboldens our hypothesis that social dreaming really is a form of historical and cultural activism, intervening on social and metaphysical levels, by returning us to a primordial practice and a forgotten science of dreams.

References

Ananthaswamy, A. (2017). "Speaking in Ripples" in *New Scientist*, April, pp. 28–32.

Auden, W.H. (1992). *In Memory of Sigmund Freud: Collected Poems*, E. Mendelson (ed.) New York: Vintage, pp. 273–276.

Beradt, C. (1985). *The Third Reich of Dreams: The Nightmares of a Nation*. Wellingborough: Aquarian Press.

Jung, C.G. (1964). *Collected Works Volume 10*, H. Read, M. Fordham and G. Adler (eds) London: Routledge and Keegan Paul, para. 317.

Rilke, R.M. (1963). "A letter by Rainer Maria Rilke", *Duino Elegies*. New York: WW Norton, pp. 128–129.

Yeats, W.B. (1990). *The Second Coming: Collected Poems of WB Yeats*. New York: Picador in association with Macmillan, p. 210.

11

SOCIAL SPACES FOR SOCIAL DREAMING

Mannie Sher

Introduction

In human society "all space is social: it involves assigning more or less appropriated places to social relations. Social space has thus always been a social product" (Brenner & Elden, 2009 p. 353). "Social space spans the dichotomy between 'public' and 'private' space … it also links subjective or phenomenological space" (Smethurst, 2000 p. 44).

"Social space contributes a relational rather than an abstract dimension; it receives a large variety of attributes, interpretations, and metaphors" (Kellerman, 2002 p. 50). Such "social space is an intricate space of obligations, duties, entitlements, prohibitions, debts, affections, insults, allies, contracts, enemies, infatuations, compromises, mutual love, legitimate expectations, and collective ideals" (Churchland, 2007 p. 123).

"In premodern societies, space and place largely coincided, since the spatial dimensions of social life are, for most of the population, dominated by presence, by localized activity. Modernity increasingly tears space away from place by fostering relations between 'absent others' locationally distant from face-to-face interaction" (Giddens, 1990 p. 18). Kellerman (2002) argues that the contemporary world is characterised by fluid identities, constantly exposed to a power struggle between local cultures and information, on the one hand, and global, virtually and economically transmitted ones, on the other. Viewing the local and the global, the real and the virtual, from the standpoint of people, rather than from the perspective of material or virtual geographic entities, influences the functioning of human beings as a result of the knowledge and information that reaches them and which is interpreted for use in daily life. Kellerman's global technological approach ignores the power of the phantasy, emotion, passion and dream to connect people beyond cognitive knowledge and information levels that make connections with "absent others" across generations, millennia and history – past, present and future. Whereas in the premodern society "everything has its assigned place in social space" (Durkheim, 1971 p. 442), postmodernists like Ermarth (1992) proclaim the need to discard the modernist discourse of historicism and representation in order to help us appreciate postmodernism, the relevant demonstration of which, for our purposes, is the multi-layered interpretation of individual dreams in a group and social context. Barthes (1977 p.142) insists that "we need to substitute for the magisterial space of the past, which is fundamentally a religious space, a less upright, less Euclidean space where no one, neither teacher nor students, would ever be *in his final place*." Similarly, spaces for social dreaming are temporary and no single dream provides a definite statement, an answer to questions; it is the democratic sharing of a multitude of dreams that offers multiple insights into social phenomena. Social dreaming can be considered as the ultimate form of the democratic ideal.

Lincoln, J.S. (1935) writing about the dream in primitive cultures, describes the custom in a Polynesian tribe of the family members telling their dreams at breakfast each day. The father, usually, mediates the dreams by telling the dreamer what the meaning of the dream is and what should be done to mitigate its negative effects. So, a son tells the family of a friend who in the dream is nasty to him and the son is frightened. The father explains that the hostility of the friend is really displaced hostility from his son onto the friend and that to prevent the relationship going bad, the son should take the friend a gift. The son does as his father bids, the friend is surprised, but pleased and relationships are restored.

Clare & Zarbafi (2009) suggest that the interior world of the novel, the capacity for play, the imagination, the dream, the unconscious and a sense of collective solidarity are disappearing from our contemporary world. In a society in which individuality and autonomy have been reduced in importance by organisational bureaucracy and mass production, it is not surprising that there is little space for the dream.

A clinical space

Dreaming and attending to dreams forms an important part of a psychotherapist's professional life. Working in a "clinical" space serves as a container that enables patients to speak of their dreams in order to better understand their hidden meanings and thereby provide the patient with relief from tensions created by their psychological disorders, depression, irrational anxieties, obsessions, phobias or fixations and their aspirations to be free of them and lead better lives. Dreams, and their analyses help patients face the contradictions, inconsistencies and paradoxes, and sometimes lies; the conflict between desire and conformity and to the enigmas of existence and the fear of annihilation. Following patients' associations as they connect with new thoughts, leads to deeper insights and understanding of their emotions and behaviour, and in many instances, to creative resolutions of their life's struggles.

In my practice I would often ponder about the relationship between association and interpretation. In the early years of my psychotherapy practice, I would think that an obvious pattern of behaviour presented by the patient required me to demonstrate my clinical competence by offering a "clever" interpretation. I noticed that I was interpreting more than was necessary. Over-interpreting implied that I had more knowledge of the patient than they had of themselves; that it was likely to lead to an imbalance in power relationships by encouraging the patient to please me by producing more and more interesting dreams and associations, rather than working on the issues contained in the single dream and facing the slow toil of uncovering each layer of meaning. I learned that by gentle questioning and waiting for associations, patients learned the art of free association and eventually reached their own conclusions. Through free association patients could accept and play with thoughts and ideas that had previously been the sources of guilt and shame. Premature interpretation would play into feelings of shame and produce defensive reactions by the patient, and set the treatment back.

Dreams are a source of "change" in emotional maturity and in life's decisions. Without always knowing what patients want to change, their dreams may be seen as requests cloaked in symbolism for change, a new order of thinking; a flexible enhanced view of a subjective experience that previously was a fixed habitual entity in the patient's mind, like a hard object.

Gordon Lawrence introduced me to social dreaming in the 1990s and I became interested in working with dreams in broader social spaces outside the consulting room. Lawrence (1998, 1991, 2003, 2007, 2011) provided a theoretical and practical framework for working with dreams in a social context. The usefulness of social dreaming became apparent; it provided opportunities for groups of people to share dreams and discover relevant unconscious social meaning from them. I was impressed by the behaviour of the matrix in its exploration of dreams, focusing on the dream, not the dreamer; becoming the property of the matrix and being played with imaginatively and used as a springboard for creating new thoughts about the social environment that the matrix was in.

Bounded and unbounded social spaces

The first social dreaming matrices I attended were events that formed a part of conferences and meetings. They were formally convened, in bounded spaces in rooms with doors with people who had assembled in that place as part of the conference. They had conscious aspirations and hopes in common and the social dreaming matrices gathered the unconscious meanings of their collective concerns. Later, I had opportunities to run social dreaming matrices in less-well organised social spaces, in public domains that allowed anyone to join (and to leave) as they wished. What would such gatherings tell us about the social milieu? Would we discover new social purposes? Would they lead to social change? What would be their impact and value? My colleagues and I took the view that social dreaming matrices are nodal points for accessing and expressing the layers of unconscious social meaning, made conscious, in ways similar to art, literature and music that could offer a window into social fantasy worlds of fear and hope, love and despair, relationship and aloneness, cooperation and competition.

It is in social spaces, bounded or unbounded, that people interact intimately in small groups or impersonally going about their business, walking, looking, breathing, anticipating, thinking, talking, reading, navigating, day-dreaming. What are the differences in content and analysis of dreams in bounded and unbounded social spaces? Helen Morgan (2007) quotes Lawrence (1998, pp. 31–33):

> To take the same thought processes as are used in psychoanalysis into a social dreaming matrix is not valid because, it is my hypothesis, a different version or even type of dream is evoked. More particularly, if the container system for receiving the dream is changed, the dream-contained will change .... What I think the social dreaming matrix questions is the ideology that dreams belong to a person and are to be interpreted as such. This is not to devalue that kind of work – so important for myself in my own psychoanalysis. All I am saying is that the matrix produces different kinds of dreams through dreamers. The context is different, that is all.

It is the different contexts and the particular dreams they produce that I wish to emphasise. Moving in several directions at once, I postulate that from social dreaming we can learn much about the social context. It is a kind of double loop phenomenon in which context, dreamers and dreams moving fluidly into and across one another and by doing so are sources of valuable social knowledge. What follows is a description of social dreaming in different social contexts and the layers of understanding that emerged from them.

Group relations conferences

The following is a dream offered to a staff meeting of a group relations conference – an accepted space for dream presentation and association:

> There are people in a room and one of them wants me to explain group relations to him. I start explaining, but a huge, long train comes trundling by and I say to him that I will continue once the train has passed. The train is made of large aluminium carriages containing a liquid gas like ammonia. The carriages are handsome, with pipes and turrets, gleaming. The train finishes passing and I tell the man and a few others that we have to move on and swim along a canal parallel to the railway line to get somewhere.
>
> We get into the water which is warm and we get carried along by the current – not unpleasant. We come to the end of the canal and getting out is difficult. There is a narrow passageway with left and right turns and we have to get around these. I am trying to ease the passageway of the people with me.
>
> We all enter a room and the final plenary of a Group Relations conference is about to start. The staff chairs are arranged in a slightly curved line, as is usual, but it is not at all clear where the director's chair is and consequently, where my seat is, as I am the

associate director. There are bags on some seats and there is general consternation among the staff. The members are themselves getting seated. Eventually, I sort out the director's seat (which is the only one with side arms, so it is pretty obvious which seat is meant for the director). I turn to the director whose name is either Larry or Lorrie – I couldn't work it out – and I tell him that we have to announce the staff fees and I show him the list of differential fees for the director (€70 + expenses), staff (less) and administrators (less). The director is smiling fatuously and he says he does not understand what I am saying and he cannot read the figures out in the plenary. Thinking on my feet – I am standing, still not having found my seat – I say in that case, we would have to have a separate meeting outside of the plenary to discuss the fees. By now, the director is becoming increasingly incoherent, two other members of staff are hectoring me to get things moving, to announce the fees and get on with the plenary. I turn to the director again and talk with him, but I can see that he is not taking anything in. I start talking to the membership to continue the plenary and I see that the director is not there. I ask a staff member where the director is, and he says 'he has gone to a place where he wants to be'. I realise I would have to conduct the closing plenary, so I stand up and announce that I am taking authority to conduct the closing plenary only, meaning that when I find out what is going on, I would return the authority to the rightful person. Everyone agrees with me, but it seems superfluous because the final plenary marks the end of the conference.

This is a detailed dream and its social context is a group relations conference in which profound learning happens about roles taken or given in groups, about leadership and organisation and many other aspects of human social interactional behaviour. Associations to the dream offered by the staff group point to the high level of anxiety experienced by the staff of group relations conferences about their competence to consult in a specialised method of education and learning for senior people, (the gleaming handsome carriages of the train). The ammonia gas represents the volatile potentially explosive nature of emotions of fear and anger and understanding and managing these which is a core function of the consultant's role. But the significant part of the dream lies in the second part with the apparent disintegration of the Director's mind and the desperate, but hopeless attempts of the Associate Director to hold things together. These dynamics, say the staff group, are present in our staff leadership as it is in leadership everywhere – that to lead people lays one open to their insane-making projections of dependency and unyielding expectation of heroic salvation coupled with the group's hatred of its dependency.

The following dream comes from a staff group of the Leicester group relations conference:

I am in a holiday house. My apartment is in a building on stilts on the 1st floor. My wife is present with a close female friend. As I am leaving, my wife goes through the pockets of my jacket and I fear she will discover a packet of cigarettes. I retrieve my coat before she gets to the 2nd pocket. My wife and her friend go down a ladder to the ground; the friend slides down the ladder on her bum and says all the steps have plastic on. I follow her down. At the bottom, I discover I have no clothes on. A friend of my wife, Bret Marie and her husband offer me a towel. I go back into the house, the lights are fused; I see a hole in middle of the floor, and I am afraid of falling through it. I go back down the ladder again. Shortly after getting down, the whole apartment block collapses like the World Trade Centre. All my suitcases tumble out. I am desperate to find my briefcase, and I discover I have someone else's. I worry about losing my diary. My wife's friend says to her, 'oh, you've lost your wedding ring'. I am more worried about my diary than about my wife's wedding ring.

Travelling, at an airport, the suitcases that tumble onto the conveyor belt are associated to the collapse of the parental couple; (and consultancy) for the maintenance of the stability of life. "Don't go naked into the council chamber" refers to the shrewdness of the Government's naked policy of carrot and stick – forcing people to comply. Brett Carr is known for his research on Winnicott and Masud Kahn and Carr's critical view of Kahn "going naked into the burial chamber". There is a hole in the middle of the floor in The Knoll (a house used by the conference) which is like the "black hole" that was described in the large study group (an event in the conference) like going down the shoot in the airplane after the bomb scare. Are Tavistock conferences going down the shoot? A diary is for keeping time and boundaries. We have our own difficulties in managing our time boundaries at the time of the pre-conference meetings.

The group notes the neglect of the dreamer's wife who needs to have him at home. A conference member had spoken of leaving their family behind. Many are torn between being wedded to the work; or wedded to the wife. Work-life (wife) balance is an issue and raises questions of cruelty in coming to the Leicester conference because of the cost to family – the wedding ring symbolising forgetting one's ties to one's wife.

Dreams at work – an industry client

A dream is spontaneously presented by a senior person in a business meeting:

*I am assessing a competitor's technology and conclude it will never provide the through-put we need to develop a product in sufficient economic volume. There is breaking news on the TV that the competitor company has met its goals of a high throughput volume worthy product. The news reports that customers had ordered dozens of the product. Everyone in my company is in shock. The CEO walks up to me, looks angry and upset and says 'and **you** always said it would never work!'.*

A second dream …

… no technology; no CEO. I am in a car driving on ice, suddenly I see a low hanging bridge and a strong wind picks up, pushing the car under the bridge, smashing its top, but I am alive and still driving. On the other side, suddenly the ice stops and we plunge into water …

The dream opens the way to understanding a complex organisational dynamic – the fear and the ambivalence of the younger generation of doing better than the revered older generation. This is a powerful unconscious dynamic present in second-level leaders in organisations that are led by charismatic people. The dream contains business content and it is offered spontaneously by an individual in a business meeting to illustrate how people in the company manage the tension between taking up their own authority and relating it to the different levels of authority in the company hierarchy. The meeting uses the dream as a springboard for new thoughts on how the group could act with greater freedom than it thought it had. Additionally, the dream provokes discussions about feelings that lie beneath the surface of the group's consciousness about the company's future growth (life) and retirement and succession of the current board members (death).

Social dreaming in the protest movement against social consequences of capitalism – Tent City

Inspired by the Tavistock Institute's Israeli colleagues who offered social dreaming matrices to the Rothschild Boulevard social protest movement in Tel Aviv in 2010 (Erlich-Ginor, 2013; Triest et al, 2015), the Tavistock Institute ran social dreaming matrices at the Finsbury Square camp of the London (St Paul's) social protest movement, called Tent City. Like the lives of the inhabitants and the living conditions in Tent City, the conditions at the venue of the social dreaming matrix are unpredictable in almost every aspect, except the mud, cold, damp and traffic noise. Furniture for sitting comprised cushions, sleeping bags, wooden pallets, and a plastic chair. Evenings are dark and light is provided by a candle or a mobile phone (Sher, 2013).

The participants of the matrix vary from day to day. There are a few "regulars", who provide continuity by taking upon themselves to explain to newcomers how the matrix is run, its purpose, etc. They seem to gain something from the regularity of the event, they present their dreams and associate freely once they get used to it. Some participants attend because they are intent on sharing their dreams; others come because they are curious about the activity going on, stay a while and leave.

Despite the instability of the process, matching in many ways, the social and personal dislocation of the people in Tent City, the matrix occurs every day, including weekends. For most people, talking about their dreams with others is a new and unusual experience. They express relief in sharing dreams, thoughts and feelings. They accept that the matrix is not intended to be a voice either for or against the aims of the social protest. They have mixed feelings about the matrix: "things won't change". Dreams are a mix of offerings of reflections of inner emotional lives, personal and family relationships and social phenomena against which the dreamers are protesting. The Occupy London social dreaming matrix challenges the facilitators because participants sometimes present dreams with profound personal trauma images; on other occasions, dreams relate to the social context of the matrix and the protest movement and links are made accordingly.

At the first social dreaming matrix (twenty people and eleven dreams), dreams fall into two categories that resonate with the social dreaming setting in Tent City – being on a journey and loss. Dreams about journeys are pleasant and exciting – being able to fly, theme parks with flashing lights and exciting rides and trains and buses. The direction and means of the journeys – literal journeys and the "journey of life" – involve history and stories and progress is made without concern.

The second cluster of dreams involves loss and these dreams are less pleasant, but are tempered by the dreams being about putting things right. There is loss of fishing equipment (the participants' search for ("fishing for") dreams?); loss of body parts (a tooth, skin peeling off a face); losing sustenance (rotting food at Tent City), loss of stability (the Japanese earthquake, tsunami and radiation); then finding mother at home, clearing and cleaning the kitchen and cooking a meal. A delivery of fresh vegetables to the kitchen is forgotten – pointing to over-looking the physical and human resources that are actually available for use and improvement. Snakes appear and although fearful, they also serve as symbols of learning (tree of knowledge) and cure (medicine), and snakes having positive meaning in many cultural mythologies.

Dream images evoke Garden of Eden scenarios where goodness is available for all, without struggle, relying on the acquisition of knowledge through magical thinking. Wild, crusty, but majestic animals, especially wolves, feature that are feared and admired. Dreams of joy and admiration are followed by dreams involving invasion and attack by burglars and abandonment of children by careless parents. The abandonment dream and dreams about politicians given to the dark arts of spin are associated to the social dimension of the brain as a recipient of information, a processing mechanism and a decision-maker that is located at the top of the organism, like governments are located at the "top" of countries. The distance from the "top" to the "bottom" is in direct relation to being thought about, heard and cared for, failures of which lead to social exclusion and threats to life. Dreams include images of dying gods, secret police and informers, suggesting the breakdown of benign authority and its replacement with tyrannical inhuman systems that rely on fear and perversion of language ("defence" means "attack" – references to "1984" and "Alice in Wonderland" – "Things mean what I say they mean").

The matrix reaches a point of acknowledging that the protesters, government and the financial systems they are protesting against, are different parts of the same social construction that both imposes its will and in which everyone shares in its shaping. This challenges the matrix to consider how the protest movement addresses questions about its role in society and making constructive use of the power it has. The dreams express fear of failing in this role – dreams of being chased or abducted, being wrapped up and given to aliens. A cluster of dreams has a theme of travel, exploration and danger – one is about cycling on a narrowing track, which eventually becomes only as wide as the bicycle wheel, the bicycle turning upside down and the dreamer falling downwards; a dreamer only just escaping an incoming tide. This is followed by a dream about vistas, climbing to the top of a mountain, bringing about the possibility of a change of perspective.

The matrix associates to a fragile Tent City and the "dead" capitalist buildings around it. They debate investments (capitalism) and vestments (religion; St Paul's). In what does one wrap oneself? The protest movement expresses something of the nakedness of humanity and about the concerns about society managing to cooperate to clothe and protect the next generation (there is a baby in the matrix). Alternatively, we are exposed and naked and adorn ourselves with Emperor's clothing.

The Wellcome Library: social dreaming in a public space

Six social dreaming matrices were held in the Reading Room, a public space, of the Wellcome Library to mark the launch of the Tavistock Institute archive at the Wellcome.

The social context of the first matrix was the UK's referendum on leaving the European Union (thirty-two people; twenty dreams). Dreams had transport associations – a London tube train where presents had been left on the seats but were actually bombs. Associations were made between ballot boxes as presents or bombs; a dream of travelling on a bus sitting between people at the front (posh men, establishment) and people at the back (tattooed, thuggish) and the people at the back turning out to be the ones who looked after her; people in a taxi on a journey to the social dreaming matrix travelling backwards.

There was a dream of a father who died in 2012 and the dreamer needing to physically care for him; wanting to talk to him about the referendum news and the earthquake-like changes.

There were a number of dreams containing rubbish and the need to clear it. "The Nazis were after me, but I still had to take the rubbish out." Rubbish has a social dimension; it is the responsibility of local government and if it is not cleared, we will die. In associating, the Nazis were heard as "nasties" and our social responsibility is to ensure the referendum does not let the nasties out. Life is dependent on maintenance; the rubbish being cleared out – dealing with nuclear waste; see what happens in Japan after the tsunami. An association is made to Thomas Crapper who invented the WC. Civilization happened when we became separated from our waste. The rubbish – the bullies in a dream are receptacles for our projected rubbish, but they turn out to be helpful – waste can be re-cycled. Dreams, sometimes dismissed as rubbish, help to process what is not processed in waking life.

There was a confluence of the tearful and joyful; the happy and the sad; in the context of the 52% – 48% European Union referendum result, 50:50 – half and half; good and bad would be preferable. The presents and the bomb; the opposing groups of the people on the bus, dreaming and not dreaming – the dreams seemed to represent wishes to restore the status quo ante and deny new realities – bombs being the new normal and the destruction of liberal integration as reflected in the different accents in the matrix.

In the review, people said they were glad they came. The matrix, they said, offered a sense of hope. A young person spoke about how she had come planning to tell her dreams but found herself unable to speak during the matrix and only able to say something after it closed. Dream presented questions on the purpose of the matrix – was it a psychological treatment? Participants spoke to how precious it had been to share their dreams with strangers.

The matrix was an "archival moment", freezing dream fragments in time and allowing thoughts and feelings about the EU referendum to be remembered – "perhaps tonight we will swap dreams with each other".

A social dreaming matrix that is part of a programme of study on Board Dynamics

A social dreaming matrix embedded in a programme of study for twelve people would naturally reflect anxieties, for participants and directors alike, about learning in a group – wanting to succeed, to be the best or favoured student and the fear of failing or being seen as failing to learn; and for the directors, anxiety about how non-traditional methods of teaching would be received; how participants would feel about being encouraged to seek their own way in a "destination unknown" learning methodology.

> *I'm in the cockpit of a large plane but I am not at the controls. The plane is going down, but it is not going to crash.*
> *I'm standing at a rose window with condensation on it that looks like a labyrinth. I am concerned about where to go and I feel uncertain.*
> *I'm in a huge field of strawberries. I start picking, but I cannot get anything done, because the field is so large. I have a machine and I work it in rows. The machine gets stuck, but I manage to repair it.*

The dreams suggest a regression to an earlier more dependent phase of life of provision for children by parents. The matrix issues symbolic calls in the dreams for the programme leaders to lead clearly, to provide more, and to ensure safety. The "strawberries" represent memories of good early experiences and the hope they will be repeated in the programme, followed by disappointment that the learning/strawberries are not easily gathered up. The dream has elements of hope of finding help; and uncertainty when the help itself falters, and is seen to be imperfect; learning to tolerate the frustration and finding alternative means to "repair". Associations to the dreams introduce ideas of the power of the matrix to help solve problems, a return to control and stability and preventing catastrophe, i.e. the shame that results from not knowing.

> *The programme directors are teaching us about social dreaming, and I am shocked that they do not tell us about the person who developed this methodology. It doesn't matter I tell myself, we will become stronger as a group. The directors are experienced, and they forgot to give all the instructions. They are human – who cares about who invented the methodology.*

The matrix becomes delinquent and views the directors as partners in crime; everyone is complicit in transcending authority, even those in authority collude, supporting a corrupt belief that the work of others who come before us can be ignored; that we can feed ourselves and avoid experiencing lack of knowledge and Bion's hatred of knowledge, minus K. "We can use what we've got. This is a tool. Do we need to think who designed it?"

There is a rock next to the seashore. I go through a beautiful beach house which belongs to a wealthy entrepreneur; his wife is with another business partner. I am surprised: it is beautiful to be in the house and see the seashore. There is no clear path to the house.

The dream intimates that learning is not what it is expected to be – teacher-taught roles are changing constantly. The dream disturbs the matrix at it realises that what is expected is not how things turn out. There is also a sense of comfort in the dream with possibilities of relationships in the group that could turn into instruments of learning – developing a new image of the directors that is less fearful; something good for the group. On the other hand, someone says, "we wait for those with knowledge to save us"; and "our directors are here to trip us up". Another association links the rose window to a cathedral, being an instrument of God – Bion's K "giving us insight into our group dysfunctionality, our collective censorship and not knowing each other's beliefs or values".

Debriefing the social dreaming matrix later, the participants talk about disappointment and the difficulty connecting to the group, but also feeling supported by it and the joy of discovering how dreams are connected to life events, how dreams belong to everyone and struggling with the tension between contributing and censoring.

Conclusion

This chapter has described the variety of social spaces in which social dreaming can take place and how different social spaces impact on the content of dreams and, in turn, how the content of dreams impacts on our understanding of the social unconscious. Social dreaming matrices happen as part of conferences, as part of daily work in organisations, as part of teaching programmes, in open public spaces and possibly in venues still untried. Dreaming can be thought of as being a representation of a social "truth" contained in the images that lies in the unconscious minds of the dreamers participating in a social space. Social dreaming allows for the fragments of dreams to be seen as a potential synthesis of confusing and frightening social phenomena, helping to brace for the cyclical arrival of new and unpredictable social realities.

Acknowledgment

The author is particularly grateful to Eliat Aram, David Armstrong, Leslie Brissett, Elena Carter, Camilla Child, Helen Morgan, Anuradha Prasad, Juliet Scott and many others with whom he has had the privilege of facilitating social dreaming matrices. He benefitted hugely from their wisdom, as they together wrestled to understand the dreams and associations made available to the social dreaming matrices. And of course, he gratefully salutes the many participants of social dreaming who willingly shared their dreams and associations that enabled him to learn.

References

Barthes, R. (1977). Writers, Intellectuals, Teachers. In: *Image, Music, Text*. Trans. Stephen Heath. Glasgow: Fontana/Collins. pp. 142–148.

Brenner, N. & Elden, S. (2009). Henri Lefebvre on State, Space, Territory. *International Political Sociology*, Vol. 3, No. 4, pp. 353–377.

Churchland, P. (2007). *The Engine of Reason, the Seat of the Soul*. Cambridge, MA: MIT Press.

Clare, J. & Zarbafi, A. (2009). *Social Dreaming in the 21st Century: The World we are Losing*. London: Karnac.

Durkheim, E. (1971). *The Elementary Forms of the Religious Life*. Mineola, NY: Dover Pubs.

Erlich-Ginor, M. (2013). "The Social Protest Movement as a Dream Matrix: Facts, Politics, Dreams." *Organisational & Social Dynamics*, Vol. 13, No. 2. The OPUS Eric Miller Memorial Lecture, 9th March 2013. pp. 160–177.

Ermarth, E.D. (1992). *Sequel to History: Postmodernism and the Crisis of Representational Time*. Princeton, NJ: Princeton University Press. p. 18.

Giddens, A. (1990). *The Consequences of Modernity*. Cambridge: Polity Press.

Kellerman, A. (2002). *The Internet on Earth: A Geography of Information*. New York: John Wiley.

Lawrence, W.G. (1991). Won From the Void and Formless Infinite: Experiences of Social Dreaming. *Free Associations*, Vol. 2. Part 2. (No. 22). pp. 259–293.

Lawrence, W.G. (ed.) (1998). *Social Dreaming @ Work*. London: Karnac.

Lawrence, W.G. (2007) (ed.). *Infinite Possibilities of Social Dreaming*. London: Karnac.

Lawrence, W.G. (2003). Social Dreaming as Sustained Thinking. *Human Relations*, Vol. 56, No. 5. pp. 609–624.

Lawrence, W.G. (2011). Intuiting Knowledge from the Social Unconscious with special reference to Social Dreaming. In: E. Hopper & H. Weinberg (eds.). *The Social Unconscious in Persons, Groups and Societies. Vol. 1. Mainly Theory*. London: Karnac. pp. 321–336.

Lincoln, J.S. (1935). *The Dream in Primitive Cultures*. pp. 3–4. Oxford, UK: Cresset Press.

Morgan, H. (2007). Shedding Light on Organisational Shadows. In: W.G. Lawrence (ed.). *Infinite Possibilities of Social Dreaming*. London: Karnac. pp. 106–112.

Sher, M. (2013). A Tale of One City: Social Dreaming and the Social Protest Movement. Occupy London at Tent City. *Socioanalysis*, Vol. 15. pp. 60–71.

Smethurst, P. (2000). *The Postmodern Chronotype: Reading Space and Time in Contemporary Fiction*. Atlanta: Rodopi. p. 44.

Triest, J., Levy, J., Mishael, I., Sharoni, Y. & Talmi, S. (2015). The Rothschild 117 Project: Dreaming in the Boulevard. In: E. Aram, R. Baxter & A. Nutkevitch (eds.). *Group Relations Work: Exploring the Impact and Relevance Within and Beyond its Network, Vol. 4*. London: Karnac. pp. 79–97.

12

PERIPATETIC SOCIAL DREAMING

St Paul's Cathedral, London UK
Oct 2011 – Jan 2012

Jacqueline Sirota

Introduction

This chapter traces a personal journey exploring and giving voice to the dreams and associations arising from the Occupy London protest tent-city in St. Paul's Square, London 2011/12 through the prism of social dreaming.

I shall describe the genesis of this endeavour which took place over five separate days. I will explain my thinking and the preparations I made prior to going solo, the name I gave to the process and how it all started. I shall then present the dreams and associations that I noted at the time while endeavouring to contextualise each day's work. Finally, I will sum up the enterprise.

Temperamentally, I have always identified with the themes of alienation and exclusion, whilst recognising how rebellion often conflicts with a desire to belong (Bion 1961). Years of psychotherapeutic practice cemented my interest in these issues. My involvement in social dreaming began in about 2003 with exposure to the work of Gordon Lawrence which in turn led me to Charlotte Beradt's seminal works, I was much moved by her endeavour and in the way the Occupy movement was being portrayed in the media. I instinctively felt a resonance with her inquiry and conjectured it might be possible to take the social dreaming matrix into spaces other than formal settings.

The Occupy movement London 2011

The Occupy movement is an international socio-political movement against social and economic inequality and lack of "real democracy" around the world. The movement's prime concerns are how large corporations and the global financial system control the world in a way that disproportionately benefits a minority, undermines democracy, and is unstable.

As part of the Occupy London a "camp" was proposed at the London Stock Exchange. As this was privately owned, Occupy's leaders chose the public space around St. Paul's Cathedral, London. The choice seemed symbolic. St. Paul represents the concept of dramatic conversion, from persecutor to follower, from hate to love. The original cathedral dedicated to him was destroyed by fire and rebuilt by an architect with the name of *Christ*opher. One of the protestors noted how the façade of the cathedral looked like a palace of power, like a fortress, against which the little "tent-city" was a striking contrast. The St. Paul's site remained a lively place from 15 October 2011 until 28 February 2012. There was a continuous flow of protesters, curious visitors, tourists and business people. Clergy, worshipers and police personnel who, while keeping an eye on things, frequently engaged in lively conversation with the occupiers of tent-city.

Seminars and meetings were held in the "University" tent. Other tents included a book stall, a free restaurant, a first aid tent and a meditation space. It rapidly became "a cool space", a place in which to "hang out" and discuss the state of the world. Throughout the protest, the weather was inclement and cold. This fact markedly constrained my activities.

On my first visit a group was gathered round a young man crouching on the pavement painting a tiny picture on dried, spat out chewing gum. It was a beautiful miniature of the Cathedral's façade. The boundaries of the gum carefully drawn to form a frame. I felt drawn into another "space". A place where ugly, unwanted waste spat from our careless mouths could be transformed, into something beautiful, through human endeavour.

Preparation

I attended a Tavistock Institute meeting in London where Mannie Sher (2013) presented his plan to offer social dreaming events to the Occupy London site in Finsbury Square. Unlike the St Paul's precinct, Finsbury Square was isolated and, as time went on and the weather became colder, fewer people engaged in what was on offer until it almost became impossible to recruit passers-by to enjoin the daily Social Dreaming Event (SDE). The Finsbury Square community dislocated itself, appearing to retreat into various degrees of apathy and despair where a sense of "community" seemed to be evaporating, but few participated in food preparation or area cleaning. It was sad to witness. I felt confirmed in my resolve to take social dreaming to the St Paul's space. Alongside my continuing involvement as a Dream Event Facilitator (DFE) with the Finsbury Square intervention, I attended their review meetings and posted my work on the Tavistock Institute blog set up to provide a forum for those who had engaged with social dreaming and shared their dreams and associations.

I sought advice from the architect of social dreaming methodology Gordon Lawrence (Lawrence 2005), as to the desirability and feasibility of working outside formal structure and practice in a room where the host creates a space or "matrix" utilising a specific arrangement of chairs – the snowflake pattern – in order to create a less threatening place than can be the case in the circle used in many groups. I wondered if stepping into participants' spaces would be a less threatening and possibly more fertile environment for dreams to be shared.

Drawing on the work of David Armstrong (2004), embracing the concept of an internalised portable "matrix" – the "*matrix in the mind*" I resolved to take this to Occupy holding hard to this cognitive structure when stepping into the spaces created by those involved in the protest on the streets. I termed this: Peripatetic Social Dreaming (PSD).

St. Paul's Square itself formed the matrix "in the mind". As the host I moved freely around this territory and, Mercury-like, holding and taking dreams and associations from place to place, like the spider weaving a "web of minds existing at any one time ... harnessed to focus on a particular topic" Lawrence (2003 p. 270). This collage or tapestry grew with time and mirrored the evolution of the move-ment in the actual physical space around St Paul's Cathedral. I presented my work at the ISPSO Annual Meeting in San Diego, USA in 2012. I have employed Peripatetic Social Dreaming (PSD) methodology in other settings since. My experiences empowering me to take social dreaming to the unstructured commu-nity and groups therein.

Method and outcomes

DREAMS collected over five days

Looking back over several months and as the "austerity" policies of the present government emerge it seems as if tent-city stood as a rehearsal for a society that will have to face increased poverty. The dreams describe a flight from the reality of this prospect. Several people said they hadn't had any dreams since joining tent-city and offered several explanations. Some felt they were already "in a dream", protected by a "psychic shield". Their sleep was continually disturbed by the bells of St. Paul's chiming every fifteen minutes, emergency service sirens and late-night drunks.

First day: 18th November 2011. (Five dreams)

The first dream came from an event "organiser" whilst waiting for the sound equipment to arrive to address the crowds in a "general assembly". His dream was: "I'm on a motorbike that is too powerful and I keep falling off". This is a powerful opening dream and seems to refer to many layers of meaning. Is it saying some-thing about the movement of Occupy that has its own momentum that feels too powerful and possibly difficult to control? It also could be understood as referring to the momentum of the banking system that throws off anyone who tries to understand let alone regulate.

A bearded man sitting on the steps of the cathedral who "has many dreams" presented a dream about a pyramid where "the top one percent was under attack by the next ten percent below. It was only when this ten percent realised they had to relinquish their hold on a desire for power could they undermine the top one percent and nourish the lower layers so that anything could be achieved". Perhaps this is the voice of the Sphinx warning of the dangers of embarking on this work alone, on a too powerful vehicle. Which seemed to be a clear reference to the Occupy movement in relation to the wealthy one percent and its physical presence in the City of London. Who are the next ten percent? Who has to give up the desire to displace and replace the one percent whilst also being prepared to attend to the lower parts of the pyramid? An association from another part of the site was to the dollar bill which has a pyramid with the Masonic "all seeing eye" on the back and a Latin reference to a "new order" linking with the aims of Occupy. The tip of the pyramid can also be seen as the conscious part of the dream, the ten percent less conscious and conflicted and the lower parts still deep in the yet to be understood unconscious realms. I carried this dream to other parts of the tent-city and other matrix-events because the pyramid is a central image of social dreaming and links with the Sphinx, the source of inquiry and mystery.

Other dreams were presented almost as part-objects rather than fully formed. They seemed to reference power and powerlessness *viz.* "a magic carpet", "teeth falling-out" and "a feeling of being lost but glimpsing 'something beautiful' so feeling compelled to go on". One man said he could "only dream about my dead father" – a reference to an order that is dead or dying?

I was cold by now and kindly offered some tea and respite in the "restaurant" tent. A young girl showed me a poem she had written in place of a dream – the poem expressed a moment of hesitation and uncertainty between the past and a future as yet unformed, a sunset over an empty plain and suggesting that we pay attention to the rhythm of life to find a way forward.

Second day: 20th November 2011. (Seven dreams)

Sunday morning. The Cathedral doors were closed until the service ended. The bells pealed out so noisily it was almost impossible to think, let alone talk. I enquired about dreams of two police officers who then walked swiftly away and a man in a "suit" who, whilst holding his iPhone between us, brusquely told me "I never dream".

Most of the seven dreams expressed "danger … vulnerability … something new or rediscovered". There were dreams of "being stuck at the top of a steep hillside with no way back up if you descend … walking on thin ice, falling in yet able to breathe under the water … a construction site that's also a quarry … a derelict ship where the singer Johnny Cash is providing music and is in charge". A young woman who'd come from Occupy Dublin offered a dream of "a baby boy and all my friends are appearing as little boys". Almost at the moment the Irishwoman had finished telling it a man came over to us and asked if she'd seen his little boy who was missing (and soon after found). This seemed to reflect something of a fragile boundary of the dreamlike quality of the place where so many said they were not dreaming because this was like a dream. The name "Cash" suggests references to the banks that are "calling the tune". The construction site is a place where things are built and a place of activity and the quarry where raw material has to be dug out but can also refer to the hunted and the possibility of eviction.

Third day: 29th November 2011. (Two dreams)

This day's intervention was a more fraught experience than the previous two. I seemed to be introjecting some of the splits and conflicts evident in the protestors camp. Was it, indeed, the "cold wind of the future" blowing through this little world?

A police officer I spoke with said he couldn't do his work if he remembered his dreams. A male protester spoke about a quote from Elizabeth Bowens book, "The Last September", "There's a chilly wind from the future". He was keen to talk about Arthur Koestler's book, "The Ghost in the Machine". Both seemed to be communications about the psyche of Occupy and the discomfort of being there, exacerbated by a bitterly cold wind. Throughout the camp people were huddled against it. I too soon felt chilled to the bone, distressed, hungry with a strong desire for warmth and food, however I was making connections and felt the urge to continue with my task

A vegan man said he had been shocked to dream of "frying a tiny little egg" having recently discovered that traces of egg can be found in a food used by vegans. "There is no avoiding signs of life", I thought. Was this referring to unwanted invasions on a micro level – that nothing is what you expect?

A man in black began shouting through a loud hailer making it difficult to hear. Drowning out others seems to be an aspect of this community. A man handing out leaflets for the Pentecostal Church began to lecture me on God. His associate spoke of dreams in which people (women?) were "much more friendly and nice than in waking life" before starting a rant about the Christians who were "all Jews" and then lectured me about the Tribes of Israel. It started to feel rather bizarre and only with difficulty did I get away. I finally escaped to one of the larger tents, the information tent.

Here a young man said he was very interested in the idea of social dreaming. He told me of all the events going on in the tent-city "University" and the space where they took place. This man said he was a bio-medical student and spoke about some research investigating "a system" in the brain that correlated with levels of empathy. He said that "the brains of higher status people don't pulsate in the way others might".

I'm not sure how my own brain was pulsating by now. Stepping onto the pavement outside the square was a vivid reminder that I was leaving the "matrix" and returning to the world where it would be inappropriate to approach passers-by to ask for dreams. I tried to run for a bus but had no power in my legs, as sometimes happens in dreams. The boundary between dreams and waking life seemed particularly permeable in this environment.

Fourth day: 27th December 2011. (5 dreams)

I walk around the site to take in the feel of the St Paul's environs. It is bitterly cold. The wind is knifing through and round the Cathedral precinct and there are very few people outside. Today I wear a badge by way of introduction and developing process. Pinning it on marked the boundary of the social dreaming role and looked more professional. It read: SOCIAL DREAMING. Share dreams and discover new meanings by telling them.

I visit the university and library tent where a meeting is about to start. The ground rules of signalling gestures in response to the speaker are being rehearsed. The meeting is about money; where to get it and how to spend it. It is a clear attempt to create a democratic process, a re-invention of a parliamentary system with its inevitable bureaucracy, leadership and organisational issues. I witnessed clear divisions appearing, whilst some protesters were huddling round the food tent, others were taking part in the meeting: some more "equal" than others.

In the library tent there is a table with a basket full of differing fabric fragments. An artist tells me she is suffering from ME. She is inviting people to choose something from this basket that evokes a memory or association and to write a brief comment on the labels she provides. She will then work on it for the next year to create a collage of all the fragments. A woman picks out a fragment that reminds her of the Welsh Eisteddfod she went to as a girl. A Persian man selects a piece of cloth that reminds him of the window blind at his lodgings when he was living in Sweden. I see a piece of embroidered table cloth and immediately remember a little private school I went to aged eight where we had embroidery classes during which stories, usually the classics, were read to us as we worked in the warmth, calm and containment of the little class. We compare social dreaming with the nature of her project. Time in tent-city "University" takes on a dream like quality. A woman wanders in with a Persian cat in her bag and on the train into London I sit opposite a woman with a little dog peering at me through its travelling box which resonated with earlier dreams presented at the Finsbury Square intervention of Mannie Sher.

I approach two Occupy women talking, across a boundary fence, to a man and a boy who are curious to learn about Occupy London. One of the women tells me that she dreams of tent-city only when she is away from it but not while there. A man joins them and reports a number of dreams, one he had three months ago. "I dreamed about a friend's ex-girlfriend and mother. There is a baby that leans across and kisses me … it is a profound experience that is hard to describe though I can feel it still". Though the dream occurred three months ago it arrives, in the telling, in this cold and humble place, like a Nativity. The baby's kiss seems like a blessing. It inspires wonder and emotion.

He offered two more dreams: "I dreamed we would be able to stay at tent-city, for another 3 weeks and it has come to pass, we heard the ruling today". The man says he has many dreams because he meditates and dreams about future events e.g. "I am in Fukushima walking with my father along the destroyed coast (in life I don't get on with my father, it's a difficult relationship). We see the mountains covered in green, all is restored and clean". The association that although things get destroyed, nature has the power of renewal

One woman describes a dream in which "I am somehow in some bushes. I can see but I am a black nothing. Then a beautiful, radiant rainbow man appears and I look in wonder and awe. Some 'machines' appear from the sky and he communicates with them in a way I can't understand". In the US many people claim to have been abducted by aliens who leave a little "hook" inside them. Someone jokes about how we should get ourselves checked for "hooks" by getting on a supermarket check-out. Strange experiences leave their mark and we can become hooked on things without realising it.

Outside the "University" tent, I see a young man gazing at the cathedral as if in some rapture. I speak to him and he says he is looking with awe at the grandeur of the building and asks if the architecture is based on Roman design. He tells me he is Kurdish and is re-setting his tent. He wants people to know about the problems of the Kurds and cannot bear to call himself Turkish. The unfinished tent has a beautiful, glowingly red carpet on the floor. He is sad because it is now soiled and wet from being there yet its beauty still shines out. He thinks it is hand-made. He has a dream that was strange because it seemed to contain a premonition of a real event.

"I was with two friends. We wanted some things from a shop that was closed but the door had not yet been shuttered. One of the friends went in and we crossed the road to look as if we were not with him. Someone shot the friend but I later saw him in the lecture hall where I am studying. I could see the base of a bullet on his chest. He seemed all right". He later heard about a real-life shooting of a relative he did not know well and said, "it seemed as if my dream had foretold this event". Real guns kill real people. Dreams and association form bridges from the yet-to-be-known to life as it unfolds as we continue to create it. The concrete quality of the gun narrative seems to shut down a flow of dreaming. My fingers are now frozen. A different form of action is called for.

Fifth day: 10th January 2012. (Six dreams)

I am surprised to see tent-city is still there after about twelve weeks. I'd had a feeling that it might have been quietly cleared away, a dream that exists only when the dreamer is there. It looks quiet and orderly as I walk across the paved area in front of the cathedral. A group of small schoolchildren approach with their teacher. She encourages a little girl in a headscarf to ask her question, "what are you doing here?" The answer comes: "To make the world a better place". The teacher quickly herds the children away.

I pin my social dreaming badge on which affords me a bit of courage to make the first request. I approach a young man and woman who are sitting talking. I introduce myself and state my question. The man asks many questions about the Tavistock Institute, its charitable status and what my connection with it is – I point them to the social dreaming blog. They were suspicious and seemed to give credence to rumours of brainwashing and social engineering. I feel some unease and a sense of the shadows cast by everything.

By way of introduction I report the dream of the pyramid and the later association, to the pyramid on the back of a dollar bill. The man brings out a dollar bill on which he has drawn round the outline of the pyramid and added an inverted triangle making a six-pointed star which, he explains, is the number of the devil: 666. Other notes are written on the bill in biro but I can't see them clearly. He speaks about "mankind", and "those who have learned their 'lessons' will rise to the fourth dimension".

The young man's dream:

> *The earth is pregnant and will soon split to give birth to a new world. (Many will be left behind but they will not suffer, just stagnate until they are ready to rise to the next level) ... I'm in the New Jerusalem. Everyone is eating lunch and I am checking to see if they are all right ... in the prophesy, London is the New Jerusalem, The city plan and grid accords with it.*

A well-dressed man approaches and greets them. He has a dream to present: "I'm at a wedding party. There's lots of lovely food but most of it has been eaten. I take the last piece of cake and it's delicious". Here are thoughts of the consequences of avarice and greed. The woman says the love of money is evil. Pregnancy which will require a painful splitting of new life. A wedding feast (often called breakfast) where there is almost nothing left but the last crumb is "delicious" and in the "New Jerusalem" people are having lunch, being fed. All the good things have been consumed or moved to a future "New Jerusalem".

A young man stayed one night at Finsbury Square and knew about the Social Dreaming Events there. Around the corner a man is selling books outside the "University Tent". He spots my badge and wants to talk. There seems to be so many dreams flying around and people are so willing to share them. Few express any surprise at being asked for dreams. Contributions come from a range across a range of ages, class, and cultures. A young woman joins saying she has many dreams:

> *People from the past keep appearing and following me around. I'm in a place I don't recognise and in a different situation. I have to go to hospital and take the heart out of my ex-boyfriend.*
>
> *Every now and then I dream I am flying, not high up but a few feet off the ground (indicates this by raising his arm just above her head), it is a lovely feeling of freedom and it helps solve problems because I have a new perspective.*
>
> *I have been gathering people in an underground house, I think it's a place of prayer. It's only meant to be for a month or so but it becomes years. Then there comes a time when they can leave and I can let them out.*

These seem to link with the concepts of pregnancy, growth and development which come to fruition at "birth" in an appropriate way, violence of the earth splitting in the dream, when the time is right or ripe: catastrophe or progress? The "heart" of what is gone has to be removed. Can we stand "a little above things" and get another perspective or are we in the grip of a battle between good and evil?

Outcomes – personal and practical

I felt nervous about engaging in this new situation but the people I approached largely welcomed the question about their dreams. Indeed, many seemed to enjoy their telling. There were a few people who seemed to be rather paranoid and others with personal agendas who could be rather insistent and some were rather threatening.

For some I seemed to represent "authority" and in the Finsbury Square camp there were those who felt that social dreaming was exploiting their dreams[1]

The whole experience may have been more enjoyable for everyone had it taken place during better weather. The weather's inclemency and the constant noise from traffic, emergency services, passers-by in various levels of intoxication as well as the booming sound of the Cathedral's tolling bells every fifteen minutes made it a real ordeal for many and certainly diminished the quality of sleep for those in tent-city. In the end, it was the physical challenge that proved most difficult for me. Finding people wanting to talk about dreams was relatively straightforward.

I thoroughly enjoyed the whole experience; except for the cold. It was invigorating to be able to take the "matrix in the mind", into a non-formal space. I felt the intervention was true to the innovative and seminal inquiry of Charlotte Beradt. I hope my experience may encourage others to explore new ways of working with social dreaming. All that is required is the will to do it. Whilst it is rather daunting approaching individuals and asking about their dreams, it gets easier. My experience is that most rather like to be asked, are welcoming and generous of spirit. In large protest groups, it is as well to be aware of a minority with individual agendas who may be less welcoming.

Given the opportunity, I would unquestionably do it again. Next time in a similar situation I would invest in printed material and a clear badge in order to give to participants more information about Social Dreaming. I would also buy warmer waterproof clothes and a larger flask.

Conclusions

On reflection, the Occupy dreams revealed to me grow in the mind and begin to feel as if they were speaking on behalf of us all and other social protests becoming manifest. There is no telling what presenting dreams had on their providers as no follow-up was feasible. Change is the only constant in life. Occupy London came and went; but left a trace.

I found peripatetic social dreaming to be a positive and empowering change of practice, situationally informed yet true to Beradt's original spirit of enquiry and embracing of the precepts and structures of the "matrix in the mind". Social dreaming is possible outside formal structures and can act to better inform our understanding and development of the discipline by creating a greater diversity of participants from across the social spectrum. Less formal locations may make an even safer space for participants as they will communicate from a space of their choosing rather than the more formal ones used in current practice.

Future directions/ possibilities

In Dublin 2016, a new opportunity for PSD presented itself at an ISPSO European Regional Meeting. I was engaged to host the morning Social Dreaming Matrix (SDM) on the two days of early morning starts. The keys to the venue had not arrived and a group of us stood in the morning chill as SDM time ticked away. Just as in St Paul's, I playfully asked for the first dream. Someone suggested we went for coffee at a nearby café where we decided to use the café space as the social dreaming venue infused as it was by warmth, taste and sound-tracked by the hissing sound of an espresso machine. Seated in the small space we held a SDM matrix with additional material provided by messages pasted on the sides of passing buses.

Footnote: What happened to the Occupy Protest in St. Paul's?

On 28th February 2012 Occupy London lost their fight to remain in St. Paul's. Bailiffs moved in just after midnight and removed the tents. Most residents had already moved their belongings. Some sat on the steps of the mighty cathedral watching the removal. Some erected a last "fortress" that had to be pulled down. There was much shouting but no physical violence. A spokesman declared that "this was just a beginning". My sense was that they had achieved recognition of their very real concerns through the challenge of their presence and conversations over the months of their occupation.

Note

1 Sher M. A Tale of One City: Social Dreaming and the Social Protest Movement – Occupy London at Tent City. *Socioanalysis* 15:2013 (60–71).

References

Armstrong, D. (2004) *Organisation in the Mind: Psychoanalysis, Group Relations and Organisational Consultancy*. London: Karnac.

Bion, W.R. (1961) *Experiences in Groups*. Lindon: Tavistock Publications.

Lawrence, W.G. (2003) *Experiences in Social Dreaming*. London: Karnac.

Lawrence, W.G. (2005) *Introduction to Social Dreaming. Transforming Thinking*. London: Karnac.

Sher, M. (2013). "A Tale of One City: Social Dreaming and the Social Protest Movement. Occupy London at Tent City". *Socioanalysis*, 15: 2013 (60–71).

13

DREAMS, SPACE, CONTEXT AND IDENTITY IN THE WORKPLACE

Franca Fubini

Prologue

The capacity to relate learning to the context wherein it takes place is an essential element of relatedness: this work focusses on the relationship with the context where human activities take place, whether geographical, historical, social or cultural.

Inspired by a clinical consultation where a *genius loci* / foundation myth catalyzed the identity of the group involved, I shall explore the connections between unconscious and space; architecture and dream; between container and contained.

Before delving into the clinical case, three interrelated areas will be mentioned, each essential to the unfolding of an organisational consultation:

1. Space looked for its quality of emptiness, in touch with the unknown where new thinking can emerge.
2. Space thought of as landscapes, mainly built ones, creating the environment, the background stage for the diverse phenomena of the life of an organisation (and of life in general).
3. Social dreaming, dreams and myths as the container – and the propeller – of culture and identity formation.

Is space empty?

We are surrounded by space but space is also the place of natural as well as man-made environments. The word "space" includes both the meaning of the element "space" (as in earth, fire, water, air and space) and space as context, the container often looked at as the *frame* or the bounded space that together with its contents, represents the prototype of fertility for creating something new: babies, products, results, thoughts, relationships. A container is also a mental space, capable of accommodating something to be contained, within a mutually transforming relationship. Here I shall look at the relationship container/contained as empty space holding all the potential for contents to appear.

When I was attempting to learn how to draw, my teacher suggested to focus on the space around an object rather than the object itself. It did not make any real sense at the time: I could simply not see it.

It has taken years to reach the capacity to see space and the realisation that the apparent emptiness is what allows the emerging matter to manifest; in fact that the two are deeply interconnected. Emptiness is the infinite potential for life to appear. Modern physicists, artists, spiritual masters, philosophers, psychoanalysts puzzle over the relationship between emptiness and the material world.

Physicists define the void as the quantum vacuum, a state out of which all matter and energy have been abstracted; yet the void is total absence and at the same time total fullness. David Peat, physicist and close collaborator of Bohm, affirms that:

> *The vacuum state is the void. It is pure silence, but it is also the bubbling sea in which elementary particles are constantly dancing in and out of existence … rather than reality consisting of molecules, and elementary particles connected to some insubstantial vacuum state, it is the vacuum state which becomes the primary reality.*
>
> *(Peat, 2000 pp. 91–93)*

To take it further, quantum mechanics hypotheses that what is regarded as objective matter is possibly just the fruit of mind, a very close vision to the statements of Buddhist philosophy that all phenomena lack inherent existence or own nature, they are merely the fruit of a complex and interdependent web of relationships (Varela, Thompson & Rosch, 2009).

Markus Aspelmeyer of the Austrian Academy of Sciences and Anton Zeilinger (Brooks, 2007) of the University of Vienna, invite us to consider that there might not be anything inherently real about what we call an object or a "measurable objective reality"; it appears that it is the act of measuring which brings matter into existence.

A statement in line with what both Schrödinger and Planck, two physicists at the centre of the discovery of quantum mechanics, support when they formulate the hypothesis that mind is what essentially creates the objective outside world (Varela, Thompson & Rosch, 2009).

Like modern physicists, many contemporary artists have looked for that void where visual and acoustic clues are missing, using it to portray the emptiness which disturbs the audience leading it to the point of doubting reality as it is normally defined.

Gordon Lawrence, when immersed in the process of developing social dreaming, wrote extensively on the concept of the infinite. From the boundaryless cosmos of the *Upanishads* to the more recent concepts of quantum mechanics where "life and matter cannot be differentiated".

"Won from the void and formless infinite" one of his first papers about social dreaming opens with a quote by Jung: "The dream is a little hidden door in the innermost and most secret recesses of the soul opening into that cosmic night which was psyche long before there was any ego" (Jung, 1953 p. 46 in Lawrence, 1998 p. 9). Lawrence postulates that dreaming is the bridge between that infinite space – empty and full of potentialities – and the world of matter we live in.

Lawrence had to contact the mental space of the unknown, free from pre-conceptions in order to find or discover a new way of thinking about dreaming, different from the penumbra of associations related to the already known dream-work of psychoanalysis. He postulated that no discovery can see the light of the day without passing through the disconcerting experience of a boundaryless space. Infinite and its relationship with creativity is central to the theory and the practice of social dreaming (Lawrence & Long, 2010). In *The Interpretation of Dreams*, Freud affirms that "There is at least one spot in every dream at which it is unplummable, a navel as it were that is the point of contact with the unknown" (Freud, 2010 p. 135).

Bion talks of the infinte, of the ultimate reality "O", which is unknowable, it is in becoming but it can never be known (Bion, 1984). He puzzles over what stands in between the possibility of being in touch with O. His theory of thinking is much concerned with the defences that limit knowledge. Time, space and causality may shift from representing useful tools for navigating the uncertain to the restrictive walls of a prison – an exoskeleton – inhabited by complacency and where the vitality that derives from contact with O, is squeezed out of existence.

I postulate that even if unmentioned, because often there is no awareness nor words to express it, every encounter – individual, group, organisation – brings the implicit request to touch on the infinite, the unknown, the empty space out of which something new can appear and unhinge mental processes which have gone stuck or stale; "to spend time on what has been discovered is to concentrate on an irrelevance. What matters is the unknown and on this (we) the psychoanalyst have to focus (our) his attention." (Bion 1984 p. 69).

Reading the landscape

It is often assumed in our forms of thinking that by definition – in itself a restrictive concept – there is an *inside* and an *outside,* that represent the implicit geometry of the mind which attempts to come to terms with the unknown.

This section looks at 'space' as an *outside* container, a holding environment, a context for living.

It manifests as territory, nature, buildings, architecture: mostly man-made landscapes and their interaction with nature and its inhabitants.

What gives a place, a country, a town, a landscape its distinctive feature and flavour?

What makes it what it is and how does it affect living beings? How do we, human beings affect the environment? Is it culture, climate, natural configuration, quality of light, architecture, history, or indeed human relationships?

I think all of the above; the questions are: how to develop one's capacity to read a landscape not with the mind only, but with one's body and senses which in fact are the main agents deeply responding to buildings, landscapes and urban shaping How to feel the character of each landscape, and their influence on one's being?

Some definitions of architecture: "Architecture is always dream and function, expression of an utopia and instrument of a convenience." (Barthes, 1967 p. 412)

"Architecture is an active participant in the interactions of people within it: to inhabit a place is to leave a footprint" (Benjamin, 1962 p. 154). People leave footprints on their environments; buildings leave footprints on the people who inhabit them. Louis Kahn, a great architecture master of the past century, affirms that:

> to create architecture implies great devotion to the well-being of mankind … Buildings have to be full of meaning … space, full of evoking capacity … buildings have the power to determine our behaviour and attitude. They must function psychologically…
> (Chinaglia & Cornoldi, 2007 p. 191; translation from Italian by the author)

Bachelard (1957) in his seminal book 'The Poetics of Space' enquires about the space where poetry is born, in the attempt to capture the subtle influences of space, from the vast horizons of nature to the intimacy of one's room and the small spaces which protect the intimacy of the soul; the sensorial perception of space, the light, the sound of the wind, darkness …; he looks at the interplay of natural elements as well as at all the elements of architecture: houses with their furniture, staircases, walls, windows, doors.

He invented a new word "topoanalysis" for the psychoanalysis of the built world and for the investigation of the minutest details of the habitat, interconnecting space and life. He advocates an architecture that should not be separated from the deepest necessities of mankind and life, including its need to dream, to develop, to create and to maintain one's distinctive identity, whether individual or of a territory or nation or region or town.

Space becomes a *site,* rather than just a place, (Heidegger, 1976) when architecture creates a living environment which offers elements of quality for the life of the people who inhabit it. In "Psychoanalysis and Architecture", Bollas (2000) explores the psycho-social-spiritual representation of human life through its built products. In the shape of a city/town/village we can find the interpretations that a collective has given to its experience of life; in the casual play of the old and of the new, we find the visionary statements of a society in becoming.

Cities are processes, mostly of the unconscious, living entities that provide a holding environment for its inhabitants, and which in their layout remind of the apparent chaos of the unconscious mind. The psychic elements of an individual mind, like those of a city, are interwoven, cross each other as they give shape to a form in movement that creates visions and organizing principles.

A very interesting concept, which Bollas actually borrows from Lynch, speaks of how a city needs to offer to its inhabitants readable and highly imaginable objects not only for the material care of their daily life, but as a form of caring for their psychic wellbeing.

Walking, or better meandering, in the streets of a city becomes an oneiric activity that might generate moments of profound reverie: dreams bear the footprint of an architectonic imagination; built structures enter the dreams, where the unconscious of the material kingdom encounters the unconscious of the individuals. Paths, edges, districts, landmarks and nodes (Lynch, 1996) are part of urban cognitive maps which release identity and recognition to its inhabitants.

Social dreaming supports culture and identity formation

Culture shares the etimological root of cult and cultivation, and represents the values and behaviours that contribute to the unique social and psychological environment of individuals, organisations, groups, nations etc. It is a foundation element of identity. "When dreaming we enter into a cultural experience ... in the deepest privacy of dreaming, the culture's ways are being developed, tested, explored and reinforced" (Lippmann, 1998 pp. 203–204).

Dreams are at the core of both our psychic life and of our cultural tradition. Psychoanalysis, anthropology, systemic studies contributed to the formulation of Lawrence's initial hypothesis about social dreaming and supported the intuition that it is a tool of cultural enquiry for illuminating the unconscious processes in systems and in society.

Social dreaming takes place in the matrix: the mental connections that lie below the surface of group life where the wide web of living relatedness and the associative unconscious (Long, 2013) can be accessed. The matrix is multifaceted: it reflects on issues regarding the many shared contexts to which the participants belong: institution, community, nation, humanity and the matrix itself. Each matrix in fact speaks also of its own process; it observes its own creation of identity and at this particular level, meaningful conversations can take place, interesting thoughts about existential questions can appear, sustained by the developing capacity for thinking and by the emotional connectedness of the dreamers.

The practice of applying social dreaming over a period of time shows that indeed the matrix both reveals the unconscious thinking of a collective and supports the development of meaning for its participants; in this way the matrix can be looked at as a structuring process at the base of identity and culture formation.

Dreams and myths are made up of the same basic psychic material, organised however according to different logic and function (Kaes, 2002). Myths have a fundamental role in the representation of a community and individuals can also have personal myths. They create a particular and distinctive mentality; they inhabit the most archaic part of the psyche. The importance of and the connection between dreams and myths has been explored by Freud, Jung, Abraham, Ranks; Kaes and Anzieu more recently, and many others. "The fact of transposing the psychoanalytical concept acquired through dream to the products of the popular imagination, such as myth and legend, would seem possible. The necessity of an interpretation of these creations has existed for some time" (Freud, 1913 pp. 414–416). The study of dreams and of their deep psychic connection to the symbolic language of myth, fairy tales, art and sense of humour is part of the legacy that psychoanalysis has offered for the understanding of the psyche. The myth renders the dream – as well as the fable, the legend and the poetic work – objective; the dream clarifies the myth.

I postulate that through the social dreaming matrix it is possible to access the foundation myth of a collective and by doing so, structural mental processes are revealed and transformed. The matrix in fact fosters the mental structuring of the collective: it reveals what is emerging, as well as it transforms the already existing mental structures. Dreamwork is mutative and foresees social changes.

A clinical case

This is the story of a consultation carried out in a large psychiatric department of the Italian NHS, after four different services merged into one department, geographically quite far from each other, but mostly distant because of the very different and distinctive cultures underlying each territory's identity. It is a story of displacement, conflicts, broken down communication and ultimately of poor service offered to the public because much of the available energy was devoted to survive the difficulties rather than to develop one's professional self-esteem by implementing better practices both for the patients and for the staff (Armstrong, 2005).

Merging departments, firms, corporations has become a common procedure, often undertaken on the ground of efficiency and hoped-for financial returns; unfortunately it is also a process which has enormous and underestimated costs for the psychic reality of an organisation: namely links, relationships, sense of worth and identity, dependency needs and recognition of roles. It affects the culture, i.e., the values and behaviours that contribute to the unique social and psychological environment of an organisation. So unique for each organisation and one of the hardest things to change. (De Gooijer, 2009).

Unskillfully managed mergers bring major disruption to the network of connective tissues of the organisation, not unsurprisingly as the map of the territories with relative boundaries gets broken down and shredded.

In the department examined here, there were sound motivations for a merger, but unfortunately it did also come with the characteristic traits of a disrupted and psychically unmanaged workplace.

The merger however is the background story: the focus of this case, is on space/territory and dreams as the containers of unconscious key elements which would support the development of identity and culture. Dreams brought the possibility to give names to perceptions, unspoken assumptions, body sensations and unconscious images which had had a major influence on the cultural identity of each service, but that, until unveiled, were remaining an "unthought known". (Bollas, 1987). Members of the staff were affected by the full immersion into a perceptive register, an undecoded world of images and sensations – often ascribed to the maternal order and powerfully dissociated from the paternal order which introduces language, names objects and offers definition. A work group which has no access to the paternal code, nor to a healthy integration of the two codes would find very difficult to recognise a line of authority and the role structure of an organisation.

Management could not recognise that each service was mourning the loss of what "was before" as well as presenting idiosyncratic difficulties which persisted in the current situation. Nobody would speak of displacement or of the fears that jobs could be lost. Those topics were swept under the carpet, and so at each corner of the carpet one territorial service stood looking suspiciously and attackingly at the other three.

Death of the previous organisational system was denied, because, as was said, "change had only been of an administrative kind", and so were depressive feelings of loss. They would surface in attacks to the management, in confusion and fragmentation, poor professional performance, persecutory anxiety and fear for one's personal survival. In the turmoil of change, management and administration had failed to see that substituting even "just an administrative structure" with another touches symbolically on the theme of death, life and the limits of one's existence.

The consultation dealt with what could be described as an archaeology of the unconscious, unearthing primordial images, well rooted in the different physical locations and which were underlying the identity of each team as well as binding the work team together.

The consultation

The director of the department was aware that the department was working poorly and asked for a staff group supervision. The first phase of the work took place with the whole group: it helped the members to get to know each other from an unseen angle, different from the one offered by regular team meetings. The methodology used a combination of social dreaming, group and clinical work. The task was to facilitate integration of the teams and to improve the work delivered to the patients.

A tentative feeling of trust developed as the group felt that there was a place where attention was focused on helping the teams to voice their concerns and to function better. However, after a time of regular meetings, the four groups were still sitting together as separate entities, each team was relating mostly to the members of one's own service and the impression was of a dissonant four voices choir.

The bottom rock of the disfunction had not been touched. Meaningless outbursts of destructive anger would still flare up far too frequently, threatening the delicate web of relationships. The hypothesis at the time was that the format of a whole group intervention could not tackle the roots of the problem.

The management was hesitant. It feared more fragmentation following the investment of a whole group consultation. But eventually the proposal of a limited number of sessions in each location was accepted with the aim to discover more of the identity of each group and what each group represented within the large system, as a starting point for the development of collaboration.

The purpose was to focus on group identity: to acknowledge, explore and reinforce identity so that each service could relate to the others from a point of strength and recognition.

A half a day supervision would take place at each service in rotation; the design of the intervention included: social dreaming matrix and dreams reflection dialogue, clinical case supervision and organisational role analysis (ORA) (Newton, Long & Sievers, 2006). The aim was to find the identity traits of each territorial service. At the end of the cycle of meetings, the groups would create an installation representing the identity of one's service for the others to see.

The first hypothesis for this piece of work was that each territorial service was bound by a foundation myth, an organizing principle/mentality, as part of its identity and it would be helpful to unearth such a myth and to name it. This was done, knowing, from the Freudian theory of the repressed unconscious, that to give a name to an object generates a large web of meanings interrelated with other objects and names which inhabit the psychic world of individuals and of groups. Dreams would help to name and to mobilise frozen, pathological and repetitive behaviour patterns.

Naming each of the four organising principles was thought as the first step towards the foundation of a hopefully collaborative department.

A second hypothesis was born out of an intuition, deeply felt in my personal experience, but without much evidence yet to support it. Social dreaming, bearer of culture and identity, is rooted in a variety of contexts: territory is one of them. Different spaces unearth different dreams: dreams related to an actual historical time and space, defining which stage for what performance.

Collective images, thoughts and beliefs revealed the foundation myths of each group culture and of its identity. Since that initial experience, I have often observed how the first social dreaming matrix in a new location would offer dreams with references to a relevant historical time and space.

The in situ consultation

During the first phase of the whole department supervision the meetings had taken place either in what was chosen as the largest room of the whole department (actually not big enough to contain the whole group, which in itself was evidence of a problem) or outside, in hired conference rooms, when it was financially viable to do so.

Service 1

It was with great trepidation and curiosity that I went for the first time to the furthest and most hostile of the four services, the one which was defined as the 'shadow management'.

It was set in a beautiful medieval town enclosed within thick stone walls and nested among hills. Leaving the car parked outside the walls, one had to go through an impressive town gate and find the building hosting the service only a few meters away. It used to be an old convent, the back door looking at a cloister and at its church. It had one meter thick stone walls; set on the ground floor, dark and behind barred windows. The entrance was up a narrow, paved street, through a small gate door which led to a domed and rather dark room, designated as the waiting room. The psychiatrist managing the service met me there, and there, supervision took place: at the border.

The work started with a social dreaming matrix. Some of the dreams spoke of the history and of the geography of the service:

- *a multitude of unknown hooded men wearing a brown robe like monks…*
- *I was in my hometown, in the Middle Ages…*
- *we go through underground tunnels and hidden passages…*
- *musketeers give me a sword so I could help the population…*

and of feeling under siege, at risk, at war:

- *men were hurting people, but it was not clear why…*
- *from a small slit I see people thrown off a rock into a huge ravine…*
- *there is war against us…*
- *I had dreamt the supervision and each one who is here now. All the others were at war against us.*

Clinical cases brought for supervision presented very disturbed patients, inhabiting pathologically enclosed and violent environments; like for example, a young man of twenty-three who had a history of repetitive rape and for the last seven years had not gone out of his family home, looked after by a mother who would dot the house, and her son's room, with pictures of herself dressed like a Madonna.

However, patients, in spite of the adverse circumstances, could improve thanks to helpful staff members and their caring dedication.

ORA reinforced what was emerging in the matrices and in the clinical work. Most of the staff in their different roles, spoke of "vocation", and in the choice of profession, of having followed a "call".

By exploring the material which emerged during the meetings the team came up with a possible unconscious image underlying their system at work.

The service is cohesive in order to face the difficulty of a hostile environment. It is committed to the care and to the salvation of its patients. The binding image is that of crusaders.

Their installation represented a medieval fortress, with gates, protection walls and only one open door with a guardian in the middle. There was something out of date: beyond individual professionality, the culture of the service seemed to look at mental illness, and its treatment, more like a Florence Nightingale's vision than a psychiatric diagnostic manual … No doubt that this culture, possibly exacerbated by the close contact and competition with the other services, was not conducive to openings nor to exchange. It supported the breeding of the culture of a shadow management within the larger system.

FIGURE 13.1 The crusaders

Service 2

The second service, a rehabilitation centre, was located within a geriatric home, set in the countryside, in the middle of nowhere, miles from the nearest town. How this geography could help psychiatric patients in their process of rehabilitation towards resuming an independent life, was one of the questions that puzzled the staff and contributed to the impression that nobody was really taking their work seriously. Staff and patients felt displaced.

The team members hosted the supervision in their best room, prepared for the occasion with flowers and snacks for the tea break. The whole group – a small one of four – was incredibly pleased that someone had bothered to come all the way to meet them in their work place.

There was a mixture of pride for what they were managing to do for the patients and shame for the shabby state of their location.

Dreams spoke of that displacement, of the uncertainty of their future:

- *Daniela – secretary of the geriatric home – announces that everybody has been made redundant: 'you should all go back home!'*
- *we walk through beautiful nature, waterfalls, water, but even if it is daytime the light is dark, dark! unreal! where are we?*

and of the dead end the patients found themselves in:

- *one of the young patients has attempted suicide;*
- *I was with the social workers and we both were holding the hands of a patient in a wheelchair. He was in the stream and we were on the banks. We walk, the stream gets deeper. Eventually the patient goes under water and drowns. We continue to walk along the river banks.*

Clinical case supervision offered hardly any hope: at first patients seemed to progress, then development would stop because there was nowhere for them to continue any realistic rehabilitation. The staff considered themselves capable and very devoted to their task – indeed they were, they were taking many worthwhile

FIGURE 13.2 The Raft

initiatives with their patients, but also rather despairing about the results because the patients were actually on the border of chronicity. The staff felt that both the physical structure and administration would not support their efforts: patients were actually blending too well with the geriatric culture of their environment.

The installation created by the staff was a raft at the mercy of the big blue sea, whilst the living beings on it – animals – were trying to find a safe haven to host them. The image, they felt, was a honest description of their state: drifting on a raft, at the mercy of the elements, pretending to be dangerous but owning only curbed weapons … looking for a safe haven and trying to build a house for ourselves. Is the value of our work recognised?

Later on in the following weeks, there were realistic conversations about the nature of chronicity and the fact that in a future mental health reorganisation, there might not be any room for a service like theirs.

Service 3

The third service had hosted the whole group supervision during the first phase of the work. By then, I could see that it was not because the group room was actually larger, but because the attitude of the people working there was more open and willing to accommodate "foreigners".

A small building with the back leaning against a nearly vertical slope full of unkempt shrubs, could be accessed by one of the main roads leading to yet another beautiful medieval town centre. Entrances and exits into the town would pass in front of the service. Its front windows looked at the most spectacular views of far distant mountains.

The first dream of the first matrix:

- *I was driving fast along a mountain road, I was happy, feeling well and healed, I did not know where I was going, but I had no fear.*

The undertone of the dreams was lively even when presenting catastrophic events "I see an airplane taking off and falling onto the church we were in: it was a catastrophe!" In the dreams there was movement: driving, being on a lift, going to visit patients at home. As though the dreams were picking the flowing nature of the service.

Indeed, the team was taking care of a large number of patients dislocated on a vast territory and was often on the move. The staff team offered good professional team work which helped the patients to progress when they could. At the same time the attitude towards chronic patients was not one of unrealistic hopes nor of self-abnegation. It looked like good, sound professional care.

The first patient presented in supervision was a borderline young man living in a small village, just about ten or fifteen houses along one road … so reminiscent of the location of the service, itself on a passageway. Staff were passionate, but not too identified with their work; learning was an important motivation, hopefully leading to further training and role development.

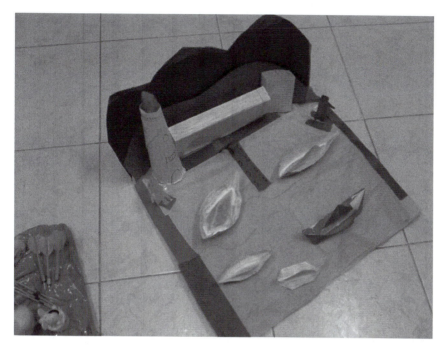

FIGURE 13.3 The sea port

The service had both a stable staff group as well as a transient one. Just during the time of the consultation four psychiatrists arrived and moved on, three nurses, one social worker. Staff learnt to cope with emergencies.

Their installation was named "a sea port". A service between stability and instability, in the middle of the other services, a "sea port" for people to pass through. A place of work, where we can stay put, but we can also go "beyond".

Service 4

The fourth service was at the outskirt of a small medieval town and hosted in one of the wings of the main hospital. The management of the whole service was located there; it had joined the whole group supervision, but kept away from this specific piece of work. The space evoked both the static quality of an institution, as well as that of a place where people were just passing by; it felt like there was nowhere to rest. The community room was small and overcrowded.

Dreams talked of toxicity (of being in the hospital, close to all sort of patients, close to the management...)

- *I was in a nice home with my own family. A new restaurant opens under my flat. The fumes are so toxic that we cannot breathe and have to call the police. The owner of the restaurant says 'I'll do what I like!'.*

The dream which was more evocative and in the end captured what the staff perceived as the essence of their service was set in their own hometown, in the old medieval centre.

- *From the town walls one could observe the teeming streets below, crowds of people moving to and fro. Some of them pushing wheel carts full of dirty clothes. 'I am worried, how will they know which garment belongs to whom?'*
- *Overcrowded and indifferentiated in an indifferent world.*

Patients were a condition to live with, they were perceived as though they had very slim chances of recovery. The case of a woman was brought for supervision: her age was unknown, as was the reason for being in care and what she actually needed. She could only be tolerated and treated as a dead weight.

- *lost in the meandering tunnels of the hospital intestines, ready to be evacuated when the time came…*

Was one of the dreams which captured the essence of the service's dilemma: evacuation or meaningful work?

The staff members did not explore much of their roles, but the feeling of weight they were carrying. The feeling of having to share the space with the patients, but not as something which could be transformed through their professional intervention. Yet most of them were extremely capable professionals. In that respect there was none of the pride the other teams had re: their roles with patients and how they looked at themselves in role. They felt weight and depression on their shoulders. They named themselves, and their service, the "tired washerwomen". Their installation portrays medieval walls overlooking into a huge basin with women washing dirty laundry.

As everyone knows, the business of keeping the clothes clean and washed is a never ending one; perhaps the tired washerwomen were picking up the gruelling, repetitive nature of mental illness.

By the time that this short cycle of meetings was completed, the consultation to the whole group resumed. It was amazing how fast the identity of each service became visible: how accessible the individuation of an organizing principle – a foundation myth – coalesced each service to its team.

Indeed the location – architecture, landscape, nature – revealed itself to be an essential component of the culture of each service and the dreams were the connecting bridge which held the process together. The vision of oneself in role and that of the patients to be treated seemed to be syntonic with each specific culture.

The four services met and shared the results of their work: each installation was presented with a few words of introduction, a quiet time of observation followed, then each team was asked to introduce a small change to the installation of the

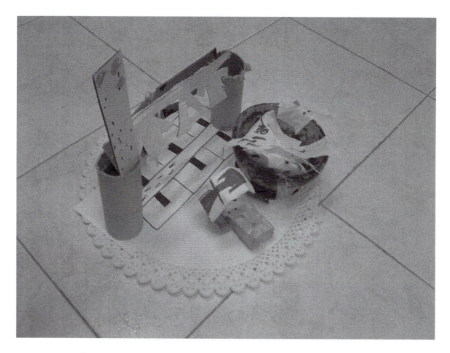

FIGURE 13.4 The tired washerwomen

other teams. I thought that it might be easier to initiate a dialogue through the objects, as it had been through the dreams in the matrix.

The first gesture was explosive: the medieval fortress (the shadow management) was torn apart; the whole of the front wall – not exactly a tiny change, in fact just the beginning of an unleashed wave of aggression to all the installations. When the results of those modifications were looked at, people were puzzled, wondering where the actual violence was coming from.

It was a starting point for communication. Through a newly found sense of identity and through the objects created it was possible to confront the difficulties that each service was facing. It was neither an easy nor a linear process: it was just a starting point. Each service had its geographical name and the name of choice: the crusaders, the raft, the tired washerwomen, the sea port. For the next phase of the work the objects of their creation were part of supervision, like the transitional objects of a newly revealed identity.

How could a seaport relate to crusaders? What did they have in common? Where would a floating raft go? Where would tired washerwomen drop their weight? And more questions related to the symbolic identity of their choice. Interaction brought changes, until the objects were resumed and a new shape given. The crusaders went underground; the washerwomen became lighter; the raft carried people; the sea port developed into a colourful larger port.

An installation was created showing the four services together.

FIGURE 13.5 Merging is chaos

Conclusions

Identities were more clearly defined. The dynamics between services were still very active, but less destructive, outspoken and under the eyes of every staff member; there was less need to voice them through conflicts amongst individuals.

Beyond individuals' professional skills, it was clear that the most functional model of work was represented by the "sea port" that was offering to the system as a whole, a culture of inclusion and movement which in time could be followed and integrated by the others.

About one year after the initial phase of the work on identity (and space), it became possible to shift the attention from territory to roles: crossing the borders of the four territories, teams could work and divide themselves according to roles (nurses, doctors, social workers etc.) in order to explore good practices, case work and role support.

FIGURE 13.6 The four services together

It looked at that point as though a model for working as a system had been found.

The supervision continued for two more years, which consolidated what was initiated by the work on identity: eventually there were both a department working as a whole, particularly when facing emergencies, and four territorial services composing the department, each one aware of what they were bringing to the system as a whole.

This piece of work highlights how searching for an absent clue, an "unknown" lead to explore the elements of the workplace identity. The connection of dreams and territory were essential for revealing deep psychic structures which lay the foundation of culture. Visions of the staff professional role as well as of patients' treatment appeared consistent and syntonic within their specific cultural identity. Transformations occurred once each of those elements found their voice.

References

Armstrong, D. (2005). *Organization in the Mind*. London: Karnac.

Bachelard, G. (1957). *La poetica dello spazio*. Deadalo: Bari.

Barthes, R. (1967). "Semiology and Urbanism", lecture given at the University of Naples.

Benjamin, W. (1962). *Angelus Novus*. Torino: Einaudi.

Bion, W. (1984). *Attention and Interpretation*. London: Karnac.

Bollas, C. (1987). *The Shadow of the Object*. London: Free association books.

Bollas, C. (2000). 'Psychoanalysis and Architecture' *International Forum of Psychoanalysis*, vol. 9.

Brooks, M. (2007). 'The Second Quantum Revolution' *The New Scientist*, n. 2609.

Chinaglia, A. & Cornoldi, A. (2007). *Architettura e Psicoanalisi Nathaniel Kahn e la ricerca del padre* in *La vitalità degli oggetti*, A. Molino, L. Baglioni, & J. Scalia (eds). Roma: Borla.

De Gooijer, J. (2009). *The Murder in Merger*. London: Karnac.

Freud, S. (1900/2010). *The Interpretation of Dreams*, J. Strachey (ed.). New York: Basic Books.

Freud, S. (1913). *The Claims of Psychoanalysis to Scientific Interest, Standard Edition of the Complete Psychological Work of Sigmund Freud*. London: Hogarth Press.

HeideggerM. (1927/1976). Essere e tempo parte prima; id., Costruire, abitare, pensare in *Saggi e Discorsi*. Milano: Mursia.

Kaes, R. (2002). *Dream or Myth? The Two Forms and the Two Fates of the Imaginary*www.funzionegamma.it/journal-in-english/catalog/, n.9.

Lawrence, W.G. (1998). *Social dreaming@ work*. London: Karnac.

Lawrence, W.G. & Long, S. (2010). "The Creative Frame of Mind" in *The Creativity of Social Dreaming*, W.G. Lawrence (ed.). London: Karnac.

Lippmann, P. (1998). *On the Private and Social Nature of Dreams*. Hillsdale, NJ: Analytic Press.

Long, S. (2013). *Socioanalytic Methods*. London: Karnac.

Lynch, K. (1996). *The Image of the City*. Cambridge: MIT Press.

Newton, J., Long, S. & Sievers, B. (eds) (2006). *Coaching in Depth: The Organizational Role Analysis Approach*. London: Karnac.

Peat, D. (2000). *Blackwinged Night*. Cambridge, MA: Perseus publishing.

Varela, F.Thompson, E. & Rosch, E. (2009). *The Embodied Mind. Cognitive Science and Human Experience in the Middle Way*. Cambridge: MIT Press.

14

WHAT NOW? FUTURE DREAMS

Julian Manley and Susan Long

Introduction

In the first chapter of his first book on social dreaming, Lawrence, taking his cue from a dream, made a virtue of being the "blind architect" of social dreaming. In the first pages of this chapter, he suggests that the true creativity that allows a person to discover what is already present but hidden, process of social dreaming, lies in being able to blind oneself to the preconceived facts and knowledge of the world as these have been assimilated by each of us (Lawrence 1998, pp. 10–12). We believe that it was indeed this ability to go "blindly" into the discovery of social dreaming that allowed Lawrence the necessary space to develop the process. Today, however, we feel the time has come to look back and reflect upon what the discovery of this process means in terms of its specific value to practitioners, thinkers and researchers who want to pursue social dreaming for their different ends according to their different needs and interests. We now feel that the time is right to lift the blindfold from our eyes and seek out further thoughts and developments for social dreaming.

In this book, therefore, we have attempted to begin the process of creating a philosophical scientific basis for social dreaming in order to refine and develop the theories of social dreaming that have been pieced together bit by bit over the last twenty-five years or so, largely through the efforts of its founder's series of publications on social dreaming, and to introduce new paradigms of philosophical framing to provide the basis for further thoughts. Our work has been to synthesise some of these original scattered thoughts into something that resembles an intellectual context that can provide a basis for the use of social dreaming in research and practice development. This process reflects the fact that ideas related to social dreaming have largely grown organically while the process of social dreaming was in development. We are now in a different phase of consolidation and reflection.

We have conceived of this book, therefore, as a bridge between those days of discovery and development of Lawrence's work and the future incorporation of social dreaming as a practical method of socioanalytic enquiry that is emerging from within the field of psycho-social studies. This edition has continued to offer a space for the recounting of praxis, but has at the same time tended towards philosophy and theory in preparation for future studies of social dreaming. In doing so, the editors and authors in this volume have explored the ways in which social dreaming is and can be used as a research method for understanding organisational and social dynamics. Important inroads have been made towards a philosophy of science for social dreaming (Long; Manley); social dreaming as research (Balogh; Agresta); theories of social dreaming related to artistic or visual perspectives (Morgan Jones; La Nave; Mersky; Fubini); social dreaming praxis, with an emphasis on community (Biran, Ezra, Netanely and Sabah-Teicher; Flynn and Jones; Sher; Sirota); and work that combines community and theory (Slade). This work is important for the growing practice of social dreaming, establishing it as a reputable and valid field of endeavour.

For those of us who work with social dreaming, it is incumbent on us as social scientists to find ways to further explore and test out the potential of social dreaming for research that leads to social understanding, community development, organisational progress, a more acute sense of democracy and a more sophisticated engagement with our human self and our relationships with others and our environments.

Where, then, can we go from here?

Informed by the work of our authors, we end this book by suggesting some of the ways in which social dreaming might be used for research, enquiry and social action. We will conclude the chapter with a substantial section on the potential of social dreaming in research, but before doing so we acknowledge and summarise our authors' developing thoughts around the application of social dreaming in contexts and environments where research is not the primary aim.

Dialogue, mediation and therapy

Our world is currently besieged by wars and violence fuelled by inequalities, discriminations, past traumas (Volkan 2001) misconceptions, fear of the other and prejudice. The processes involved include the escalation of hostilities, violent incidents, mass destructions, closure of hostilities, rebuilding, restoration and reconciliation. As well as engaging in fighting and protecting themselves during hostilities, communities have later to work hard at allowing mourning, rebuilding themselves and eventually reconciling their differences with others to allow normal relations to recommence. Social dreaming, in the way it circumvents the immediacy of horror, trauma, and anxiety, by sharing similarities rather than difference in dreams that can be shared and felt as belonging to all – the oft cited emphasis in social dreaming on the dream and not the dreamer – has sometimes been used as a therapy for violent troubles and mourning and consequently as an effective tool for mediation. There have been examples of this throughout the social dreaming literature of the past (see for example the social dreaming work that has emerged in Israel, where circumstances have produced an imperative need for a space for mediation and trust building, (Elrich-Ginor 2003; Biran 2007)). In these examples, dialogue has been opened out where it would otherwise have been difficult to express feelings and ideas, suggesting that social dreaming could be considered by mediators and therapists who work with groups as a helpful, supportive method for their work. In our current edition, the work of Sher, Sirota, Biran et al. and Flynn and Jones – all working in contexts where dialogue is felt as being necessary but difficult to find – supports the use of social dreaming in environments of struggle, pain, frustration and lack of trust. Examples of these contexts have been the Occupy movement struggling against what they see as neo-liberal oppression; the traumatic context of nation building in Israel; or simply as opening spaces for dialogue in London. It seems to us that at each of these stages, social dreaming allows insight into the experiences of the communities involved. In particular, dialogue between hostile groups is critical to stem violence and build or rebuild trust (Bar-On 2000; Boccara 2014).

Beyond dialogue, we have the potential of the associative unconscious for introducing relief from repression and trauma and therefore moving towards a form of therapy for participants: the "talking cure", so to speak, but in a shared space, something similar to a combination of Bion's work on psychodynamic group processes and Freud's dyadic free association. In this book, we have shown the great scope of social dreaming ranging from research to its potential use in a therapeutic context. Although these two worlds cannot meet – on the one hand, therapy brings up unwanted ethical issues in research, and on the other hand the use of social dreaming in a therapeutic setting will also cause difficulties in admitting that patients' situations can be used as data – the work of La Nave, Morgan Jones and Slade show how the potential of social dreaming might be used in such contexts. We believe that the use of free association and dreams in social dreaming – becoming associative thinking within the shared associative unconscious of the participants in the containing matrix – can develop the therapeutic work of the dyadic relationship of the analyst/analysand to that of the shared social dreaming matrix in an inter-subjective and mutually empathic way. Whether used deliberately or not, we have often noted the sense of enjoyment and wellbeing that arises in participants to a social dreaming matrix. It seems to us that this might be an area worthy of further exploration.

Work with organisations

Gordon Lawrence had a strong desire to establish social dreaming as a tool or method that could be used in organisational consultancy. In fact, the first edited publication on social dreaming was titled *Social Dreaming @ Work* (1998). In that book, there are various attempts to demonstrate the use of social dreaming in a working organisational context (Eisold 1998; Lawrence 1998; Lawrence, Maltz and Walker (1998)). It has to be said that Lawrence was largely unsuccessful in the endeavour, and that the idea of introducing the sharing of dreams into the culture of the western neo-liberal workspace has proved to be problematical. It might be that Lawrence's own insistence on this was due to his own needs at the time of his personal biography, since at that time he was moving out of the world of the Tavistock Institute into unchartered waters, joining Shell International as a consultant and trying to make a difference in that context while pursuing his interest in social dreaming. In our current volume, Franca Fubini describes her work with a government health organisation using social dreaming as part of her design, aiding the organisation to bring disparate parts with different cultures together.

Research and an epistemological framework

Ruth Balogh and Domenico Agresta have shown how social dreaming can be used in research that is psycho-social in *attitude* (Clarke and Hoggett 2009) and as such can be used for data collection and receive validation from academic peers who pursue research from this perspective. We are convinced that social dreaming will be used more frequently in psycho-social research and we are aware of both current and future research that uses social dreaming in research: examples include Gosling and Case (2013) who consider the use of social dreaming in the context of climate change catastrophe; Karolia and Manley (2018) who use social dreaming to uncover the complexities of British Muslim identity in the face of terrorism; and Berman and Manley (2018) who explore trauma in South Africa. These uses of social dreaming are especially appropriate where the subject matter is so complex or hidden from dialogue or debate that the access to the shared associative unconscious thinking that is offered by social dreaming can be used to uncover data that would otherwise have remained concealed or "unthought".

The psycho-social, in its attempt to address the balance between the psycho-analytically informed researcher and the social scientist, is potential territory for social dreaming as a research method and the pursuit of new kinds of data and a new way of approaching knowledge. As Balogh says in this edition, there is a "tension between clinical practice and the use of psychoanalysis as a culturally situated interpretive approach". In his chapter, Agresta combines a psycho-analytically informed approach with anthropology, where the dreams are the research data that enables an enquiry into the nature and the perception of time for a traditional Italian community. In both cases, the use of social dreaming as a research method is essential to the data and the outcomes.

There are various aspects of social dreaming that are relevant to the research endeavour and to future work on the use of social dreaming in research: the application of social dreaming as a way of gathering research data that would be difficult to collect using other methods; research into social dreaming as a research method in itself, its strengths, weaknesses and challenges, its place in the range of qualitative research methods available to the researcher and its credibility as a method; the use of further research and other research methods to explore and develop themes, thoughts and affect that have arisen from the use of social dreaming, for example the use of the triangulation of data gathered via different methods that would add to the value and meaning of the original social dreaming data; research into the epistemology implied or enacted through the use of social dreaming and its location in the framework of research paradigms available to the researcher. We are hopeful that this book has made a start in the systemic analysis of these various perspectives as a basis for future development.

As indicated above, there is a developing interest in the nature of the data that can be collected through the use of social dreaming research. The method as a research method is justified by the difficulty and complexity of the subject matter, whenever this verges on the inexplicable and inexpressible. This is as true of the application of social dreaming as a tool for mediation as it is for research. As we have already noted, examples of these include the situation in Israel, climate change, Muslim identity and South African trauma. It seems that this is at least one legitimate area of application for social dreaming as a research method.

In order to support this legitimate use of social dreaming in research, there is a concurrent need to continue investigating the inherent and essential nature of what is happening when we use social dreaming as a method. In doing so, we need to remember that aspects of social dreaming have been morphed into other related methods, such as the social photo-matrix (Sievers 2008), social dream-drawing (Mersky 2008), the visual matrix (Manley et al. 2015), and the use of art therapeutic methods to complement social dreaming (La Nave 2010 and Berman and Manley 2018). Lawrence himself associated social dreaming with the Listening Post (Khaleelee and Stapley 2013). There is a need to understand what these methods share and in what ways they differ. As a method, it is also true to say that most of the focus has been on the social dreaming matrix itself (Manley 2014), and there is as yet an undefined, or at least unconsolidated, area of thought available to us from the session that immediately follows the social dreaming matrix, whether this is a dream reflection dialogue, a process of "quickening" as described in Australia, or creative role synthesis; whether it uses pro-active facilitation around a flipchart or some other way of making meaning of the matrix for the participants. Indeed, there is a central question, for research purposes, about whether or not the material that is gathered by the participants after the matrix itself is indeed data; and if so, what kind of data is it and how can it be used? In addition, to these specific questions regarding social dreaming as a research method, there is (and always will be?) the question of the reliability of the data itself. Questions about to what extent someone's own subjectively experienced dream can be relevant – even if it were completely understandable, given the fact that dreams are by their very nature intrinsically difficult to understand – to someone else's life and thoughts, let alone relevant to a social milieu, will be asked of the empirical researcher. We are convinced that despite our interest and respect for social dreaming as a research method, there will be a contingent of researchers, especially those who tend to the "social" side of the psycho-social, who will find it difficult to agree that dreams can in any sense be regarded as empirical data. This question, therefore, cannot be left or taken for granted but must be pursued, argued for and backed up with freshly conceived ideas about what might reasonably constitute research data.

What might give validity to social dreaming data is further work into what other methods should be used to either consolidate findings that have emerged from social dreaming or to extend and develop those initial findings through the use of other methods. Triangulation – the use of other methods to support apparent findings or for the purposes of providing a more rounded and complete picture of those findings – would be a good way of doing this, and would add considerably to the acceptance of social dreaming data as being valid as well as interesting. The question remains as to what would be the best methods to employ for such triangulation of data.

Finally, and most importantly in our view, there is a pressing need to develop an epistemology for social dreaming that places this way of working firmly into a paradigm of research thinking that can then be seen and recognised as a method that can be used alongside others that are used by researchers to tackle specific research questions on topics. Clearly, this area is what is called psycho-social or socioanalytic research. Social dreaming, therefore, needs to find its defined place in this ambit of research practice. It is worth pointing out, however, that the field is in itself not quite a discipline and somewhat undefined, with researchers who are interested and involved in the field not necessarily agreeing among themselves about the exact nature or focus of the "psycho-social" or "socioanalytic" (Various 2008). Whatever can be thought about and clarified in terms of an epistemology for social dreaming might not easily find a place within a framework that is itself slightly unstable. This is why, in part, research into the philosophical underpinnings of social dreaming is such a necessary and interesting venture.

We have attempted to make a start on this journey in this book, as well as in previous publications. We do believe, however, that this is just a start. The problem is complex and warrants a sustained effort in thought, argument and reflection. On the one hand, we have the tradition of Gordon Lawrence's own thought on social dreaming, much of which was centred around Bion and group relations thinking. This has been summarised in Manley (2014). We feel, however, that Lawrence's initial thoughts and findings, while they merit the respect and admiration due to the discoverer of social dreaming, are in themselves insufficient. This is why Long has worked on bringing Peirce's theories of abductive reasoning to bear upon social dreaming, and Manley is developing epistemological connections between social dreaming and Deleuzian thought. Long's (2013 and in this volume) work on the associative unconscious shows how Peirce's semiotic approach can be applied to social dreaming, reducing the need for the reductionist scientific approach and giving value to an abductive logical position. Manley's work (this volume) similarly places an emphasis on associative thinking that moves towards the validation of data through a Deleuzian epistemology, where the tendency for social dreaming data to be apparently only loosely and sometimes randomly interlinked through association can be given meaning by adopting a rhizomatic and nomadic perspective on the research data. In these areas, and those begun by Lawrence, we feel there is much that remains to be discovered and enunciated, and from these research examples and the development of a philosophy of science for social dreaming, we hope that researcher will be encouraged to further develop the use of the social dreaming matrix in academic research.

Our present future dreams

At the same time as Gordon Lawrence was beginning his journey of exploration of social dreaming, we witnessed the collapse of the Berlin Wall. Many of us had hoped to interpret its fall as a new beginning, almost a dream symbol of freedom and democracy. We see, ironically, that new walls are proposed and built today to limit such freedoms. In reflecting upon the rich tapestry of dreams, associations and images that have emerged from this book, we suggest that social actions and changes for the good in our lives could benefit from the sharing of those aspects of our beings that truly, essentially bind us together as a human race. We all dream, and we all dream together. Maybe our hopes for the future can be dreamed of today, and maybe we can do this through the practice of social dreaming and create a future of dreams that become realities.

References

Boccara, B. (2014) *Socio-Analytic Dialogue: Incorporating psychosocial dynamics into public policies.* New York: Lexington Books.

Bar-On, D. (2000) *Bridging the Gap: Storytelling as a way to work through political and collective hostilities.* Hamburg: Korber Stiftung.

Berman, H. and Manley, J. (2018) Social Dreaming and creativity in South Africa: Imagi(ni)ng the unthought known. In: Adlam, J., Gilligan, J., Kluttig, T. and Lee, B.X. (eds) *Creative States: Overcoming Violence.* London: Jessica Kingsley.

Biran, H. (2007) The Dreaming Soldier. In Lawrence, W.G. (ed) *Infinite Possibilities of Social Dreaming.* London: Karnac.

Clarke, S. and Hoggett, P. (2009) (eds.) *Researching Beneath the Surface.* London: Karnac.

Eisold, K. (1998) Vision in organisational life. In Lawrence, W.G. (ed) *Social Dreaming @ Work.* London: Karnac.

Elrich-Ginor, M. (2003) Sliding Houses in the Promised Land: Unstable reality worked through dreams. In Lawrence, W.G. (ed) *Experiences in Social Dreaming.* London: Karnac.

Gosling, J. and Case, P. (2013) Social Dreaming and Ecocentric Ethics: Sources of non-rational insight in the face of climate change catastrophe. *Organization*, pp. 1–17.

Karolia, I. and Manley, J. (2018) '1 in 5 Brit Muslims' Sympathy for Jihadis': An insight into the Lived Experience of UK Muslims following the Terror Attacks in Paris'. In: Adlam, J., Gilligan, J., Kluttig, T. and Lee, B.X. (eds) *Creative States: Overcoming Violence.* London: Jessica Kingsley.

Khaleelee, O. and Stapley, L. (2013) OPUS Listening Posts: Researching society. In Long, S. (ed) *Socioanalytic Methods.* London: Karnac.

La Nave, F. (2010) Image: Reflections on the treatment of images and dreams in art psychotherapy groups. *International Journal of Art Therapy*, Volume 15, pp. 13–24.

Lawrence, W.G. (1998) Social Dreaming as a Tool of Consultancy and Action Research. In Lawrence, W.G. (ed) *Social Dreaming @ Work.* London: Karnac.

Lawrence, W.G. (ed) (1998) *Social Dreaming @ Work.* London: Karnac.

Lawrence, W.G., Maltz, M. and Walker, E.M. (1998). In *Social Dreaming @ Work.* London: Karnac.

Long, S.D. and Harney, M. (2013) 'The Associative Unconscious' in S. Long (ed) *Socioanalytic Methods.* London: Karnac.

Manley, J. (2014) 'Gordon Lawrence's Social Dreaming Matrix: Background, origins, history and developments'. *Organisational and Social Dynamics*, Volume 14, Issue 2, pp. 322–341.

Manley, J., Roy, A. and Froggett, L. (2015) Researching Recovery from Substance Misuse Using Visual Methods. In L. Hardwick, R. Smith and A. Worsley (eds) *Innovations in Social Work Research*. London: Jessica Kingsley.

Mersky, R.R. (2008) 'Social Dream-drawing: A methodology in the making'. *Socio-analysis*, Volume 10, pp. 35–50.

Sievers, B. (2008) 'Perhaps it is the Role of Pictures to get in Contact with the Uncanny': The social photo matrix as a method to promote the understanding of the unconscious in organizations. *Organisational and Social Dynamics*, Volume 2, Issue 21, pp. 234–254.

Various authors (2008) Special Issue on British Psycho(-)social Studies. *Psychoanalysis, Culture & Society*, Volume 13, Issue 4.

Volkan, V. (2001) 'Transgenerational Transmissions and Chosen Traumas: An aspect of large group identity'. *Group Analysis*, Volume 34, Issue 1, pp. 79–97.

INDEX